NEW DEAL OR RAW DEAL?

"Page by page Folsom peels away the parchment wrapping the Roosevelt myth to reveal the flawed figure beneath. Like other recent works, most notably Amity Shlaes's *The Forgotten Man*, this enjoyable and eye-opening revisionist account seeks to separate fact from folklore, and correct common misperceptions about the New Deal and its economic legacy."

—*National Review*

"Folsom argues that Roosevelt's role in creating jobs is vastly overstated; that he increased taxes too much, particularly on wealthier Americans; and that his spending saddled Americans with debt for years."

—*The Boston Globe*

"An intriguing theory."

—*Barron's*

"*New Deal or Raw Deal?* is a careful documentation and analysis . . . that allows us to reach only one conclusion: While President Roosevelt was a great man in some respects, his economic policy was a disaster. . . . Folsom has produced a highly readable book and has done a yeoman's job in exposing the New Deal."

—Walter E. Williams, John M. Olin Distinguished Professor of Economics, George Mason University

This title is also available as an eBook

ALSO BY BURT FOLSOM

Urban Capitalists

The Myth of the Robber Barons

The Industrial Revolution and Free Trade

Empire Builders

No More Free Markets or Free Beer

NEW DEAL OR RAW DEAL?

HOW FDR'S

ECONOMIC LEGACY

HAS DAMAGED AMERICA

Burton W. Folsom, Jr.

THRESHOLD
EDITIONS

New York London Toronto Sydney

Threshold Editions
A Division of Simon & Schuster, Inc.
1230 Avenue of the Americas
New York, NY 10020

First Threshold Editions trade paperback edition November 2009

THRESHOLD EDITIONS and colophon are trademarks of Simon & Schuster, Inc.

For information about special discounts for bulk purchases,
please contact Simon & Schuster Special Sales at
1-866-506-1949 or business@simonandschuster.com.

The Simon & Schuster Speakers Bureau can bring authors to your live event.
For more information or to book an event contact the Simon & Schuster Speakers
Bureau at 1-866-248-3049 or visit our website at www.simonspeakers.com.

Manufactured in the United States of America

11

Library of Congress Cataloging-in-Publication Data

Folsom, Burton W.
    New Deal or raw deal? : how FDR's economic legacy has damaged America /
by Burton W. Folsom, Jr.
    Includes bibliographical references and index.
        p.   cm.
    1. Roosevelt, Franklin D. (Franklin Delano), 1882–1945.   2. United States—
Economic Policy—1933–1945.   3. New Deal, 1933–1939.   4. Depressions—
1929—United States.   5. United States—Politics and government—1933–1945.
6. United States—Economic conditions—1918–1945.   I. Title.

E806.F64   2008
973.917—dc22   2008020381

ISBN 978-1-4165-9222-8
ISBN 978-1-4165-9237-2 (pbk)
ISBN 978-1-4165-9631-8 (ebook)

To
Ron Robinson
and
Larry Reed,
two friends indeed

ACKNOWLEDGMENTS

The New Deal is the landmark event in the political history of the last century. Franklin Roosevelt, the architect of the New Deal, is one of the most significant presidents in U.S. history. In keeping with the importance of this president and his program, this book has been almost ten years in the making.

Over the last decade, I owe thanks to many people for helping me research and think through the momentous Roosevelt presidency. My starting point is Gary Dean Best. His books, his insights, and his knowledge of primary sources were very helpful to me at different points in my research. In particular, he pinpointed for me key collections and key documents within those collections in both the Library of Congress and the Franklin D. Roosevelt Presidential Library. My many visits to these libraries, which are the central repositories of materials on Roosevelt and the New Deal, were greatly illuminated by Professor Best's guidance. Also, I thank John Braeman, a longtime expert on the New Deal, who read this manuscript twice and with his critical eye has saved me from many errors. Mark Leff is the foremost authority on tax policy during the New Deal and I appreciate his reading my chapters on taxes, and offering friendly advice. Paul Moreno, a superb colleague and labor historian, critiqued several chapters and advanced my understanding of labor and the New Deal. George Nash alerted me to several key sources and shared his wide knowledge of the New Deal period with me.

My students, especially those at Hillsdale College, have come to my aid as well. Jennifer Keenan Harrell did great work for me on the WPA in the National Archives. Brennan Brown effectively researched the beginnings of the federal minimum wage law in the 1930s. Other students, especially Christina Kohn, Jennifer Bryson, and David Morrell, wrote excellent papers on the New Deal and engaged me in thoughtful discussions. Ryan Walsh and Ben Stafford did fact-checking and valuable proofreading. Roseli van Opstal compiled the index.

Special thanks go to the staffs at the Franklin Roosevelt Presidential Library, the Library of Congress, the Kansas State Historical Society, and the Hoover Institution. In particular, Robert Parks at the RPL helped me find sources and shared his insights on Roosevelt with me.

I benefited from discussions on Roosevelt and the New Deal with Aileen Kraditor, Arthur Ekirch, Fred Luebke, and my father, Burton W. Folsom, Sr. All of them lived through the New Deal. I have also been helped in different ways by other scholars: Richard Jensen, Robert Higgs, Jim Couch, Jim Powell, Amity Shlaes, Joseph Rishel, Larry Schweikart, Gordon Lloyd, Will Morrisey, Robert Eden, and Tom Krannawitter.

Lawrence W. Reed, president of the Mackinac Center for Public Policy, has been a fine friend and constant source of ideas on politics in general and the New Deal in particular. My five years on his staff was time well spent. Winston Elliott, president of the Center for the American Idea, supported this project during my time with him. Ron Robinson, president of the Young America's Foundation, has been a friend for almost thirty years. His friendship I treasure and he has given me a regular forum every summer to discuss the New Deal before student audiences and on C-SPAN.

My agent, Alexander Hoyt, is a superior negotiator and a great encourager. He is a constant source of support. Kathy Sagan at Simon & Schuster/Threshold edited this book and has made many valuable suggestions. I have profited from her advice. William F. Buckley, Jr., and Evan Galbraith, both now deceased, believed in this project from the beginning. Seven years ago they began funding my research with a personal grant. Mr. Buckley argued that often the greatest contribution a scholar can make is to examine and challenge the central ideas of his age.

My last debt is my greatest. My wife, Anita Folsom, has been an indispensable part of getting this book written and finished. She is a good editor and thoughtful student of history, and she has discussed FDR and the New Deal with me for more years than either of us care to admit. Her wise counsel has kept me on balance and has helped set the right tone for the book. My son, Adam, has also listened patiently to many dinner conversations about the 1930s.

BURTON W. FOLSOM, JR.
February 29, 2008

CONTENTS

INTRODUCTION

The greatest and most enduring economic myth of the twentieth century is the idea that Franklin Roosevelt's New Deal pulled America out of the Great Depression. This fantasy is so prevalent even today that liberal Democratic leaders in Congress call for a "new" New Deal to lift the incomes of the middle class and shelter American workers from the anxieties attached to the competitive forces of a global economy.

We are now informed that free market ideas have become old-fashioned, and that what Americans need are new government regulations, guard rails, and twenty spending programs to correct for the excesses of capitalism, such as the housing bubble.

An April 13, 2008, story in the *New York Times* told a tale that went like this: Once upon a time free market champion Milton Friedman taught us that it was the botched performance of government and politicians that created and then deepened the Great Depression, which became the prevailing view in recent decades. But now, "a bipartisan chorus has decided that unfettered markets are in need of fettering. Bailouts, stimulus spending, and regulations dominate the conversation." Never mind that in 2007 there were $3 trillion in spending programs, and a record ninety thousand pages of federal rules and ten thousand commandments that are supposed to be doing that already.

Burt Folsom impressively details the massive catalog of governmental failures that were launched in Washington by the New Deal in the 1930s. The list ranges from the creation of Social Security, to the minimum wage, to farm subsidies, to the birth of the modern-day welfare system, to the Securities and Exchange Commission, to high rates of tariff and income taxation.

As Dr. Folsom points out, the Depression lasted eight years *after* FDR was elected and his first hundred-day assault on free markets was launched. The unemployment rate averaged greater than 12% during all of FDR's first two terms in office. In the decade of the 1930s, U.S. industrial production and national income fell by almost one-third. The stock market never fully recovered from Black Tuesday in October of 1929 until the 1940s.

The most damning indictment of FDR's New Deal agenda is that it did not do what it set out to do: end the Great Depression. Ask anyone over eighty, and he or she will probably say that FDR cared about the working man and gave the country hope. Maybe so, but that is not a sound economic plan—to declare, much as Bill Clinton would do sixty years later, "I feel your pain." Empathy is all well and good, but it does not create jobs or businesses or wealth.

Burt Folsom rigorously reviews the history and leaves no doubt to anyone with a clear and open mind that the New Deal was in every objective way a failure. Here is what Folsom tells us:

The minimum wage increased unemployment in the 1930s. Taxes and tariffs triggered the great stock market collapse in 1929, then held the head of the economy underwater for another dozen years. The Smoot-Hawley tariff of 1930 (signed by Herbert Hoover), which raised the import tax to the highest level ever, may have been the single most economically destructive law to pass the U.S. Congress in all of the twentieth century—maybe even worse than Roosevelt's WPA, NRA and AAA. The top tax rate under Roosevelt soared to almost 80 percent and then 90 percent, thus smothering any possibility of a recovery—a history lesson that Democrats would be wise to memorize.

Even the programs that are said to be the glittering examples of public policy success don't shine so brightly any longer. Social Security was built as a Ponzi scheme where future generations would pay for the costs of the expansive benefits paid to earlier ones. "Pay as you go" worked like a dream when there were forty workers per retired person, but now looks like an Enron accounting fraud to today's young workers—every two of whom will eventually subsidize every one retiree. The system's massive deficits get larger every year. To declare Social Security a great success is to say that the *Titanic* had a glorious maiden voyage until it hit the iceberg.

The wonder is that our free enterprise system was resilient enough to withstand all these body blows and still have the remaining strength to eventually pull out of the Depression. It's a testament to the American spirit of entrepreneurship, grit, and determination that prosperity was not lost forever.

The Democrats' current laundry list of "new" New Deal programs—from cap and trade anti–global warming regulations, to 52 percent marginal tax rates, to socialized health care, to $300 billion of new spending programs every year appear to be almost intentionally designed to torpedo the U.S. economy. Voters may find the recent Barak Obama chant, "Change we can believe in," mighty appealing. But if we adopt this "new" New Deal, the economy will almost certainly crater.

One incident recalled in Folsom's truthful and indispensable history book reminds me of how economically counterproductive some of the New Deal laws were. Folsom recounts the tax time bombs FDR signed into law: "On April 27, 1942, he signed an executive order taxing all personal income over $25,000 at 100 percent. Congress balked at that rate and later lowered it to 90 percent at the top level, but the president and Congress approved of withholding taxes and also of a 20 percent rate on all annual income starting at $500." *Yikes.* Clearly the New Dealers had forgotten the benefit of the 1920s tax cuts. We had to rediscover that tax lesson decades later with the Laffer Curve, which suggests that cutting high tax rates will generate more revenue than hiking taxes.

The irony of the New Deal is that this agenda, based on good and honorable intentions to help the poor and unemployed, caused more human suffering and deprivation in America than any other set of ideas in the twentieth century. And this book proves it.

Democrats make many of the same lofty promises today: They promise to put equality above growth. Yet they are likely to discover, as we learned from the New Deal, that this redistributionist agenda produces neither.

—Stephen Moore, Senior Economics Writer,
the *Wall Street Journal* editorial board,
and coauthor of *The End of Prosperity*

1

THE MAKING OF THE MYTH:
FDR AND THE NEW DEAL

On May 9, 1939, Henry Morgenthau, Jr., the secretary of the treasury and one of the most powerful men in America, had a startling confession to make. He made this remarkable admission before the influential Democrats who ran the House Ways and Means Committee. As he bared his soul before his fellow Democrats, Morgenthau may have pondered the irony of his situation.

Here he was—a major cabinet head, a man of great authority. The source of his power, of course, was his intimate friendship with President Franklin Delano Roosevelt. Morgenthau was the president's longtime neighbor, close confidant, and—would be for over a decade—his loyal secretary of the treasury. Few men knew the president better, talked with him more, or defended him more faithfully. Eleanor Roosevelt once said Morgenthau was one of only two men who could tell her husband "categorically" that he was wrong and get away with it. Roosevelt and Morgenthau liked to banter back and forth at cabinet meetings, pass each other secret notes, meet regularly for lunch, and talk frequently on the phone. Morgenthau cherished a photo of himself and the president in a car, side by side, friends forever, with Roosevelt's inscription: "To Henry," it read, "from one of two of a kind."[1]

But in May 1939, Morgenthau had a problem. The Great Depression—the most devastating economic catastrophe in American history—was not only persisting, in some ways it was getting worse. Unemployment, for example, the previous month had again passed the 20 percent mark. Here was Morgenthau, the secretary of the treasury, an expert on finance, a fount of statistics on the American economy during the 1930s; his best friend was the president of the United States and the author of the New Deal; key public policy decisions had to go through Morgenthau to get a hearing. And yet, with all this power, Morgenthau felt helpless. After almost two full terms of Roosevelt and the New Deal, here are Morgenthau's startling words—his confession—spoken candidly before his fellow Democrats on the House Ways and Means Committee:

> We have tried spending money. We are spending more than we
> have ever spent before and it does not work. And I have just one
> interest, and if I am wrong . . . somebody else can have my job. I
> want to see this country prosperous. I want to see people get a job.
> I want to see people get enough to eat. We have never made good
> on our promises. . . . I say after eight years of this Administration
> we have just as much unemployment as when we started. . . . And
> an enormous debt to boot![2]

In these words, Morgenthau summarized a decade of disaster, especially during the years Roosevelt was in power. Indeed average unemployment for the whole year in 1939 would be higher than that in 1931, the year before Roosevelt captured the presidency from Herbert Hoover. Fully 17.2 percent of Americans, or 9,480,000, remained unemployed in 1939, up from 16.3 percent, or 8,020,000 in 1931. On the positive side, 1939 was better than

1932 and 1933, when the Great Depression was at its nadir, but 1939 was still worse than 1931, which at that time was almost the worst unemployment year in U.S. history. No depression, or recession, had ever lasted even half this long.

Put another way, if the unemployed in 1931 under Hoover would have been lined up one after the other in three separate lines side by side, they would have extended from Los Angeles across the country to the border of Maine. In 1939, eight years later, the three lines of unemployed Americans would have lengthened, heading from the border of Maine south to Boston, then to New York City, to Philadelphia, to Washington, D.C., and finally into Virginia. That line of unemployed people from the border of Maine into Virginia was mostly added when Roosevelt was president.[3]

We can visualize this hypothetical line of unemployed Americans, but what about the human story of their suffering. Who were some of them, and what were they thinking? In the line at Chicago, we would encounter salesman Ben Isaacs. "Wherever I went to get a job, I couldn't get no job," Isaacs said of the prolonged depression. "I went around selling razor blades and shoe laces. There was a day I would go over all the streets and come home with fifty cents, making a sale. That kept going until 1940, practically." Letters to President Roosevelt tell other stories. For example, in Chicago, a twelve-year-old Chicago boy wrote the president, "We haven't paid the gas bill, and the electric bill, haven't paid grocery bill for 3 months. . . . My father he staying home. All the time he's crying because he can't find work. I told him why are you crying daddy, and daddy said why shouldn't I cry when there is nothing in the house." In our hypothetical unemployment line at Latrobe, Pennsylvania, we might see the man who wrote in 1934, "No home, no work, no money. We cannot go along this way. They have shut the water supply from us. No means of sanitation. We cannot keep the children clean and tidy as they should be." From Augusta, Georgia, in 1935 came this letter to the president: "I am eating flour bread and drinking water, and no grease and nothing in the bread. . . . I aint even got bed[d]ing to sleep on. . . ." But even he was better off than the man from Beaver Dam, Virginia, who wrote the president, "We right now, have no work, no winter bed clothes. . . . Wife don't even have a winter coat. What are we going to do through these cold times coming on? Just looks we will have to freeze and starve together."[4]

High unemployment was just one of many tragic areas that made the 1930s a decade of disaster. The *Historical Statistics of the United States*, compiled by the Census Bureau, fills out the rest of the grim picture. The stock market, which picked up in the mid-1930s, had a collapse later in the decade. The value of all stocks dropped almost in half from 1937 to 1939. Car sales plummeted one-third in those same years, and were lower in 1939 than in any of the last seven years of the 1920s. Business failures jumped 50 percent from 1937 to 1939; patent applications for inventions were lower in 1939 than for any year of the 1920s. Real estate foreclosures, which did decrease steadily during the 1930s, were still higher in 1939 than in any year during the next two decades.[5]

Another disaster sign in the 1930s was the spiraling national debt. The United States had budget surpluses in 1930 and 1931, but soon government spending ballooned and far outstripped revenue from taxes. The national debt stood at $16 billion in 1931; by the end of the decade the debt had more than doubled to more than $40 billion. Put another way, the national debt during the last eight years of the 1930s, less than one decade, grew more than it had in the previous 150 years of our country's existence. From 1776 to 1931, the spending to support seven wars and at least five recessions was more than offset by the debt acquired during the 1930s. Put yet another way, if Christopher Columbus, on that October day when he discovered the New World, could have arranged to put $100 a minute in a special account to defray the American debt, by 1939 his account would not yet have accumulated enough cash to pay for just the national debt acquired in the 1930s alone. In other words, if we were to pay $100 a minute (in 1930s dollars) into a special '30s debt account, we would need more than 450 years to raise enough money to pay off the debt of that decade.[6]

The economic travail of the New Deal years can also be seen in the seven consecutive years of unbalanced trade from 1934 to 1940. Much of our government spending during the decade went to prop up prices of wheat, shirts, steel, and other exports, which in turn, because of the higher prices, made them less desirable as exports to other countries. From 1870 to 1970, only during the depression years plus the year 1888 did the United States have an unfavorable balance of trade.[7]

Hard times are often followed by social problems. The United States in the 1930s was no exception. For example, the American birthrate dropped sharply, and the country's population increased only 7 percent in that decade. During the more prosperous 1920s, by contrast, the birthrate was higher and the country's population increased 16 percent.[8]

For many Americans, the prolonged Great Depression of the 1930s became a time of death. As one eighty-year-old wrote, "Now [December 1934] there are a lot of us [who] will choose suicide in preference to being herded into the poor house." Apparently, thousands of Americans agreed with her, because suicides increased from 1929 to 1930 and remained high throughout the 1930s. Equally sad were the people who gave up on life after prolonged despair and took their lives more subtly, through an accidental fall, reckless driving, or being hit by a train. All three of these categories hit record numbers of deaths per capita during the New Deal years.[9]

The loss of the will to live was also reflected in life expectancy during the 1930s. When Franklin Roosevelt became president in 1933, life expectancy in the United States was 63.3 years. Since 1900, it had steadily increased sixteen years—almost half a year each year of the first third of the twentieth century. In 1940, however, after more than seven years of the New Deal, life expectancy had dropped to 62.9 years. Granted, the slight decline during these years was not consistent—two of the seven years showed an increase over 1933. But the steady increase in life expectancy from 1900 to 1933 and from 1940 to the end of the century was clearly interrupted only during the New Deal years.[10]

The halt in improved life expectancy hit blacks even harder than whites. In 1933, black Americans could expect to live only 54.7 years, but in 1940 that had dropped to 53.1 years. Both before and after the Great Depression, the gap in life expectancy between blacks and whites had narrowed, but from 1933 to 1940 it actually widened. Strong indications are that blacks suffered more than whites during Roosevelt's first term as president.[11]

Someone might survey the wreckage from the 1930s and say, "Okay, maybe the whole decade of the thirties was a disaster. But since the Great Depression was a worldwide catastrophe, doesn't that diminish America's blame for its bad numbers?" The Great Depression did, of course, rock most of the world, but some nations performed better than others in limiting damage and restoring economic growth. Fortunately, the League of Nations collected data from many nations throughout the 1930s on industrial production, unemployment, national debt, and taxes. How did the United States compare with other countries? The answer: in all four of these key indexes the U.S. did very poorly, almost worse than any other nation studied. Most nations of Europe weathered the Great Depression better than the United States did.[12]

In a decade of economic disaster, such as the 1930s, a decline in morality is a significant danger. If record numbers of people are hungry, out of jobs, and taxed higher than ever before, will the charity, honesty, and integrity necessary to hold a society together begin to crumble as well? The *Historical Statistics of the United States* offers some help in answering this question. Homicides increased slightly during the 1930s. There were more than 10,000 murders a year only seven times from 1900 to 1960, and all seven years were in the 1930s. Arrests during this decade roughly doubled: almost 300,000 were made in 1932, and this steadily increased, reaching a peak of almost 600,000 in 1939. Divorce rates increased as well, especially during the late 1930s, and the number of cases of syphilis treated almost doubled, although cases of gonorrhea were roughly constant.[13]

Statistics can't tell the whole story of the changing mores of the 1930s. Many persons openly threatened to steal—or thought about stealing—to make ends meet during the Great Depression. Joblessness also led to "jumping trains" either to find work elsewhere or just to roam the country. R. S. Mitchell of the Missouri Pacific Railroad testified before the U.S. Senate that young men who jumped trains often encountered "hardened criminals" on these rides, who were a "bad influence" on the character of these youths. The *Historical Statistics* further shows that deaths to trespassers on railroads were at their highest ever during the depression years of 1933 to 1936.[14]

ROOSEVELT AND THE HISTORIANS

Did the New Deal, rather than helping to cure the Great Depression, actually help prolong it? That is an important question to ask and ponder. Almost all historians of the New Deal rank Roosevelt as a very good to great president and the New Deal programs as a step in the right direction. With only a few exceptions, historians lavish praise on Roosevelt as an effective innovator, and on the New Deal as a set of programs desperately needed and very helpful to the depressed nation.

An example of this adulation is the appraisal by Henry Steele Commager and Richard B. Morris, two of the most distinguished American historians of the twentieth century. Commager, during a remarkable career at Columbia University and Amherst College, wrote over forty books and became perhaps the bestselling historian of the century. From the first year of Roosevelt's presidency, Commager lectured and wrote articles in defense of the New Deal.

Richard Morris, his junior partner at Columbia, was a prolific author and president of the American Historical Association. Here is Commager and Morris's assessment of Roosevelt and the New Deal:

> The character of the Republican ascendancy of the twenties had been pervasively negative; the character of the New Deal was overwhelmingly positive. "This nation asks for action, and action, now," Roosevelt said in his first inaugural address, and asked for "power to wage war against the emergency." . . .
>
> It is the stuff of good history, this—a leadership that was buoyant and dynamic; a large program designed to enable the government to catch up with a generation of lag and solve the problems that crowded upon it; a people quickened into resolution and self-confidence; a nation brought to realize its responsibilities and its potentialities. How it lends itself to drama! The sun rises on a stricken field; the new leader raises the banner and waves it defiantly at the foe; his followers crowd about him, armies of recruits emerge from the shadows and throng into the ranks; the bands play, the flags wave, the army moves forward, and soon the sound of battle and the shouts of victory are heard in the distance. In perspective we can see that it was not quite like that, but that was the way it seemed at the time.[15]

Commager and Morris's assessment highlights four main points of defense for Roosevelt and the New Deal that have been adopted by most historians for the last seventy years: first, the 1920s were an economic disaster; second, the New Deal programs were a corrective to the 1920s, and a step in the right direction; third, Roosevelt (and the New Deal) were very popular; and fourth, Roosevelt was a good administrator and moral leader.

These four points constitute what many historians call "the Roosevelt legend." Since the works of Arthur M. Schlesinger, Jr., and William Leuchtenburg have been essential in shaping and fleshing out this view of Roosevelt, I will quote from them liberally. Schlesinger twice won the Pulitzer Prize and was probably the best-known historian in America. His three volumes on the rise of Roosevelt and the early New Deal became landmark books. Leuchtenburg, a professor at Columbia University and the University of North Carolina, wrote the standard one-volume history of the New Deal. Leuchtenburg studied and wrote his Ph.D. dissertation under the direction of Commager. The seasoned Commager was pleased with Leuchtenburg's devotion to Roosevelt because Commager gave Leuchtenburg the opportunity to write his history of the New Deal for the prestigious New American Nation Series. Leuchtenburg, in his career, trained scores of New Deal historians, who later wrote books and major articles on the New Deal. No one has ever, and maybe will ever, train more New Deal historians than William Leuchtenburg.[16] Here, in more detail, are the four myths that Commager, Morris, Schlesinger, Leuchtenburg, and most historians have promoted.

First, as Commager and Morris state, "The character of the Republican ascendancy of the twenties had been pervasively negative; the character of the New Deal was overwhelmingly positive." In other words, the 1920s was an economic disaster that helped lead to the Great Depression, from which Roosevelt with his New Deal provided useful tools of relief, partial recovery, and reform for the American economy.

To promote this view, both Schlesinger and Leuchtenburg support the underconsumption thesis, which states that the Great Depression was accelerated because workers did not have adequate purchasing power during the 1920s to buy the products of industrial America. According to Schlesinger, "Management's disposition [in the 1920s] to maintain prices . . . meant that workers and farmers were denied the benefits of increases in their own productivity. The consequence was the relative decline of mass purchasing power." President Calvin Coolidge and his treasury secretary, Andrew Mellon, contributed to great income disparities by enacting tax cuts for the rich. "The Mellon tax policy," Schlesinger says, "placing its emphasis on relief for millionaires rather than for consumers, made the maldistribution of income and oversaving even worse." Along similar lines, Leuchtenburg argues, "Insofar as one accepts the theory that underconsumption explains the Depression, and I do, then one can say that the Presidents of the 1920's are to blame. . . ."[17]

Second, "the character of the New Deal was overwhelmingly positive." Its intentions were excellent, and its results tended to be positive. Historians cite statistics to support this point: unemployment was 25 percent in 1933, Roosevelt's first year in office, and dropped steadily to about 15 percent by the end of his term in early 1937. The New Deal, then, did not solve the Great Depression, but it was a move in the right direction. William Leuchtenburg writes, "The New Deal achieved a more just society by recognizing groups which had been largely unrepresented—staple farmers, industrial workers, particular ethnic groups, and the new intellectual-administrative class." Samuel Eliot Morison, longtime professor at Harvard University, echoed this view: "The New Deal was just what the term implied—a new deal of old cards, no longer stacked against the common man." Textbook writers often pick up this theme. Historian Joseph Conlin concludes, "The greatest positive accomplishment of the New Deal was to ease the economic hardships suffered by millions of Americans. . . ."[18]

Third, Roosevelt was a popular and beloved president. He received unprecedented amounts of fan mail and he won reelection by a smashing 523 to 8 landslide in the electoral college—and then won two more terms after that. His fireside chats on the radio uplifted Americans and mobilized them behind his New Deal. "He came through to people," Schlesinger wrote, "because they felt—correctly—that he liked them and cared about them." Conlin writes, "Where Teddy [Roosevelt] had been liked and enjoyed, however, FDR was loved and adored." There were, of course, pockets of opposition to Roosevelt, especially among some selfish and greedy businessmen, who resented the regulations and taxes in the New Deal programs. "Roosevelt," Leuchtenburg writes, "was also determined to regulate the practices of high finance, and it was inevitable that this would cost him business support." But most Americans were enthusiastically behind the president. In fact, in his first midterm election of 1934, his party gained seats in both the House and Senate—something only Roosevelt did between 1902 and 1998. By 1936, his Democrats dominated Congress more than any party has in the last 150 years.[19]

Fourth, Roosevelt was an admirable executive and a good moral leader. Schlesinger, like all historians, concedes that Roosevelt "made mistakes both in policy and in politics," but he was a great president nonetheless. "Roosevelt had superb qualities of leadership, superb instincts for the crucial problems of his age, superb ability to select and manage vigorous subordinates, enormous skill as a public educator, and enormous ability to lift the spirits of the republic and to mobilize national energies." According to Morison, "Roosevelt reasserted the presidential leadership which had been forfeited by his three predecessors and promoted the growth of federal power, which had halted since the First World War." Leuchtenburg concludes that "if the test of a good administration is not an impeccable organizational chart but creativity, then Roosevelt must be set down not merely as a good administrator but as a resourceful innovator." What's more, "Franklin Roosevelt re-created the modern Presidency. He took an office which had lost much of its prestige and power in the previous twelve years and gave it . . . importance. . . ." Moral leadership is important, and Leuchtenburg writes that "essentially he [Roosevelt] was a moralist who wanted to achieve certain humane reforms and instruct the nation in the principles of government." "The presidency," Roosevelt himself said, "is not merely an administrative office. . . . It is predominantly a place of moral leadership."[20]

These four parts of the Roosevelt legend have a strong cumulative effect and historians regularly place Roosevelt among the top three presidents in U.S. history. In fact, the most recent Schlesinger poll (1996) ranks Roosevelt and Lincoln as *the* greatest presidents in U.S. history. FDR and his New Deal have become American idols. As Conlin writes, "From the moment F. D. R. delivered his ringing inaugural address—the clouds over Washington parting on cue to let the March sun through, it was obvious that he was a natural leader." Even before Roosevelt died, Conlin notes, "he was ranked by historians as among the greatest of the chief executives. . . . No succeeding generation of judges has demoted him." Leuchtenburg concludes, "Few would deny that Franklin Delano Roosevelt continues to provide the standard by which every successor has been, and may well continue to be, measured."[21]

Of course, historians are often nigglers and all students of Roosevelt and his presidency have some complaints. What's interesting is that most of these complaints are that Roosevelt should have done more than he did, not less. "The havoc that had been done before Roosevelt took office," Leuchtenburg argues, "was so great that even the unprecedented measures of the New Deal did not suffice to repair the damage." Therefore, to Leuchtenburg and others, the New Deal was only "a halfway revolution" that should have gone further. Some historians say FDR should have done more deficit spending during the recession of 1937; some chide him for not supporting civil rights more strongly; some point to abuse or corruption in some of the programs; and some say he should have done much more to redistribute wealth. The New Deal was, many historians conclude, a conservative revolution that saved capitalism and preserved the existing order. Some New Deal historians of the 1980s, 1990s, and 2000s—loosely called the "constraints school"— argue that the New Deal did promote many needed changes, but that Roosevelt was constrained in what he could accomplish and therefore he did as much reform as circumstances would permit.[22]

These recent criticisms of Roosevelt and the New Deal slightly alter but do not diminish the Roosevelt legend. The four points of defense are currently intact, and are usually found in most histories of the New Deal and in virtually all of the American history text-books today.

Two examples will help illustrate this point. David Kennedy and George McJimsey, both of whom loosely fit in the "constraints school," have written recent books on the Roosevelt presidency. Kennedy's book won the Pulitzer Prize in history and McJimsey's is part of the distinguished American Presidency Series. Kennedy praises "the remarkable generation of scholars" who did "pioneering work on the New Deal era." He cites Leuchtenburg, Schlesinger, and four other similar historians and writes, "Though I sometimes disagree with their emphases and evaluations, they laid the foundation on which all subsequent study of that period has built, including my own." Kennedy, like these predecessors, concludes, "Roosevelt's New Deal was a welcoming mansion of many rooms, a place where millions of his fellow citizens could find at last a measure of . . . security. . . ." McJimsey, also like his predecessors, praises Roosevelt: "No president in our history has faced such critical problems with the courage, vision, and stamina that Roosevelt displayed." McJimsey concludes that "one of Roosevelt's major achievements was to create an institutional structure for the modern welfare state. . . . Subsequent presidents," McJimsey notes approvingly, "were freer than ever to use government in creative ways."[23]

The durability of Roosevelt's popularity among historians was noted by Arthur Schlesinger, Jr., who himself was sometimes criticized for his Roosevelt books. Schlesinger remarked in 1988 that the rapidly increasing historical scholarship has more polished than tarnished the Roosevelt legend. In 1988, almost thirty years after Schlesinger's major works on Roosevelt were published, he surveyed the avalanche of recent books on the New Deal and observed that "a very considerable literature has appeared on many facets of the age of Roosevelt. I do not believe that the outpouring of scholarly books, monographs, and articles changes the main outline of the story told in these volumes, but some float ingenious theories and others add valuable details."[24]

After his 1996 presidential poll, Schlesinger was more confident in Roosevelt than ever. Of the thirty-two experts consulted, thirty-one gave FDR the highest rating of "Great" and one ranked him "Near Great," the second highest rating. "For a long time FDR's top standing enraged many who had opposed his New Deal," Schlesinger wrote. "But now that even Newt Gingrich pronounces FDR the greatest president of the century, conservatives accept FDR at the top with stoic calm." Along these lines, historian David Hamilton, who edited a book of essays on the New Deal, observed, "Conservative critiques [of the New Deal] have drawn less attention in recent years. . . ." In other words, according to Schlesinger and many historians, the debate is over as the Roosevelt legend is established even among conservative historians.[25]

The historical literature tends to support Schlesinger. The books and articles on Roosevelt and the New Deal are now so extensive, however, that it is almost impossible to read it all. Historian Anthony Badger has come as close as any modern historian to mastering the New Deal literature, and his book *The New Deal: The Depression Years, 1933–1940* is an essential tool to the modern historian trying to sort out all the writing on the subject. Badger looks fondly at Schlesinger and Leuchtenburg, the two key historians to shape the historical writing on the New Deal:

> At a time when there were few specialist monographs, both authors [Schlesinger and Leuchtenburg] displayed a remarkably sure touch in identifying the critical issues at stake in the most diverse New Deal activities. Both demonstrated an enviable mastery of a vast range of archival material. No one is ever likely to match the richness of Schlesinger's dramatic narrative. No one is ever likely to produce a better one volume treatment of the New Deal than Leuchtenburg's.[26]

Thus, the Roosevelt legend seems to be intact. And as long as it is intact, the principles of public policy derived from the New Deal will continue to dominate American politics. As historian Ray Allen Billington noted, the New Deal "established for all time the principle of positive government action to rehabilitate and preserve the human resources of the nation."[27] Yet, as we have seen, there is that nagging observation in 1939 by Henry Morgenthau, the secretary of the treasury, the friend of Roosevelt's and the man in the center of the storm. With great sadness, he confessed, "We are spending more than we have ever spent before and it does not work.... We have never made good on our promises."

Since national unemployment during the previous month of April 1939 was 20.7 percent, Morgenthau's admission has the ring of truth to it.

Is it possible that the Roosevelt legend is really the Roosevelt myth?

FDR'S RISE TO POWER:
POLITICAL SKILL, AMBITION, AND DECEPTION

For many people today, Franklin D. Roosevelt is still an American icon. But what kind of man was he? The basic facts of his life are clear. He was born an only child into a wealthy Democrat family in Hyde Park, New York. He married Eleanor Roosevelt, a distant cousin, who was the favorite niece of President Theodore Roosevelt. Franklin's connection with his famous relative was one he cultivated and one that stirred his own interest in politics. He was attractive, a good speaker, a clever politician, and well connected—all of which he used to launch his political career. He was elected twice to New York's state senate and served a stint as assistant secretary of the navy during World War I. Twice Roosevelt was defeated in politics—once in a primary race for the U.S. Senate in 1914 and once as the Democrats' vice presidential candidate in 1920. He contracted polio in 1921 and lost the use of his legs. But he continued his political career from his wheelchair and thereafter he won six elections, two as governor of New York and four as president of the United States. These are the bare facts, but there is so much more to the story.[1]

Roosevelt, as his battle with polio suggests, displayed great perseverance and skill to become president. His teachers and peers insisted he was no intellectual, but he learned quickly, either from others or from experience. He had a retentive mind that ranged widely, and he was an eager talker always on the search for listeners. He liked to be the center of attention and would exaggerate and stretch the truth to hold and impress an audience. He was very confident in his abilities and, like many successful politicians, he was charismatic. He attracted people to him, and people liked to be with him.

Given Roosevelt's wealth and opportunity, it is surprising to discover that he was not gifted in the field of economics in general, or in business in particular. In part, his family's wealth immunized him from having to learn how business worked or how to earn money. "Money was never discussed at home," his mother, Sara, revealed, "living as we did in the country there was no opportunity for spending it. . . . All his books and toys were provided for him." She added, "We never subjected the boy to a lot of don'ts."[2]

Even if his parents had wanted to teach their son about finance, it's not clear what wisdom they could have imparted. His father, James, had inherited his fortune, and through a series of poor investments in southern railroads and a canal through Nicaragua, he barely maintained it. On his mother's side, his grandfather, Warren Delano, made his money selling opium illegally to Chinese addicts. "I don't pretend to justify . . . the opium trade in a moral and philanthropic point of view," Delano said, but he persisted in it even when China declared war to stop it. When Delano finally retired to his mansion in New York, his legitimate business investments there seem to have done no better than James Roosevelt's. Strapped for cash, Delano went back to the opium trade and Sara spent several of her youthful years in China with her family while her father rebuilt his finances.[3]

From 1865 to 1910, the United States became the major industrial nation of the world, but the Roosevelts, despite their inherited wealth, did little to increase or decrease their fortune during this period. Others, often poor men, and sometimes immigrants, took the risks that made America preeminent in railroads, oil, and steel. For example, from another Dutch New York family came Cornelius Vanderbilt, who controlled the remarkably successful New York Central Railroad and became the wealthiest man in the nation. Immigrant Thomas Dickson, who started work as a mule driver, became a manufacturing giant and president of the Delaware and Hudson Railroad. As a vice president of the Delaware and Hudson, James Roosevelt worked with both of these men, or more accurately, under both of these men. Thomas Dickson was the boss, and the gentlemanly Roosevelt must have chafed at taking orders from an uneducated immigrant. When Vanderbilt's grandson Frederick moved nearby, Roosevelt refused to accept a dinner invitation at the Vanderbilt home because, as he told his wife, "If we accept, we shall have to have them at our house."[4]

Young Franklin enjoyed this story immensely and retold it with gusto often, but he was not a snob like his father. It's true, as Eleanor noted, that "Franklin finds it hard to relax with people who aren't his social equals." But in politics, he would develop superb skills in persuading and leading those who were not born into wealth or social position.[5]

Growing up in the sheltered and secure atmosphere of a huge mansion in Hyde Park, Roosevelt was sent to be with his "social equals" in prep school at Groton and in college at Harvard. He struggled at both schools and had many disappointments. At Groton, he confessed years later, "I always felt entirely out of things." His academic work was competent, but "not brilliant," as the rector noted. And in sports his feeble efforts won no respect from his more capable peers. He was "always a little the outsider," he told Eleanor. He was not good enough to make the football team; in baseball he played on "a new team which is called the BBBB, or

Bum Base Ball Boys," which attracted, according to Roosevelt, "about the worst players in the school." So he took boxing lessons. In his first and last boxing match, played out before his classmates, Roosevelt was ignominiously pummeled in two rounds. The victor, Fuller Potter, later said, "I can't understand this thing about Frank. He never amounted to much at school."[6]

Much of Roosevelt's Harvard experience was a replay of Groton. He did not make the football team again, and was relegated to the cheering section. His grades were mediocre, a C to C+ average. He tended to avoid the academic world of homework, study, and research; instead he focused on the social-political world of clubs, public debates, and journalism. His record was again mixed. He was accepted into membership of "The Fly," a prominent social club, and he did become editor of the *Crimson*, the school newspaper. But he was rejected for membership in Porcellian, the oldest and most elite social club at Harvard. Since his father had made Porcellian—as did Teddy Roosevelt and his two sons—that public failure was especially galling to him. Fifteen years later he confessed to a relative that his rejection by Porcellian was "the greatest disappointment of my life."[7] But Porcellian members were future entrepreneurs, bankers, and corporate lawyers; Roosevelt was a future politician.

Young Roosevelt had high ambitions and he was sensitive to the gap between his expectations and his performance in school. He sometimes chose to handle his failures by evasiveness, exaggerations, and small lies. It's hard to tell when his habit of stretching the truth started, but it was well developed at Groton. For example, when he fared poorly in a race with one hundred students, he told his parents he finished fourth—knowing his deception would be undetected because the school newspaper (which they would see) only listed the top three finishers. Geoffrey Ward, who has studied Roosevelt's early years perhaps more carefully than any other scholar, has described his regular efforts to manipulate the evidence to explain his shortcomings: "The boys who outran or outboxed or outkicked him were invariably [according to Roosevelt] too experienced or too big to have provided fair competition; if he slipped in the academic standings it was because of the arrival of two 'horribly clever' new boys. And if he thought distorting the truth would go undetected, he did not hesitate to try that, either."[8]

After graduating from Harvard, Roosevelt tried to find his niche in law school at Columbia. But his record again was not one of distinction. According to one of his professors, Jackson Reynolds, "Franklin Roosevelt was not much of a student [at Columbia] and nothing of a lawyer afterwards. . . . He didn't appear to have any aptitude for law, and made no effort to overcome that handicap by hard work. He was not a worker and he flunked." Although he did pass Jackson's course, he flunked two others. He never did finish law school, but he passed the bar exam, and was thus open for employment in one of New York's law firms. Roosevelt married his cousin Eleanor during this time—President Theodore Roosevelt gave away the bride—but the marriage was one of convenience.[9]

In Roosevelt's generation, most graduates of Groton and Harvard went into banking, law, or business. The problem, of course, is that Roosevelt did not have aptitude in those areas. Searching for his niche, he became a law clerk for the New York firm of Carter, Ledyard, & Milburn. Lewis Ledyard, the senior partner, described Roosevelt as "utterly worthless" and complained about the quality (and quantity) of his work. But young Franklin's mind was elsewhere. He didn't like law or business and he had enough family wealth that he didn't need to please Lewis Ledyard, Jackson Reynolds, or anyone else, except, perhaps, his doting and recently widowed mother. Roosevelt's much older stepbrother, James R. Roosevelt, Jr., was a "gentleman" and never held a full-time job. Franklin could have done the same thing, and if he had his mother would probably have subsidized and encouraged him.[10]

But young Franklin was developing a burning interest in politics. What he lacked in aptitude and desire for business and law, he was developing in political skills. He was slowly learning how to influence men. Even as a young man of twenty-five, with no ideas of his own, Franklin had set his eyes on the presidency. At Ledyard's law firm, when Franklin and some of the other clerks would discuss their futures, he explained to them in detail how he planned to win the presidency someday. With persuasive charm, Roosevelt mapped out his strategy of following in his famous cousin's footsteps: He would first run for the state legislature, then he would advance to assistant secretary of navy, and then win election as governor of New York. From a base as head of the largest state in the union, he would launch a successful bid for the presidency. Over the next twenty-five years, he would in fact follow every step of that path.[11]

As improbable as Roosevelt's ambitions were to his fellow law clerks, his choice of a career in politics would fit his skills perfectly. When he switched his thinking from how to earn money to how to influence voters, he was playing to his natural strength. Oliver Wendell Holmes later observed of Roosevelt that he had "a second-class intellect. But a first-class temperament." Given that stark distribution of talent, the world of smiles, handshakes, and speeches fit Roosevelt much better than the world of ledgers, lawsuits, and investments. He preferred to use his mother's money—and she supplied him regularly and generously—to run for office rather than to fund a business. Throughout his life, he depended on largesse from his mother to make ends meet.[12]

In 1910, at age twenty-eight, the well-financed Roosevelt chose to launch his political career with a run for the New York state senate. Unlike his mediocre efforts in the classroom, he found he could sway voters in speeches and in conversation. He campaigned diligently from town to town for five weeks throughout the whole Hyde Park district. The crowds, the speeches, and the politicking were all salve to his ego, and a fresh relief from the world of business. And he was actually good at it—so good that he became the first Democrat in decades from his district to capture a seat in the New York Senate. Two years later he overwhelmingly won reelection. When Roosevelt, with his magnetic charm and famous name, showed himself to be a vote-getter he attracted even more notice and won a larger audience. President Woodrow Wilson therefore plucked him out of the legislature and placed him into the cabinet as assistant secretary of navy, where FDR would serve during the First World War. Roosevelt had finally achieved distinction, and was following his path to the White House. Dozens of Roosevelt's peers had received A's in economics classes; dozens more were successful lawyers and corporate executives. But only Roosevelt was winning tough political races and consulting with the president.[13]

Many who have studied Roosevelt's remarkable ascent in politics have noted that his rise is all the more spectacular because in achieving the White House he had to overcome the crippling disease of polio. Indeed, when Roosevelt contracted polio at age thirty-nine, after a chilling swim at his summer home in Canada, his career in politics seemed over. He had to persevere with boldness and political skill to establish himself among New York Democrats as a viable candidate.[14]

But Roosevelt had some good luck as well. First, when he was just a state senator, Louis Howe, a newspaper reporter, was attracted by Roosevelt's magnetic charm and quit his job, joined Roosevelt's staff, and dedicated his life to making him president. Howe regularly addressed his boss as "our future and beloved president." When Roosevelt was hit by polio, Howe always stood by him, still called him "future president," and personally nurtured Roosevelt's political contacts throughout New York. Second, Marguerite "Missy" LeHand joined Roosevelt's staff a year before his polio attack, and she, like Howe, was swept into his personal orbit. She absorbed her life into his. She became his loyal secretary, efficient maid, lifelong companion, and (with Howe) his most enthusiastic booster. Together she and Howe cared for Roosevelt, nurtured his dreams, and constantly helped him adjust to life in a wheelchair. Third, Roosevelt still had access to his mother's money (even though she tried to maneuver him out of politics). This regular source of cash meant that Roosevelt could spend most of his time away from home, with Louis Howe and Missy LeHand to help him, while his mother and Eleanor raised his five children from their households in Hyde Park and New York City.[15]

A final piece of Roosevelt luck was the timing of the polio. It occurred during a Republican decade when Democrat victories in New York and elsewhere were few and far between. If Roosevelt had been perfectly healthy, he no doubt would have been tempted to try to win a major Democrat nomination in New York, and might have suffered a trouncing that would have squelched his political ambitions forever. With polio, no Democrat expected him to run for office again; he had seven years to get used to life in a wheelchair and plan his next political race. Meanwhile, the team of Howe and LeHand, by signing Roosevelt's name to hundreds of letters and articles, regularly kept his name before the public. And Roosevelt himself—with leg braces and an escort—made nominating speeches for Al Smith for president at the Democrat conventions in both 1924 and 1928.[16]

That still left Roosevelt with many years to adjust to polio, and to seek elusive cures for it. He bought a used houseboat, which he named the *Larooco*, and lived much of the 1920s on it—swimming, planning, and enjoying the company of old friends. Eleanor and his children were excluded, and rarely joined him; mostly he spent time with Louis Howe, Missy LeHand, and friends from college and political life. "I imagine it is as well you are far away from all entanglements," Eleanor wrote him. But his children did not agree. "Those were the lonely years," his eldest son, James, lamented. "For a long while during this time of illness and recovery we had no tangible father, no father-in-being, whom we could touch and talk to at will—only an abstract symbol, a cheery letter writer, off somewhere on a houseboat. . . ."[17]

Such a family living arrangement was very peculiar, but there was a reason for it. Franklin and Eleanor had become emotionally separated from each other because of a three-year sexual affair he had with Eleanor's secretary, Lucy Mercer. Eleanor confronted Franklin about the affair after she discovered a set of love letters Lucy had written him. "The bottom dropped out of my own particular world," Eleanor lamented to a friend. Franklin, meanwhile, saw himself in a bind: if he divorced Eleanor, as Louis Howe quickly pointed out, that would end his run for the presidency. Also, and perhaps even worse, Sara entered the picture and apparently threatened to cut her son off without a penny if he disgraced the family with a divorce. So Roosevelt decided to stay married to Eleanor, and promised not to see Lucy anymore. But Lucy was drawn to Roosevelt's charm—"his beloved presence" she called it twenty-five years later. Even after she married someone else, she saw him from time to time. Lucy Mercer was present at each of his presidential inaugurations, and she, not Eleanor, was with him when he died.[18]

Therefore, Franklin and Eleanor, in their marriage of political necessity, were apart more than they were together. On the *Larooco* for sometimes months at a time, Roosevelt would dream about the presidency but then look at the reality of his useless legs, which he tried hard to nurse back to use. Missy LeHand was there with him and, she observed, "There were days on the *Larooco* when it was noon before he could pull himself out of depression and greet his guests wearing his lighthearted facade." But other days his optimism prevailed and he would be the center of conversation. He and Louis Howe talked politics for hours, and to keep busy, he invested in a variety of business ventures. The shift from politics to business, however, was unfortunate. It put him back where he had no patience or talent.[19]

The 1920s was an entrepreneurial boost for America, but not for Roosevelt. During this decade, those with a talent for enterprise, some of whom lived very close to Roosevelt, changed the habits of the nation by producing radios, air-conditioning, zippers, vacuum cleaners, and Scotch tape. But not Roosevelt. He missed these investments. Instead he pursued futile schemes to drill oil in Wyoming, buy ships to cross the Atlantic, and sell stamps that were premoistened. He and Howe tried to corner the live lobster market, but they were the ones pinched; Roosevelt lost $26,000 before bailing out. Often his ideas were impulsive and whimsical. For example, he assumed airplanes were only a passing fad, and he invested in a line of airships, called dirigibles, to fly from New York to Chicago. "I wish all my friends ... would keep out of aeroplanes ... ," he wrote. "Wait until my dirigibles are running. ... " But they never did. Meanwhile, not far away, Igor Sikorsky was inventing the helicopter, with no help from Roosevelt. Instead, FDR tried buying and selling German marks, planting thousands of trees, and making cash with vending machines, but he never hit the jackpot. Toward the end of the 1920s, he lost money in his resort for polio patients in Warm Springs, Georgia—and then, to top that off, he lost more money farming the land nearby.[20]

Roosevelt's string of business failures did not surprise those who knew him well. One friend, Franklin Lane, Wilson's secretary of interior, concluded, "Roosevelt knows nothing about finance, but he doesn't *know* he doesn't know." Therefore, he tried one scheme after another, pursuing whims not research, always thinking the next idea would be a winner. Henry Wallace, who would become Roosevelt's vice president, liked his boss in politics but not in business. Wallace had published a newspaper in Iowa and knew the patience and tenacity needed to earn a profit. "I reached the conclusion," Wallace said after watching Roosevelt in action, ". . . that I would under no circumstances, ever have any business dealings with him."[21]

Perhaps as Roosevelt contemplated the red ink on his ledgers, he regretted not paying closer attention to the study of business in his economics classes. But Lane and Wallace would probably have argued that Roosevelt simply had no sense for business—for the patient study of products and markets. He was intuitive and impulsive, not systematic and cautious. Albert de Roode, who watched Roosevelt flounder as a lawyer, said, "I feel sorry for him. . . . He [quickly] comes to conclusions. He hasn't got the patience to work things out." Marquis Childs, a prominent newspaper reporter, studied Roosevelt as president and agreed with Roode: "He did not seem to arrive at conclusions in methodical ways. . . ."[22]

Roosevelt's son Elliott was also fascinated by his father's poor knack for business. Like Roode and Childs, Elliott pointed to his father's intuitive and impatient ways. "His handling of his own finances was like the draw poker he liked to play, with one-eyed jacks and deuces wild. He firmly believed in his luck. That was part of the broad streak of superstition in him." He had "lucky numbers, lucky days, lucky clothes," and even a lucky hat and lucky shoes.[23]

Yet Elliott also went on to say of his father, "Promoters were drawn to him like bees to honey. . . ." He was so congenial, so charismatic, and so optimistic that he always had people believing he could succeed in whatever he undertook to do. Henry Wallace believed that those traits of intuitive boldness that made FDR so inept in business made him successful in politics. His engaging smile, his confident voice, his hearty laugh, and his gregarious ways may have failed to sell his lobsters from Maine, his marks from Germany, or his coffee from South America, but he attracted voters by the millions. Even after Roosevelt was confined to a wheelchair, Van Lear Black, the president of Fidelity & Deposit, a surety bonding firm that hired him, continued to pay Roosevelt his salary of $25,000 because his winning ways continued to capture clients for the company. And Al Smith, the governor of New York for most of the 1920s, had expressly asked Roosevelt to nominate him for president at the Democrat conventions of 1924 and 1928.[24]

Before looking at Roosevelt's crucial campaign to become governor of New York in 1928, it might be useful to review the 1920 presidential campaign, in which he ran as the Democrats' nominee for vice president. That was Roosevelt's first national campaign and it showcased both his strengths and weaknesses. Since his party was caught in the midst of a recession after the First World War, he and Governor James Cox of Ohio were running a near hopeless campaign to succeed President Wilson. The Republican candidates, Warren G. Harding and Calvin Coolidge, were resonating with voters, and many Democrats were sitting the election out.

Not Roosevelt. With some of his own money, and lots of his mother's, he crisscrossed twenty states making hundreds of speeches, twenty-six in one day alone. "[Roosevelt] gets the last ounce of appeal-power out of each sentence," wrote a reporter for the *New York Post*. He was "the figure of an idealized college football player, almost the poster type in public life," he added. Roosevelt "speaks with a strong clear voice, with a tenor note in it which rings—sings, one is tempted to say—in key with . . . [an] intangible, utterly charming and surely vote-winning quality." Those who met him did not forget it. Emily Smith, Governor Al Smith's daughter, gushed after meeting Roosevelt and called him "so handsome, so debonair, and with a family name so universally known."[25]

With such responsive crowds and such flattering news clippings, Roosevelt soon began stretching the truth. On August 18, in Deer Lodge, Montana, Roosevelt defended Wilson's League of Nations before a group of farmers. He suggested that American influence on the proposed league would be great, and that the Central American countries would follow their neighbor to the north. "Does anyone suppose that the votes of Cuba, Haiti, Santo Domingo, Panama, Nicaragua, and the other Central American states would be cast differently from the vote of the United States? We are in a very real sense the big brother of these little republics. . . ." Then he bragged, "You know I have had something to do with running a couple of these little Republics. The facts are that I wrote Haiti's Constitution myself and, if I do say so, I think it a pretty good Constitution." Since the farmers in Deer Lodge were impressed and cheered him on, Roosevelt talked about his constitution writing in his next speeches in Butte and Helena. The problem is that Roosevelt was never even remotely involved in writing Haiti's constitution, and had never run a republic (although he did visit Haiti once as assistant secretary of the navy).[26]

When the Republicans heard about Roosevelt's falsehood,

Harding called it (with exaggeration of his own) "the most shocking assertion that ever emanated from a responsible member of the government of the United States." The Republicans pounded away at this error. Roosevelt's response to his exposure is interesting: he denied ever making the statement, and denied it years afterward every time the issue was brought up. He specifically blamed the Associated Press for misquoting him, after which thirty-one citizens of Butte signed a document swearing they heard Roosevelt boast that he had indeed written Haiti's constitution. But Roosevelt simply continued to deny it, and shifted to other issues.[27]

The 1920 presidential campaign was Roosevelt's first venture on the field of national politics. After contracting polio the next year, he spent most of the 1920s on the sidelines. By 1928, Roosevelt would be ready but not anxious to make his next political move. Al Smith, who had been New York's governor for four terms, won the Democrat nomination for president, and he wanted Roosevelt to follow him in the governor's chair. Roosevelt and Smith, a second-generation Irish Catholic, always had an awkward relationship. Smith grew up poor in lower Manhattan and won support from Tammany Hall, the urban political machine in New York. He had worked his way up to speaker of the New York legislature by 1912, the year Roosevelt joined him as a freshman legislator.[28]

Smith loved to tell the story of the first time he came to Roosevelt's house to call on him. Smith rang the doorbell of a very large house, rented for Roosevelt by his mother, and a butler came to the door to greet Smith and escort him to Roosevelt. Since the rent for the mansion was more than three times a legislator's salary, Smith knew at once he was meeting a different type of Democrat. The two men never developed close personal ties, but had a good political relationship because they needed each other. Both appealed to different groups of voters, and together they made the Democrats hard to beat.[29]

Smith, as the Democrats' candidate for president, wanted Roosevelt on the ticket in New York as a candidate for governor because he could bring out upstate Protestant voters to go with the urban ethnic Catholics whom Smith hoped to attract in New York City. The calculating Roosevelt was worried about a strong Republican trend, but he agreed to run for governor and did, in fact, use his skills effectively to eke out a win against Republican state attorney general Albert Ottinger. Since Smith lost the presidency to Herbert Hoover, Roosevelt, as governor of the largest state in the union, was well positioned for a run for the White House. The next phase of his political plan had indeed come to pass.[30]

While Roosevelt was governor, the Great Depression struck America. The stock market collapsed and investment capital rapidly disappeared. With factories closing, unemployment soared more than 20 percent—the worst economic disaster in U.S. history. President Hoover tried a variety of programs but none seemed to work. His presidency was in shambles. Roosevelt, who aspired to Hoover's job, had to develop an economic plan. And here was the irony: Roosevelt had neglected the study of economics in order to study politics and now, when his big chance for the presidency came, it was during a crisis that required a thorough knowledge of economics. He formed a brains trust in New York. He needed advice. What had caused this ever-deepening depression and what course of action should he recommend?

3

WHAT CAUSED THE GREAT DEPRESSION?

What caused the Great Depression? That question would not only perplex the general public of the 1930s, but the experts then as well. Even today the debate is not yet resolved, but economists and historians have pointed to three credible causes that help explain how Americans slid into their worst economic crisis ever.

The first cause highlights the negative consequences of the Great War. World War I was a financial and social catastrophe. The Versailles Treaty, which ended the war, resolved little and increased bitterness throughout a devastated Europe. Here at home, the United States saw its national debt balloon from $1.3 billion to $24 billion in three short years. A large chunk of that debt—almost one-half—consisted of Allied loans. The United States had lent over $10 billion to European countries during the war; they were obligated to pay it back. Many nations did begin small payments during the 1920s, and this "intent to pay" helped stabilize American finances. America may have a large debt, the investors reasoned, but there is Treasury Secretary Andrew Mellon whittling it away.

From 1929 to 1932, however, almost all of Europe (Finland was an exception) balked at repayment and, in fact, soon repudiated their debts to the United States. One argument in their repudiation was that America passed a high tariff; if we wouldn't let Europeans trade with us, how could they raise the cash to repay us?[1] That leads to cause number two, the tariff.

The Smoot-Hawley Tariff Act, which was debated and passed during 1929 and 1930, instituted the highest tariff ever in U.S. history. This new tariff taxed 3,218 imported items, and on 887 of them the tax was sharply increased. Foreigners were understandably outraged. In Switzerland, for example, the leading industry was watch (and clock) making, and the leading customer for these timepieces was the United States. But the sharp increase in the tariff made Swiss watches less competitive than the inferior American brands. What the United States may have gained in shutting out the Swiss and selling American watches was more than lost when Switzerland passed retaliatory tariffs and refused to import U.S. cars, typewriters, or radios. Our high tariffs on other European goods (for example, on wool for the British and on olive oil for the Italians) resulted in anti-American rhetoric, more retaliatory tariffs, and a repudiation of war debts across the European continent. Our exports, therefore, dropped from $7 billion in 1929 to $2.5 billion in 1932.[2]

At another level, the Smoot-Hawley tariff was a direct attack on our own home economy. When we pay more for American-made watches and wool blankets than for quality foreign substitutes, we are able to buy fewer American-made radios, cars, or telephones. But the problem goes even deeper than this. We needed imports to help make our own industrial products. A tariff hike, therefore, crippled our own leading industries. The tariff on tungsten, for example, hurt steel; the tariff on linseed oil damaged the paint industry. General Motors and Ford were the premier carmakers of the world, but the Smoot-Hawley tariff increased the duty on over eight hundred items used in making cars. U.S. automakers, then, took a double hit. First, they sold fewer cars because Europeans slapped retaliatory tariffs on the United States. Second, they had to pay higher prices for hundreds of items needed to make cars. No wonder American car sales plummeted from over 5.3 million in 1929 to 1.8 million in 1932.[3]

The Smoot-Hawley tariff, some scholars argue, did something else perverse—it helped cause the stock market crash of October 1929. This argument is tentative, but has enough merit to mention. As this record high tariff was being debated in the House and Senate, investors watched with worry. They sensed that such a high tariff would hurt their stocks. During those periods when the high tariff looked as though it might be defeated, the stock market rose; during those periods when the tariff made headway in Congress, the market tended to fall. In late October, when the stock market did its worst, the Senate voted to open the tariff bill to include all goods, not just farm products. Sixteen key members of the low-tariff coalition switched sides and it became apparent that the bill would probably pass. President Hoover received urgent messages exhorting him to veto the tariff bill; over one thousand economists signed a petition urging him to wield the veto pen. Hoover seems to have been skeptical of the high tariff, but he concluded that signing it would fulfill the Republican campaign pledge. He did so in June 1930, and by July the stock market had lost one-third of its value in ten months.[4]

The third cause of the Great Depression was the poor performance of the Federal Reserve. The Constitution gives the government power to coin money and regulate its value. The Federal Reserve was created in 1913 to control the money system by regulating interest rates and lending money to banks. The idea was that the Fed, by setting interest rates and lending cash to needy and worthy banks, would help prevent a banking collapse. The Fed would get this cash by buying bonds in the open market or by discounting assets of the member banks. That was the theory.[5]

In practice, the Fed had raised interest rates four times, from

3.5 to 6 percent, during 1928 and 1929. That made it harder for businessmen to borrow money to invest, which hindered economic growth. This contributed to the October 1929 stock market crash, the race by customers to get their money out of their banks, and the closing of many banks. In the early 1930s, the Fed dithered and let the runs on banks continue. Bankers keep about 3 to 10 percent of their deposits on reserve for customers who want to withdraw money from their savings accounts. Then the bankers lend out the rest to investors, home buyers, or other bankers. If too many customers choose to withdraw their funds, the bank will run out of cash, and fail. Or if bank loans are not repaid, a bank can also fail. Bank failures can be contagious; when one bank fails, insecure depositors of other banks sometimes rush to get their money out before their banks fail.

On December 11, 1930, the prominent Bank of the United States failed. This triggered a series of runs on other banks, and hundreds of banks throughout the country either failed or were on the verge of failure. The Federal Reserve could have slowed or possibly even have halted this crisis by lending money to cash-hungry banks. Instead the Fed let the runs continue; it let hundreds of banks collapse. And by 1932, the quantity of money in the United States had fallen by about one-third in three years. The money, like the unpaid loans, simply vanished. As banks failed, their assets disappeared. Many advisors in the Federal Reserve system urged the Fed to intervene, but they did not prevail; the Fed, which was created to prevent a banking crisis, helped create one.

The Great Depression is complex, and those three causes do not explain everything, but they explain a great deal. They help show why we had a banking crisis, a stock market decline, vanishing exports, angry trading partners, economic uncertainty about the national debt, and a collapse of key industries such as car manufacturing. Moreover, all three causes involve problems created by government, not the free market. War debts, high tariffs, and failed monetary regulation were all government blunders.

One theory of the cause of the Great Depression, strongly proposed by many intellectuals during the 1930s but rejected today, did point the finger at free enterprise. The underconsumption thesis, briefly described earlier, concedes that the 1920s was a decade of industrial growth. But the prosperity, it insists, was not evenly divided. The rich got richer and the poor got poorer. Class divisions sharpened, and the tax cuts initiated by Mellon and Coolidge funneled more money to the rich. Because middle-class America was largely walled off from the prosperity of the era, most people could not afford to buy what they produced. We soon had overproduction, and too few buyers for too many goods. The Great Depression was the inevitable result; careful government planning and regulation were the proposed cure.[6]

At a superficial level, some evidence does seem to support underconsumption ideas. Many successful entrepreneurs became millionaires, and the Mellon tax cuts helped this happen. The farmers of the decade did overproduce, and when the Great Depression hit, the United States had a lot of unsold cars, refrigerators, and telephones. But a few scattered facts do not a theory make, any more than a white sauce and a pinch of sugar make a soufflé. The eggs are missing, and with the underconsumptionists, the statistical support is missing.

The underconsumption thesis can only be sustained if the answers are "yes" to the following three questions. First, during the 1920s, were the rich really getting a significantly larger proportion of the national income? Second, were employees receiving a smaller share of corporate income? Third, were consumers consuming less of the gross national product (GNP) in the late 1920s than in 1920? If we look at the historical evidence, we discover that the answer to all three questions is a resounding "no."

First, the top 5 percent of the population earned 25.47 percent of the nation's income in 1921; in 1929, the top 5 percent earned 26.09 percent of the national income. Yes, that is an increase, but not a significant one. Second, corporate profits in the United States averaged 8.2 percent from 1900 to 1920, and remained at 8.2 percent from 1920 to 1929. There was no upsurge of corporate profits during the decade. However, the wages going to employees actually rose during the 1920s from 55 to 60 percent of corporate income. In other words, employees were capturing a larger share of corporate dollars during the 1920s than before. Third, the percentage of GNP that went to consumption expenses did not fall, but actually rose from 68 percent in 1920 to 75 percent in 1927, 1928, and 1929.[7]

A more accurate picture of the 1920s would show Americans buying more and more radios, telephones, cars, vacuum cleaners, and refrigerators. The 1920s was more a decade of overconsumption than underconsumption. Demand outstripped supply. According to Peter Temin, an economist at the Massachusetts Institute of Technology, "The concept of underconsumption has been abandoned in modern discussions of macroeconomics." He explains this simply: "The ratio of consumption to national income was not falling in the 1920s. An underconsumptionist view of the 1920s, therefore, is untenable."[8]

This analysis of underconsumption is important because Roosevelt, who was anxiously groping for economic ideas, latched on to underconsumption and made tackling it part of his presidential campaign. He would present it as an alternative to Hoover's programs. It is not clear whether Roosevelt discovered underconsumption ideas on his own or was led to them by his "Brains Trust." As governor of New York, Roosevelt regularly hosted a group of professors from Columbia University—they became his "Brains Trust"—and they presented Roosevelt with a variety of economic ideas fashionable in academic circles. Some of these advisors, especially Rexford Tugwell, championed an underconsumption perspective, and Roosevelt soon cited "underconsumption" by name in his speeches, which the Brains Trust helped him write.[9]

Underconsumption theory especially appealed to intellectuals. If the rich were wrecking American industry, exploiting tax cuts, and using their economic power to impoverish farmers and laborers, then capitalism was failing. Government, by implication, needed to step in and appoint "experts" to planning boards to jumpstart the American economy, promote consumer spending, and redistribute wealth. This was a recipe for massive government intervention, and many college professors, as educated experts, would have roles to play on the planning boards that would tinker with, and manage, the American economy. In retrospect we can see that the historical statistics often refute the underconsumption view. Perhaps, therefore, it is not surprising that its strongest advocates were not actually trained in economics. Almost all businessmen, and many economists, such as Benjamin Anderson, Henry Hazlitt, Isaac Lippincott, and Irving Fisher, sharply opposed it. If Roosevelt had only balanced his Brains Trust by including a businessman, he might have thought through his ideas more carefully.[10]

In Roosevelt's quest for the presidency, he established himself as the Democrats' front-runner by handily winning reelection as governor in 1930. Then, in early 1932, he entered several Democrat primaries and won many party leaders to his cause by his victories there, by his personal charm, and by the confidence he projected that he could lead the Democrats to victory in November.

When Roosevelt was campaigning from state to state he was often shrewdly cryptic in his comments on the Great Depression. At one level, Roosevelt promised a free-market approach to economic growth: cut federal spending, reduce taxes, and lower the Smoot-Hawley tariff. He hit these three points frequently and no doubt won many votes because of that. In other speeches, however, he expressed his underconsumption views. On May 22, at Oglethorpe University in Atlanta, Roosevelt described low wages, insufficient purchasing power of consumers, and the need for government intervention "to inject life into our ailing economic order" and to create a "more equitable distribution of the national income."[11]

On July 2, Roosevelt came to Chicago to accept the Democrat

nomination for president. At this time, he outlined his economic views for the delegates. "Ours must be a party of liberal thought, of planned action," Roosevelt urged. He then asked the delegates to "look a little at the recent history and the simple economics" of the Great Depression.

> In the years before 1929 we know that this country had completed a vast cycle of building and inflation; for ten years we expanded on the theory of repairing the wastes of the War, but actually expanding far beyond that, and also beyond our natural and normal growth. Now it is worth remembering, and the cold figures of finance prove it, that during that time there was little or no drop in the prices that the consumer had to pay, although those same figures proved that the cost of production fell very greatly, corporate profit resulting from this period was enormous; at the same time little of that profit was devoted to the reduction of prices. The consumer was forgotten. Very little of it went into increased wages; the worker was forgotten.... [12]

These four sentences, which reflect underconsumption ideas, are riddled with errors. Inflation during the 1920s was low, not high, and the "cold figures of finance" show that employees received an increasing share of the corporate dollar, that corporate profits were constant, and that the prices of cars, radios, and other consumer and industrial goods were steadily falling, not rising. By 1929, therefore, most factory workers had an easier time buying what they produced than ever before. There is almost no accurate economic information in his analysis.

But from this analysis, Roosevelt concluded that government would have to step in to undo the damage from bad investment decisions by businessmen. About his specific program, he was somewhat vague, but in his acceptance speech he did describe a plan for public works, by which "employment can be given to a million men," a need for "aid to agriculture," and "when we get the chance, the federal government will assume bold leadership in distress relief." Also key to Roosevelt was redistributing the wealth that businessmen, with their "obeisance to Mammon," had so poorly handled.[13]

Some who heard this speech may have wondered where Roosevelt would get the money for his massive public works, his "aid to agriculture," and his "bold leadership in distress relief," among other promises. It may have been especially perplexing because Roosevelt, while he was promising a more active government, was also promising to cut government in size by 25 percent and to balance the budget in each year of his presidency.[14]

But how could Roosevelt expand federal programs and cut government and balance the budget at the same time? We are back again to Roosevelt's lack of economic training. It can't be done. Arthur Ballantine, who was undersecretary of the treasury under Herbert Hoover, knew Roosevelt well and was a classmate of his at Harvard. Ballantine must have squirmed when he heard Roosevelt's remarkable economic statements. He later said, "As I watched [Roosevelt's] extraordinary career, there were times when I wished that Franklin Roosevelt had managed to spend more time in college on some of our excellent instruction in economics and government."[15]

Ballantine's boss, President Hoover, did in fact challenge the contradictions in Roosevelt's economic program again and again. It would in no way balance the budget, Hoover fumed, but instead would "mean the enormous expansion of the Federal government" and the "growth of bureaucracy such as we have never seen in our history." The problem here is that Hoover was discredited with the voters. In his own acceptance speech four years earlier, he said, "In America today we are nearer a final triumph over poverty than in any land. . . . We shall, with the help of God, be in sight of the day when poverty will be banished from this nation." Hoover's sense of the timing was no more reliable than Roosevelt's sense of economics. But the latter was not clearly known and the former, with the Great Depression, stood open for public criticism.[16]

Furthermore, Hoover's response to the Great Depression was thoroughly repudiated. First, he supported and signed the Smoot-Hawley Tariff Act, which, as we have seen, was one of the causes of the Great Depression. Roosevelt, by contrast, attacked that tariff repeatedly in his campaign and on that point his economic understanding was better than Hoover's. Second, Hoover endorsed the Federal Farm Board, which placed the government perversely into the farm business. The Farm Board wasted $500 million subsidizing the price of wheat and cotton, and then dumped the surplus on an oversaturated world market. Third, Hoover supported the Reconstruction Finance Corporation (RFC), which spent over $1.5 billion on loans (or gifts) to failing banks and industries. But which of the many troubled banks and industries would win the government's help? Inevitably, the decisions were political, and those who were close to the Hoover administration were often first in line for taxpayer dollars.[17]

This last point needs emphasis: When Hoover used $1.5 billion of taxpayer money to pick winners and losers of special government loans, the process was quickly and inevitably politicized. Those with the right political connections found themselves at the head of the line. For example, the treasurer of the Republican National Committee received a loan of $14 million for his bank in Cleveland. In one of the worst cases, Charles Dawes, the head of the RFC (and a former Republican vice president) resigned from the RFC just in time to win a $90 million loan for his Chicago bank. Hoover's administration, therefore, was so mired in questionable economic decisions that it had no credible offensive against Roosevelt.[18]

On the campaign trail, then, Hoover, the incumbent, was the object of special scrutiny and Roosevelt was relatively free to present in some speeches his traditional ideas of cutting spending and in other speeches his underconsumption ideas for increasing spending. Roosevelt, especially in his underconsumption speeches, presented businessmen as villains and government as the hero in the story of the Great Depression. He peppered his speeches with attacks on businessmen: "5,000 men in effect control American industry," Roosevelt told a Boston audience, and "some of these 5,000 men who control industry are today invading the sacred political rights of those over whom they have economic power." [19]

Roosevelt correctly anticipated that Hoover would attack his underconsumption ideas as leading to increased government and massive spending. Roosevelt was thus vague on how he would implement his plans "of adjusting production to consumption." Also, to deflect criticism, he artfully promised to balance the budget; he then put Hoover on the defensive as heading the greatest peacetime spending administration in the history of the world—his four years in office were "the most reckless and extravagant past that I have been able to discover in the statistical record of any peacetime government anywhere, any time." [20]

Roosevelt never explained how he would cut "the cost of current federal government operations by 25 percent," which he promised in Pittsburgh, and reorganize industry, adjust wages, and redistribute wealth, which he pledged to do in San Francisco and Chicago. It was an impossible promise. Of course, he may also have been artfully playing politics, and knew full well he could not fulfill his promises. Louis Howe, Roosevelt's chief advisor for twenty years, helped put together many of his boss's speeches. In a speech of his own to a group of students, Howe confessed, "You can't adopt politics as a profession and remain honest." Howe reiterated, "If you are going to make your living out of politics, you can't do it honestly." [21]

Hoover was frustrated beyond measure with Roosevelt's campaign of contradictory promises. Hoover concluded that the real Roosevelt was not the budget balancer, but the government reorganizer. At Madison Square Garden on October 31, Hoover gave his clearest and hardest-hitting speech of the campaign. "This campaign," he said, "is more than a contest between two men. It is more than a contest between two parties. It is a contest between two philosophies of government." Hoover became more specific:

> In order that we may get at the philosophical background of the mind which proposed profound change in our American system and a new deal, I would call your attention to an address delivered by the Democratic candidate in San Francisco on September 23rd. . . . "Our task now is not the discovery of natural resources or necessarily the production of more goods, it is the sober, less dramatic business of administering the resources and plants already in hand . . . establishing markets for surplus production; of meeting the problem of underconsumption; distributing the wealth and products more equitably and adapting the economic organization to the service of the people."

Hoover continued, "If these measures, these promises . . . mean anything, they mean the enormous expansion of the Federal government; they mean the growth of bureaucracy such as we have never seen in our history." Hoover observed that such a growth in government would create incentives for congressmen to secure benefits for their constituents and pass the expenses on to the nation as a whole: "Our legislative bodies cannot delegate their authority to any dictator, but without such delegation every member of these bodies is impelled in representation of the interest of his constituents constantly to seek privilege and demand service in the use of such agencies." He concluded on a prophetic note: "This election is not a mere shift from the ins to the outs. It means deciding the direction our nation will take over a century to come."[22]

Hoover's problem was not the content of his speech, but the content of his presidency. He failed to ameliorate the Great Depression. He had signed the Smoot-Hawley Tariff Act while Roosevelt opposed it. Hoover wasted $500 million on a Farm Board that merely encouraged surpluses and then dumped them abroad; he spent three times more than that on loans to failing businesses, but the loans were often politicized and therefore discredited. Roosevelt may have had glaring contradictions in his promises, but Hoover had glaring failure in his policies. His critique of Roosevelt, therefore, did not carry weight. On election day, Roosevelt won in a landslide. He began a crucial presidency that would, in Hoover's words, decide "the direction our nation will take over a century to come."

On inauguration day, FDR displayed his charm, his sense of drama, and his inclination—as Hoover predicted—to use the powers of government, not cuts in spending and tax rates, to attack the Great Depression. "First of all," the new president announced, "let me assert my firm belief that the only thing we have to fear is fear itself. . . ." As an antidote to fear, Roosevelt said, "I shall ask Congress for broad executive power to wage a war against the emergency. . . ." During Roosevelt's first term, that broad executive power would be highlighted by nine letters: NRA, AAA, and WPA.

THE NRA:
WHY PRICE-FIXING DAMAGED AMERICAN BUSINESS

Let's start with the New Deal's effort to promote industrial recovery: the National Industrial Recovery Act (NIRA), which became law in 1933 and was soon shortened to NRA. Of that act, Roosevelt said, "History will probably record the National Industrial Recovery Act as the most important and far-reaching legislation ever enacted by the American Congress."[1] The president was right: the NRA was revolutionary. It allowed American industrialists to collaborate to set the prices of their products, and even the wages and hours that went into making them. Leaders in all industries, from steel and coal to shoulder pads and dog food, were invited to sit down together and write "codes of fair competition" that would be binding on all producers in their industry. Laborers were often allowed to organize, and antitrust laws were suspended.

America's traditional free market system, where businesses compete and innovate to sell products of varying price and quality to choosy customers, was overthrown. With the NRA, a majority in any industry had government approval and legal force to determine how much a factory could expand, what wages had to be paid, the number of hours to be worked, and the prices of all products within the industry. According to law, a businessman in that industry might or might not help write the code for his industry, but whether he did or not, he would be bound by the terms of the code and subject to a fine or jail term if he violated the code.[2]

Adam Smith in 1776 explicitly warned against such a price-fixing system and observed what would happen if it were to occur. "People of the same trade seldom meet together, even for merriment and diversion, but the conversation ends in a conspiracy against the public, or in some contrivance to raise prices." Smith went on to conclude, "But though the law cannot hinder people of the same trade from sometimes assembling together, it ought to do nothing to facilitate such assemblies; much less to render them necessary."[3]

Smith, then, would not have been surprised to hear the initial reaction of many businessmen to the arrival of the NRA. "Washington hotels rejoice and Cabinet members groan," wrote one observer, "over the wild rush of business men to the capital to find out about the new industrial plan. They want to know everything, but mostly how to punish the rascal who has been cutting prices in their industry, and how to fix some nice new prices." In other words, the more than 540 codes that were written into law had the strong tendency to raise prices, raise wages, reduce working hours, and remove competition—as well as innovation of industrial products.[4]

Why would Roosevelt and certain New Dealers be so eager to see higher wages and prices, without an increase in productivity, and with less competition? As part of their faith in the underconsumption theory, they believed that artificially higher wages meant greater purchasing power, which they believed would help Americans out of the Great Depression. If people earned more, they could buy more, and that would stimulate industrial and economic recovery. In this "high wage" theory, the efficient businessman, the innovator and price cutter, was evil because he was believed to contribute to lower wages and therefore diminishing purchasing power. He was a violator of "fair competition." His gain was not just the loss of his competitors, but of the whole country. The NRA, by encouraging codes of "fair competition," was giving all existing businesses a chance to make profits, to pay high wages, and to survive the price cutter and innovator. As Roosevelt said, the NRA "was passed *to put people back to work*, to let them buy more of the products of farms and factories and start our business at a living rate again." [5]

Hugh Johnson, the man Roosevelt put at the head of the NRA, called it a "Holy Thing . . . the Greatest Social Advance Since the Days of Jesus Christ." The fifty-one-year-old Johnson was a gruff West Point graduate who grew up on the Indian frontier of the Oklahoma Territory. He had experience in government during World War I working for Bernard Baruch and the War Industries Board. Nicknamed "the General" or "Old Iron Pants," Johnson was muscular and heavyset with a roundish face, a strong chin, and a full head of dark hair with occasional graying on the sides. Emotional and impetuous, Johnson had a strong temper. He was a boisterous, hard-drinking man with a cigarette on one side of his mouth and profanities often coming from the other side. "May God have mercy on the man or group of men," Johnson threatened, "who attempt to trifle with this bird." [6]

Like Roosevelt, Johnson failed in his business ventures during the 1920s. Their faith in the NRA was not based on the laws of economics, on knowledge of supply and demand, or on human nature. "I think industry can both run itself and govern itself," Johnson announced. Even economist John Maynard Keynes, who often advocated massive government intervention, disagreed with Johnson. The NRA "probably impedes recovery," Keynes wrote in the *New York Times*, and "has been put across too hastily." Economics professor Edward S. Mason of Harvard concluded, "The provisions for limitation of output and the raising of prices, if effective, can result only in the further curtailment of our already seriously reduced national income." What some laborers gain by being employed at high wages, others lose by not getting a job at all in a stagnant economy. If wages fell to their natural market level, more people could be hired and the products produced might expand its market share—which would then provide more jobs. What's more, as Edward Chamberlin, another Harvard economist, pointed out, "There is no doubt that the tendency to substitute machinery for labor is strengthened by artificially high wages. . . . A rate of wages which is too high may work positive injury to the class it is supposed to benefit."[7]

The whole NRA, by carving up markets among existing producers and by fixing prices and wages, assumed all industry was stagnant and unchanging. In fact, almost no industry fit that model. In steel, for example, when Andrew Carnegie founded what became Carnegie Steel, in 1872, he was the smallest producer in America—and England far outsold the United States in the world steel market. Rails were the main steel product, and the price of rails was about $56 a ton. In 1872, however, unlike in 1933, markets, prices, and wages were not fixed; they were fluid and the American customer was the winner. Carnegie, for example, cut costs by using the Bessemer process and open-hearth method of making steel; he innovated in accounting with double-entry bookkeeping; he was daring in sales by bidding for contracts and assuming that economies of large scale could help him fulfill contracts profitably. Unlike his competitors, if Carnegie found a cheaper way to make rails, he would rip out a factory and rebuild the improved version immediately. As a result, in 1900 Carnegie was the largest steel producer in the United States and larger than all the major steel producers in England put together. He could make steel rails for $11.50 per ton. Competition in price and product helped Carnegie and all consumers of steel.[8]

In 1901, Carnegie sold his company to help create United States Steel, a billion-dollar behemoth that controlled over 61 percent of the American steel market. U.S. Steel, however, without

Carnegie at the helm, was not innovative. Elbert Gary, the chairman of the board, had an NRA mentality: U.S. Steel was on top; let's keep things the same. "Prices should always be reasonable," Gary said. "What we want is stability." But what is a reasonable price for steel rails? It was $56 per ton in 1872, and less than half of that in 1900. Would the stability of 1872 have been good for Carnegie? Would it have been good for the users of steel anywhere in the world? Would it have been good for the United States, which came to dominate the world market for steel after 1872 through innovation and competition?[9]

In 1925, Gary said, in words that could have been spoken by Hugh Johnson ten years later, "We believe in competition, in vigorous, energetic, unyielding competition.... But we do not believe, or certainly most of us do not believe, in unfair, destructive, unrighteous competition, which is calculated to ruin the competitor. We believe ... that stability and just dealing are desirable and beneficial to all. . . ."[10] What Gary is saying is, "Let's compete, but let's not try too hard and let's make sure we keep prices high enough to give business to every steel company." If Carnegie had believed that, and if the United States had instituted an NRA in 1872, steel rails fifty years later would probably have been priced at over $50 per ton and England and Germany would have continued to be the dominant world producers of steel. Rail and trolley travel for all Americans would have been more expensive, and the millions of poor immigrants to America would have paid more for rail travel and had less for food and shelter.

Under Gary's philosophy, steel prices ceased to decline and innovation was almost halted. Finally, at Bethlehem Steel, under the management of Charles M. Schwab, real competition in steel began again around 1910. Schwab, with almost no support from the other contented steel producers, invested in structural steel to build bridges and skyscrapers. He innovated with the "Bethlehem beam," which allowed for the constructing of steel beams directly from an ingot as a single section, instead of riveting smaller beams together.

Schwab's astonishing success transformed the steel market. Structural steel became a popular product. The *New York Times* called Bethlehem Steel "possibly the most efficient, profitable, self-contained steel plant in the country." Officers at U.S. Steel, meanwhile, spoke of idle factories and a demoralized workforce. Its market share declined from 61.6 to 39.9 percent from 1901 to 1921. If only Gary could have had an NRA in 1901, U.S. Steel's domination would have been fully protected by law. Schwab, with a fixed market share assigned to him, would have had no incentive (and possibly no legal grounds) to risk his capital in the nascent structural steel market. American progress in structural steel would have been almost nonexistent; the United States would have had fewer bridges and skyscrapers or would eventually have had to import that steel from abroad, where no limit existed on output, innovation, and market share.[11]

Cheaper steel meant cheaper cars, and Henry Ford took advantage of that. He took the cheaper steel, and the increasing varieties of steel, and built an assembly line and began making Model Ts. Ford, by about 1920, had captured over one-half of the American car market and had cut the cost of a car from $3,000 to about $300. But General Motors, under competitive pressure from Ford, showed the ability to improve its own product. Chevrolet innovated with an ignition starter and a gas tank gauge. By 1928, Ford had abandoned the Model T and began working on the Model A, with a new and improved V-8 engine. Competition brought out the best in Ford and in William Durant at GM. American travelers were the winners.[12]

If we had had an NRA in 1905, we would have had higher-priced steel, no assembly line, and a small car market with few Americans able to afford the expensive vehicles built then by Buick, Oldsmobile, and Ford. If an NRA had been instituted in 1905, many in the transportation business would have been delighted—the makers of carriages and buggy whips would have attracted more capital; the makers of expensive Packards and Pierce-Arrow cars may have been able to stay in business; street cleaners, especially the ones who cleaned 1.3 million pounds of horse manure daily in New York City alone, all would have had protected jobs. These and others would have liked Johnson's call for "fair competition" to escape the price-cutting Ford, who was following a vision to put a car in every garage. But most Americans would have been poorer with their high-priced carriages and more expensive traveling. Beyond all that, Ford even innovated with high wages and massive increases in employment. In 1910, 140,000 people in the United States worked in the auto industry. By 1930, with better and cheaper cars, there were 380,000 doing so.[13]

The story of the dynamic nature of the steel and car industries shows three things. First, competition is necessary for new and cheaper products to appear on the market. Second, competition is also a sensible way to set prices and wages. Third, many businessmen want to avoid competition—to them "fair competition" is letting them set prices, wages, hours of work, and market share. Like Hugh Johnson, they will talk soothingly about the need for codes of fair competition to hold price cutters like Henry Ford in check. If that happens, innovation declines and customers pay more.

When the NRA went into effect in 1933, Senator William Borah (R-Idaho), who opposed the bill, received about nine thousand complaints from businessmen and entrepreneurs who were damaged by the law's restrictions. That was more letters than he received when he had fought the League of Nations almost fifteen years earlier. Reading some of these thousands of letters reveals the damage done to the American economy when it was strapped in the NRA straitjacket.[14]

The tire industry is a good place to start because it is closely linked with the steel and auto industries. When the major tire makers, Goodyear, Goodrich, and Firestone, got together and wrote the NRA tire code, the price of tires immediately soared. That meant, first of all, that the price of cars had to be raised. That hurt America's export market in cars and it also meant that fewer Americans could afford to pay the increased cost of a new car in the Great Depression days of 1933. Not surprisingly, American car sales continued to decline, and in 1933 were only one-third of what they were in 1929.[15]

But the problem of fixing high tire prices went further. Within the tire industry, high fixed prices meant that large companies could easily seize business from smaller producers. Larger companies, with national networks of stores, could promise buyers service for their tires almost anywhere in the nation. From these "great master stations," Goodyear, Firestone, and Goodrich advertised heavily and hired salesmen to publicize their companies and sell their tires nationwide.

Among those damaged was Carl Pharis, the general manager of Pharis Tire and Rubber Company in Newark, Ohio. Pharis employed over one thousand people, mainly in the Newark area. His company grew because, in Pharis's words, "we would make the best possible rubber tire and sell it at the lowest price consistent with a modest but safe profit." He and his employees had survived the grim Great Depression years because they had lower prices, a good tire, and solid support in central Ohio from buyers who knew the company because it was local and because it priced its tires lower than the larger firms. As Pharis said, "It is obvious that they cannot make as good a tire as we make and sell it at the price at which we can sell at a profit."[16]

Then came the NRA with its high fixed prices for tires. As Pharis said, "Since the industry began to formulate a Code under the N. R. A., in June, 1933, we have at all times opposed any form of price-fixing. We believe it to be illegal and we know it to be oppressive." He added, "We quite understand that, if we were compelled to sell our tires at exactly the same price as they sell their tires, their great national consumer acceptance would soon capture our purchasers and ruin us. Since we have so little of this consumer publicity when compared with them, our only hope is in our ability to make as good or a better tire than they make and to sell it at a less[er] price. . . ."

Since Pharis and other small companies were no longer allowed to sell tires at discounted rates, Goodyear and Firestone "could go out just as they have gone out," Pharis noted, "and say to prospective customers that, since they had to pay the same price, it would be wiser if they bought the nationally advertised lines."

In a nutshell, Pharis put it this way: "The Government deliberately raised our prices up towards the prices at which the big companies wanted to sell, at which they could make a profit, . . . where more easily, with much less loss, they could come down and 'get us' and where, bound by N. R. A. decrees, we could not use lower prices, although we could have lowered them and still made a decent profit."

Pharis was on the verge of closing down and having to lay off all of his one thousand employees. His company, with its low prices and quality tires, could weather the Great Depression, but not the NRA. "If we were asking favors from the Government," Pharis concluded, "there would be little justice in our complaints. . . . And so, if the big fellows, with their too-heavy investments and high costs of manufacturing and selling, cannot successfully compete with us little fellows without Government aid, they should quit."

Pharis was far from alone in objecting to higher selling prices for tires. Montgomery Ward, one of the country's largest retailers, reluctantly decided to obey the NRA code. In doing so, the company issued the following statement to customers in newspapers throughout the country:

> The NRA, through the Retail Tire Code, effective Monday, May 14, is requiring approximately twenty percent price increases on Ward's Rambler Tires. We would prefer to continue the low prices made by our economical method of selling tires. We regret that we cannot do so after the NRA order fixing these prices becomes effective next Monday.[17]

Other sellers wrote Borah with the same complaint—how could they stay in business if they were not allowed to sell more cheaply than the bigger companies? J. R. Isaacson of the Toledo Tire Corporation noted that fewer tires were being sold because fewer people could "afford to pay the code prices on new tires." Therefore, Isaacson noted, "since the price fixing code has gone into effect . . . there has been a very large demand for used and rebuilt tires." Such a trend, Isaacson concluded, was unprofitable and even unhealthy. "As a rule," Isaacson wrote Borah, "the man who is forced to buy used and rebuilt tires not only pays proportionately much more, for less service, but also jeopardizes himself, his family and the safety of others on our public highways." [18]

Sometimes a smaller tire seller would refuse to sign the NRA code, refuse to sell tires at such high prices. F. H. Mills, Jr., the president of Master Tire and Service, Inc., in Youngstown, Ohio, was one such businessman. When he did so, Frank Blodgett, an NRA administrator, came to Youngstown and visited Mr. Mills. "When I explained my conditions," Mills wrote, "and showed where it would be impossible to stay in business and comply with his request he demanded that he be given the right to go over my books and to run my business according to his ideas." Mills refused. "I have not signed the President's agreement for a blue eagle [the NRA symbol] and never will or any other code agreement. The furious Mr. Blodgett then stated that he would put his heel upon the neck of our little company and twist it with all the force at his command." [19]

Not all men who refused to sign the code could be easily intimidated. In the auto industry, Henry Ford refused to sign the NRA code and jack up his car prices, as his competitors were doing. "I do not think that this country is ready to be treated like Russia for a while," Ford wrote in his notebook. "There is a lot of the pioneer spirit here yet." However, General Motors, Chrysler, and the smaller independents eagerly signed Blue Eagle codes, which, under penalty of fine and imprisonment, regulated their production, wages, prices, and hours of work. Ford was astounded: his colleagues preferred stability and government regulation to competition and free trade. He was especially irked when Pierre S. DuPont, the former head of General Motors, urged him at a party to sign the code.[20]

In the face of strong pressure from the NRA, Ford refused to sign the auto code. He defied the law, pronouncing it un-American and unconstitutional. Hugh Johnson, the NRA chief, and President Roosevelt, however, wanted government control as well as compliance. They tried to pressure Ford into signing the code, and when he refused they tried force. Ford would receive no government contracts until he signed—and with the large increase in government agencies during the 1930s, that meant a huge business. For example, the bid of a Ford agency on five hundred trucks for the Civilian Conservation Corps was $169,000 below the next best offer. The government announced, however, that it would reject Ford's bid and pay $169,000 more for the trucks because Ford refused to sign the auto code. As Roosevelt announced at a press conference, "We have got to eliminate the purchase of Ford cars" for the government because Ford has not "gone along with the general [NRA] agreement."[21]

Ford's assertion of freedom and independence gave hope to those who wanted to return to competition. When Hugh Johnson was asked what would happen to those "who won't go along with the new code," Johnson threatened, "They'll get a sock in the nose."[22]

Although Johnson refrained from applying his fist to Ford's nose, he did use the arm of the law to jail many men who refused to jeopardize their businesses by complying with NRA codes. In York, Pennsylvania, for example, Fred Perkins manufactured and sold storage batteries for factories and lighting equipment for farms. He had for ten years built up a business in York, eventually hiring about twenty unskilled laborers, all of whom insisted he was an excellent boss and had paid them fairly. However, the wages Perkins paid were lower than the 40 cents per hour demanded by the NRA Battery Code wage scale. Perkins operated on a small profit margin and could not pay 40 cents per hour. Even paying lower wages, Perkins had to lay off almost half of his workers. Thus, when the NRA Battery Code became law, Perkins had the choice either to close his business, or pay his remaining employees less than 40 cents per hour and try to squeak out a profit. Perkins and his employees all preferred to remain in business with the lower wages. He, therefore, personally appealed to Hugh Johnson for an exemption, but did not receive one.

When NRA officials came to York and threatened Perkins, he refused to close his shop and also refused to raise wages. Within two months, Perkins was in the York County jail for violating the NRA code. Running his storage battery business from his jail cell, Perkins talked regularly with his secretary and his son to advise them on daily business decisions. His employees quickly defended him to reporters. J. B. Jones, for example, said, "We asked him for work and he gave it to us at a time when we were in distress. The wages he was paying were fair. . . ." Jones added that Mr. Perkins "was interested in our welfare outside the shop. Often he aided us when we had sickness in the family. When our creditors pressed us he came to our assistance." The letters and newspaper clippings on Perkins in the Borah Papers at the Library of Congress end on July 3, 1934, with Perkins still in jail.[23]

Others were jailed for giving discounts to customers. For example, Sam and Rose Markowitz, who operated the Community Dry Cleaners in Cleveland, were jailed, according to a newspaper article in Borah's file, "because they cleaned suits for 5 cents less than the NRA code provides." Initially, Judge George Baer fined the couple fifteen dollars each; then he sentenced them to jail for not paying the fine within three days.[24]

Many dry cleaners argued that offering discounts to customers was essential for survival. "Our plant is located some several blocks from the main part of town," explained R. W. Johnson, a dry cleaner in Meridian, Mississippi. "We have always maintained prices slightly lower than the larger, downtown cleaners, because of our more or less inconvenient location." The price-fixing requirements in the NRA code for the cleaners and dyers trade hurt Johnson's business. "Since . . . the establishment of minimum prices by the government, our business has steadily decreased . . . until, now, it is scarcely 35% of what it was before." [25]

A more dramatic jailing was that of forty-nine-year-old Jacob Maged of Jersey City, New Jersey. Maged had been pressing pants for twenty-two years and his low prices and quality work had kept him competitive with larger tailor shops in the better parts of town. The NRA Cleaners and Dyers Code demanded that 40 cents be charged to press a suit. Maged, despite repeated warnings, insisted on charging his customers only 35 cents. "You can't tell me how to run my business," Maged insisted. When threatened with jail, he said, "If you can send me to jail, go ahead." [26]

Not only was Maged thrown in jail, he was also slapped with a hundred-dollar fine. "We think that this is the only way to enforce the NRA," said Abraham Traube, a director of the NRA code authority for the Cleaners and Dyers Board of Trade. "If we did the same thing in New York City we would soon get the whole industry in line." Many editorialists, however, sided with Maged. "It didn't matter," the *Washington Post* said, "if Maged had to charge less than the bright and shiny tailor shop up the street if he wanted to continue to exist. The law said he couldn't." "For a parallel," the *New York Herald Tribune* said, "it is necessary to go to the Fascist or Communist states of Europe. . . ." [27]

No merchants wanted to pay fines or go to jail, but the more than five hundred NRA codes often imposed such quirky regulations that it was hard for many to comply. The officers of the Oneida Cedar & Lumber Company in Rhinelander, Wisconsin, noted, "Our large competitors planned and drafted their particular codes and are now administering [them]; naturally they fitted the Code regulations according to their business." What was especially galling to the Oneida company was the NRA's "official report forms," which, the officers complained, now "require[d] the listing of our customers' names. . . . It discloses what we small concerns consider as our trade secrets to our already powerful competitors."[28]

C. J. Gilbert, an investment securities analyst, complained that in the Code of Investment Bankers he could "not call on a person to sell securities without the written permission of that person. . . . There is also a [$500] fine in sending a letter to a prospective customer. . . ." "Are we," Gilbert asked, "during our lifetime, going to get back to a constitutional form of government? . . ."[29]

Armand Friedlander, a jeweler in Houston, was astonished to learn that under the Jewelry Code he "absolutely cannot advertise any prices on watch repairing." Five large jewelers in Houston, according to Friedlander, were working with Dick Golding, an NRA official, to clamp down on any discounts Mr. Friedlander and others were attempting to offer customers. "Today," Mr. Friedlander complained, "we received a bill to pay $6.00 or more for the Blue Eagle's cost of keeping up this office of Mr. Golding." Friedlander wanted to avoid the fate of Fred Perkins and Jacob Maged. "We have quit advertising prices because we feel we cannot allow ourselves to be dragged into courts," he said. Bakers, coal operators, lumbermen, vegetable sellers, all sorts of small businessmen wrote to Borah describing how the NRA was in the process of putting them out of business, or, in some cases, how it had already done so.[30]

Even data compiled by the NRA itself showed how dismally it failed to help the U.S. economy recover from the Great Depression. The Consumers' Advisory Board of the NRA reported huge price hikes, price fixing, regulation of output, and persecution of efficient businessmen—all to the disadvantage of consumers. The Research and Planning Division of the NRA noted that wages were up nationally, but that retail prices were up even more. Real wages in January 1935, they concluded, were actually below those of June 1933 when the NRA became law. The National Recovery Review Board, headed by lawyer Clarence Darrow, investigated a flood of complaints against the NRA. The committee had some internal disagreements, but their first report was highly critical of the NRA. Many codes, they observed, spurred "the exit of the small enterprises" and led to "the always growing autocracy of the greater" corporations. Yale economist Irving Fisher analyzed the impact of the NRA and told Roosevelt "the NRA has *retarded* recovery and especially [has] retarded re-employment."[31]

Roosevelt, despite the growing contempt for the NRA, remained supportive of the blue eagle. He did replace Hugh Johnson with lawyer Donald Richberg, but that move was designed to make the NRA more palatable to critics. Other cosmetic changes came as well—some businesses in small towns were allowed specific exemptions from NRA enforcement, and women could be paid less in some of the codes. But these changes simply raised new questions: Could businesses move to small towns to avoid code restrictions? Could men be fired and women be hired in their place to save costs on wages? The more tinkering that Roosevelt did with the NRA, the more complex and convoluted it became.[32]

The Schechter brothers, who sold kosher chickens in Brooklyn, provided the court case that finally overturned the NRA in May 1935. The Schechters were doing some of the same things that landed Fred Perkins, Rose Markowitz, Sam Markowitz, and Jacob Maged in jail. To avoid their fate, the Schechters hired an excellent legal team, headed by attorney Joseph Heller, to keep them out of jail and try to have the NRA declared unconstitutional. When their case came before the Supreme Court, NRA prosecutors alleged that the Schechters were paying wages below the code minimum, selling sick chickens, and allowing customers to choose the chicken they wanted to buy rather than demanding that customers select their chickens randomly from the coop.[33]

This last point was so astonishing to the justices of the Supreme Court that Joseph Heller had to clarify it repeatedly. Under the NRA code, he explained, "the customer is not permitted to select the ones [chickens] that he wants. He must put his hand in the coop when he buys from the slaughterhouse and take the first chicken that comes to hand. He has to take that." According to the transcript of the trial, that response produced a rarity—open laughter in the Supreme Court chamber. After more discussion, Justice George Sutherland elicited more guffaws when he asked, "Well, suppose, however, that all the chickens have gone over to one end of the coop?" After the laughter ceased, the justices met and voted 9–0 that the NRA was unconstitutional. After almost two years of massive promoting by President Roosevelt and thousands of hours of work writing millions of details into 546 codes— all of it was so patently unconstitutional in the Court's opinion that not even one of the nine justices would condone it.[34]

The defeat of the NRA was a cause for celebration. "The Constitution has been re-established," Senator Borah rejoiced. "Impulsively adopted without mature consideration," journalist Frank Kent said, "it [the NRA] was fastened on the people by the most blatant ballyhoo ever promoted by a Government, and it ends in a horrible mess." Many Democrat politicians seemed glad to be rid of the NRA albatross; reporters noted that the Supreme Court had removed a good campaign issue from the hands of Republicans.[35]

Four days after the Supreme Court verdict, Roosevelt defended the NRA and denounced the decision. He said the Court was taking the country backward with a "horse and buggy" interpretation of the Constitution's Commerce Clause, which gives Congress the power to regulate commerce. So attached was he to the industrial regimentation of the NRA that he promoted smaller versions of the law before Congress. For example, Roosevelt endorsed the Guffey-Snyder Act, which applied the NRA ideals to the coal industry. When that bill was considered by Congress, Roosevelt wrote the relevant House committee: "I hope your committee will not permit doubts as to constitutionality, however reasonable, to block the suggested legislation."[36]

When the Guffey bill passed, it was back to price fixing. For the coal industry, the prices to fix were so complicated—by different types of coal, different sizes of coal, and different destinations for the coal—that 350,000 prices for coal had to be fixed. Unfortunately, when that arduous labor was accomplished, the higher price of coal made oil, natural gas, and electricity increasingly popular as alternate sources for power and fuel. The coal industry thus stumbled into lower sales, further decline, and the specter of setting up a police state in Pennsylvania to regulate the buying and selling of coal.[37]

Roosevelt always believed that the NRA was an excellent idea and would have worked well had it not been for selfish businessmen, on one hand, who discredited some of the codes by greedy manipulation, and nitpicking lawyers on the other hand, who focused on occasionally flawed methods instead of the ideal results that might have been achieved. Five months before the *Schechter* decision, Roosevelt said, "There may be half a dozen more court decisions before they get the correct language and before they get things straightened out according to correct constitutional methods."[38]

Even after *Schechter*, Roosevelt would have liked to have reinstated the NRA (after bringing in some new Supreme Court justices). In fact, he envisioned "having an international cartel in different commodities," a type of worldwide NRA, in which Roosevelt himself would organize, systematize, and help resolve world problems. "Let me give you my big idea," as Roosevelt explained it to Henry Morgenthau, Jr. According to Morgenthau, Roosevelt

> pictures himself as being called in as a consultant of the various nations of the world. He said, "Maybe I can prescribe for their ailments or, after making a study of their illnesses, I will simply turn up my nose at them and say, 'I am sorry—I cannot treat them.' For example I would tell England that she had too many people and she should move out ten million of her population. I would take a look at each country and, of course, when we made them disarm we would have to find new work for the munition workers in each country and that is where this international cartel would come in and your job would be to handle the finances."[39]

5

THE AAA:
HOW IT HURT FARMING

The Agricultural Adjustment Act (AAA), which was Roosevelt's plan for farmers, also passed Congress in 1933 with expectations almost as high as those for the NRA. "I tell you frankly," Roosevelt said of the AAA, "that it is a new and untrod path. . . ."[1] During the president's busy first hundred days in office in 1933, that was his opening salvo in restructuring the whole American farm program.

The AAA was very complicated, but in a nutshell here is how it worked. First, some farmers would be paid not to produce on part of their land; second, farm prices would be pegged to the purchasing power of farm prices in 1910; third, millers and processors would pay for much of the cost of the program. What's more, power would be centralized through the secretary of agriculture, who would set the processing taxes, target the price of many commodities, and tell farmers how much land to remove.[2]

Why would Congress pass such a strange law in the first place? The origin was in the severe farm crisis after World War I: overproduction of crops and the low prices received for those crops. Of course, in a sense that was the perennial problem of the American farmer. In 1790, about 80 percent of Americans made their living as farmers. In the 1800s and 1900s, mechanization of crops (especially the major crops of wheat, corn, and cotton), improved seeds, and improved fertilizers meant that each farmer could feed more and more people. The economics of supply and demand typically worked against the farmer. The more he produced, the lower his price was, and, therefore, the more that farmers moved to the city and took up jobs there in the expanding factories and businesses.[3]

By the 1930s, urbanization was well under way. Only 30 percent of Americans made their living as farmers in 1933. But selling the farm and moving to the city—the traditional response to low prices and overproduction—did not happen in the 1930s, and for three reasons. First, because the Great Depression was nationwide, few businesses were expanding and few jobs, therefore, were available in the city. Second, the Smoot-Hawley tariff, the highest tariff in U.S. history, created retaliatory tariffs. Few Europeans were buying American farm exports and thus foreign markets—the traditional outlet for overproduction—were shut off. Third, both Hoover and Roosevelt were more willing to experiment with government solutions to farm problems, even though the Constitution made no provision for direct farm relief.[4]

The Federal Farm Board was Hoover's futile effort at intervention. He picked two major crops, wheat and cotton, both of which had strong political constituencies. He pegged the price of wheat at 80 cents/bushel and cotton at 20 cents/pound. Those were price floors, minimum prices. The government promised these prices for every bushel of wheat and every pound of cotton that American farmers produced. That way, two large groups of farmers would be protected from falling prices. Disaster quickly resulted. Wheat and cotton farmers, with prices guaranteed, expanded acreage and grew as much as possible. Farmers of other crops shifted to wheat and cotton, where their prices could then be guaranteed. Soon Hoover's

Farm Board was building grain elevators to store wheat, and warehouses to store surplus cotton. After about two years of wild overproduction, the government had spent the $500 million allocated to the Farm Board. They stopped the programs and gave away or sold at huge losses about 250 million bushels of wheat and 10 million bales of cotton.[5]

To many Americans, the Farm Board showed the damage created when government interfered with supply and demand. If more farmers would have moved to the city, which was an expanding job market before the 1930s, less would have been produced and prices would have risen for the more efficient farmers who remained on the farm. But few of the 30 percent of Americans who remained as farmers wanted to leave the land. The Farm Board gave them a precedent for government intervention and the high tariff gave them a reason to complain that others were getting help from the government. Why not farmers as well? Since farmers were a potentially strong political group in many states, politicians emerged to argue for more intervention. Hence Roosevelt and others made the case for the AAA, paying farmers not to produce. The AAA, as strange as the program sounds when it is explained, did satisfy two immediate problems. First, it curtailed production by paying farmers not to produce. Second, it raised farm prices by linking them to what they were in an earlier, more prosperous era.[6]

The concept of parity was invented by economists and farm leaders to rationalize using government to fix higher prices for them. Farm prices, of course, tend to go up or down depending on supply and demand. The farmers chose 1909–14, a period when farm prices were high. Their argument was that prices in the 1930s, and thereafter, should be pegged to the purchasing power of farm prices during 1909 to 1914. If, for example, the price of wheat averaged $1.00 per bushel from 1909 to 1914, and if the cost of living had doubled in the next twenty years, then wheat farmers should receive $2.00 per bushel in 1933. The government should guarantee it. That way, the farmer is protected from falling prices of farm products. His purchasing power is thus kept in "parity" with the prices of other industrial and consumer products.[7]

But if farmers should be protected by parity, why not everyone else? Some economists of the New Deal era asked that question. Henry Hazlitt, for example, looked at what would result if General Motors and Alcoa had parity.

> A Chevrolet six-cylinder touring car cost $2,150 in 1912; an incomparably improved six-cylinder Chevrolet sedan cost $907 in 1942; adjusted for "parity" on the same basis as farm products, however, it would have cost $3,270 in 1942. A pound of aluminum from 1909 to 1913 inclusive averaged 22.5 cents; its price early in 1946 was 14 cents; but at "parity" it would have cost, instead, 41 cents.[8]

One reason Chevys improved in both quality and price from 1912 to 1942 was that Billy Durant and Alfred P. Sloan—leaders at GM—did not have parity. They had to compete in the marketplace. They had to improve their cars, and did so with ignition starters, adjustable front seats, automatic engine temperature control, and hydraulic shock absorbers, for example, which helped them sell more cars than Henry Ford. They did not receive from the government a fixed price and a fixed market share; therefore, they did research, improved their Chevys, and sold more of them. American consumers, of course, were winners. And so were farmers, who also had the cheaper cars along with better tractors, chemical fertilizers, hybrid corn, and mechanical cotton pickers from the 1930s on. In the 1930s, for example, before serious development of hybrid corn, farmers produced about 26 bushels of corn per acre; thirty years later that figure was up to 84 bushels per acre. Other crops had similar improvements.[9]

Farming, like industry, is dynamic. Competition and improved efficiency and sometimes even price cuts make better, cheaper food, industrial products, and consumer goods increasingly available to

Americans. But American farmers in the 1930s under the first AAA (and the second AAA, which followed after the first was declared unconstitutional) were able to secure parity, or near parity, for farmers.

The second key ingredient in the AAA was paying farmers not to produce. Not all farmers were allowed to participate: only those in major crops and those crops with strong political support—wheat, corn, cotton, and hogs, for example. Different crops had different reductions in acreage; processors—for example, flour companies, textile companies, and meat companies—paid the tax to support these farm payments, and these cost increases were then passed along to consumers.[10]

When the AAA came before the Supreme Court in 1936, Justice Owen Roberts made the following parallel:

> Assume that too many shoes are being manufactured throughout the nation; that the market is saturated, the price depressed, the factories running half-time, the employees suffering. Upon the principle of the statute in question Congress might authorize the Secretary of Commerce to enter into contracts with shoe manufacturers providing that each shall reduce his output and that the United States will pay him a fixed sum proportioned to such reduction, the money to make the payments to be raised by a tax on all retail shoe dealers or their customers.[11]

That analogy is a thoughtful one. Roosevelt, however, endorsed the AAA, not just as an emergency program but as the basis for full-time government control of farming. He wanted parity, and payments not to produce, to be a permanent part of American farm policy. In October 1935, Roosevelt announced: "But it never was the idea of the men who framed the [Agricultural Adjustment] Act, of those in Congress who revised it, or of Henry Wallace or [AAA director] Chester Davis that the Agricultural Adjustment Administration should be either a mere emergency operation or a static agency. It was their intention—as it is mine—to pass from the purely emergency phases necessitated by a grave national crisis to a long-time, more permanent plan for American agriculture."[12]

The AAA, as it operated in practice, was fluid and sometimes hard to describe. Much discretionary power was centralized in the secretary of agriculture, and the specifics—parity prices, which crops to subsidize, how much acreage to set aside—could vary from crop to crop. These were issues that the secretary of agriculture strongly influenced. Henry Wallace, Roosevelt's man for that job, made sure the bill was written that way. Wallace later wrote: "To make provision for flexibility in the bill; to give the Secretary of Agriculture power to make contracts to reduce acreage with millions of individuals, and power to make marketing agreements with processors and distributors; to transfer to the Secretary, even if temporarily, the power to levy processing taxes; to express in legislation the concept of parity—all these points, and a thousand others, were unorthodox and difficult to express even by men skilled in the law."[13]

What this meant was a huge expansion in the Department of Agriculture. More bureaucrats were needed to determine which crops needed to be reduced, how much reduction should be made, what should be the parity payment for each crop, and what should be the processing tax for the flour millers and textile companies. Beyond this, the department of agriculture used the 3,000 county agents and hired about 100,000 men from farming counties (at three and four dollars per day) all over America to help enforce and determine the correct acreage each farmer would be allowed to set aside for cash. Under the AAA, farmers could refuse to be paid not to plant, but most farmers found it more profitable to farm taxpayers, not their soil. The 110,500 county committee men employed by Agricultural Adjustment Administration collected information on local farmers and tried to keep them honest.[14]

In 1933, for example, a wheat farmer could remove 40 of his 200 acres from cultivation and be paid about $10 an acre not to produce on that land. He was not allowed to plant—secretly or overtly—on any of the 40 acres he had set aside. However, he could pick his worst 40 acres to set aside—even land he normally didn't plant on. Also, he could use his government subsidy to buy fertilizer to improve his yield on the land he did cultivate. In fact, the huge increase in the sale of fertilizer in 1933 and 1934 reveals that many farmers did that—which, of course, forced those federal bureaucrats to recalculate the set-asides for various crops based on ever-increasing yields per acre. The supervising and regulating of millions and millions of farmers so expanded the Department of Agriculture that it became, with the possible exception of the Post Office (and later the Defense Department), the largest employer in the federal government.[15]

H. V. Kaltenborn, a national radio commentator and an admirer of Henry Wallace, described how he visited Wallace and "saw the size and scope of the bureaucratic machinery set up under the new Agricultural Adjustment Act." According to Kaltenborn:

The amount of regulatory machinery essential to administer A. A. A. was a fearsome thing to behold for anyone who believed in the American farmer as master of his own domain. Thousands of inspectors had to be sent into the fields. Thousands of accountants had to keep track of what each inspector reported about, what each farmer was growing, and what benefits every grower or nongrower was entitled to receive. As soon as the A. A. A. helped one group of farmers, other groups were affected and called for similar benefits and protective regulations. If one particular crop was controlled, the farmer would plant excessively in other crops. If acreage was controlled he would use only his best acres. That produced a new surplus, which also had to be controlled. Farmers were paid millions of dollars *not* to produce crops while President Roosevelt was telling us that one third of our people were ill fed. For every problem that was solved two or three new problems were created.[16]

How well did Wallace and his army of bureaucrats do in their regimentation of production, their efforts to coordinate supply and demand on a national scale? They compiled mountains of data on many crops, acres in production, average yield per farm, world production, prices of crops, and so on. Yet their performance, as the chart below shows, was a disaster. With millions of acres out of production, American farmers had underproduced in many crops in 1935. The United States had, for almost the first time in its national history, become a major food-importing nation. In 1933, the U.S. was plowing under 10 million acres of cotton and killing 6 million piglets; in 1935, the U.S. was importing 36 million (bales) of cotton and 2 million pounds of ham and bacon. We were also importing other basic commodities—butter, corn, and even wheat.

What went wrong?[17]

Food Imports into the United States

	1934	1935
Beef and veal (lbs)	138,283	7,684,637
Ham, bacon (lbs)	626,148	2,846,005
Butter (lbs)	535,144	21,948,458
Corn (bu)	816,694	34,809,120
Wheat (bu)	3,330,188	13,446,009
Raw cotton (lbs)	7,328,084	36,353,324

Source: Frank Kent, *Without Grease: Political Behavior, 1934–1936* (New York: William Morrow and Co., 1936), 250.

The bureaucrats in the Department of Agriculture were quick to blame the weather, especially a drought in part of the Midwest, for their inaccurate crop projections. But their projections were inaccurate even in areas without weather problems. In any case, varying weather is always a problem in farming, and it is one of many variables that make it almost impossible to pinpoint accurately what prices are reasonable and how much land should be reduced in any given year. Farming is a dynamic and fluctuating enterprise. Paying farmers not to produce, as we have seen, gave many an incentive to use fertilizers to increase their yields. Other farmers refused to be "bought off" by government and used all of their land for production. But other farmers saw the low prices in the crops subsidized by the government and shifted to other crops. More farmers were buying tractors; others were experimenting with hybrid corn; others abandoned their farms. World overproduction of some crops and underproduction of others also affected prices and made it hard for the department to anticipate which crops would be in demand. By the late 1930s, many of these crops imported were again being overproduced.[18]

Much of what Wallace had dealt with as secretary of agriculture was the unintended consequence of government control of farming. When politicians decided to manipulate the price of food, the farmers gained, the consumers lost. The price of food and clothes increased in the years after the AAA became law. With Americans still deep in the Great Depression, that meant many impoverished Americans had to go hungry and wear tattered pants and shirts. With fewer shirts, steaks, and loaves of bread being sold, that meant textile companies, meatpackers, and millers had to lay off workers—which led to more unemployment. With the demand down, say, for shirts, then future cotton purchases were down as well—and the bureaucrats at the Agriculture Department would have to revise the acreage that should be planted for cotton. Those calculations were flawed, and by 1937 the government had in storage enough cotton to supply the nation even if no one grew cotton in 1938.[19]

With cotton in strong supply, the Department of Agriculture worked to reduce the acreage planted to cotton. In international terms, that meant a decline in the American market share of cotton. Before the AAA, the United States had about a 60 percent world market share of cotton. With the steady reduction in cotton acreage, Brazil, among other countries, increased its share. In

1933–34 alone, Brazil more than doubled its land planted in cotton from 1.3 to over 2.6 million acres.

Another unintended consequence of the AAA was the massive eviction of tenants from southern cotton plantations. When cotton growers were being paid to remove as much as 40 percent of their land from cultivation, they set aside their worst acreage and expelled the tenant farmers, who were often farming that less desirable land. Wallace and others did not want these evictions to happen, and according to AAA rules, tenants were supposed to share somewhat in the federal largesse; but hundreds of thousands of tenant farmers were, in fact, thrown off the land into unemployment.[20]

As the tenant farmers left the southern countryside, Roosevelt began to tinker with federal programs to relocate them, along with farmers on marginal lands, into special urban settlements elsewhere. Very few of these new model communities were actually under way in 1935 when they were consolidated into the Resettlement Administration (RA), headed by the undersecretary of agriculture, Rexford Tugwell. Tugwell, a Columbia University professor, was popular with Roosevelt and was a member of his Brains Trust. The youthful, curly-haired Tugwell was excited about creating planned societies for those in need. "If one arm of the Department, [the] Triple-A, worked for the advantaged element in the farm population" Tugwell argued, "it was the Department's responsibility equally to advance effective programs to improve the lot of the disadvantaged."[21]

The visionary Tugwell was skeptical of capitalism and even the ownership of private property. "I personally have long been convinced that the outright ownership of farms ought to be greatly restricted," Tugwell explained.[22] "My own view," Tugwell added, is "that under intelligent state control it should be possible to introduce a planned flexibility into the congestion and rigidity of our outdated economic system."[23] Tugwell was anxious to head the RA and begin his experiment in planned societies. With a staff of

13,000 and a mammoth $250 million to spend, Tugwell made plans for resettling thousands of tenants and marginal farmers into new model communities.

The result was a disaster. "It was all done awkwardly and wastefully," Tugwell later confessed about the work of the RA. Even Roosevelt himself conceded, "I don't think we have a leg to stand on," when confronted with the high costs of the model towns Tugwell was building. Drawing model communities on paper was one thing, but it was another thing to relocate real tenant farmers into affordable houses far away in real towns with functioning services. One of Tugwell's model communities was Arthurdale in West Virginia. A major problem there was that the ready-made houses could not fit their foundations. Once that problem was solved, the planners discovered that most residents, people from poor backgrounds, could not afford to live there. That protest became a common one in model communities all over the nation. Finding meaningful and profitable work for unskilled laborers was another recurring complaint.[24]

What that meant was that sometimes the RA had communities built, but no residents either willing or able to move in. An example of this was Ak-Sar-Ben (Nebraska spelled backward), a "dream city" of thirty-eight green-shuttered houses, each on seven acres of land twenty miles west of Omaha on the Platte River. The problem was that no one wanted to move in. Ak-Sar-Ben became deserted. Nearby farmer Henry C. Glissman observed this project and drew this conclusion: "I predict that in time these homes will all be abandoned and stand as a gruesome monument to a government's inefficiency and folly in fostering a movement that to a practical mind has the earmarks of failure from the start."[25]

Another venture, Project No. 32, was the transplanting of two hundred families in Alaska at a cost estimate of $5 million. Some critics faulted the choice of location because the 117 families already living there were struggling to earn a living. Moving two hundred new families into the area, without knowing whether their skills fit the environment, proved to be a leap of faith. Rex Beach, an expert on Alaska, saw Project No. 32 unfold and decided to research and write about it. After watching the new families struggle, Beach predicted that three-fourths of them would soon abandon the area. "No wonder," Beach wrote, "Alaskans speak with contempt of these new-fangled schemes for 'social betterment' and 'rural rehabilitation.'" To illustrate his point, Beach quoted an Alaskan observer, who said, "The whole project is socially and economically unsound. It was conceived in ignorance and has been ludicrously mishandled."[26]

Most of the other model towns did not do much better; FDR, under a barrage of complaints, muzzled Tugwell during the 1936 presidential election, accepted his resignation from the RA shortly after the election, and merged the controversial RA into the newly created Farm Security Administration in 1937. But Roosevelt continued to invite Tugwell's ideas, and the president "on many occasions" told financier Bernard Baruch, "You know Rex wants me to do over night what it is going to take years for me to do."[27]

One of Tugwell's most persistent critics was Senator Harry Byrd of Virginia. The origin and development of their dispute is illuminating. Byrd came from an old Virginia family, which had fallen on hard times by the early 1900s. In 1902, at age fifteen, Byrd quit school to take over his father's failing newspaper, the *Winchester Evening Star*. Byrd worked long days to get the paper out of debt, but he learned good business techniques while doing so: "A good many days we were a little late in getting the paper out because I had to scour the town scraping up the six dollars to get the newsprint out of hock." But Byrd made the paper profitable, and at age nineteen, he leased an apple orchard and made it profitable as well. During the next two decades he began buying apple orchards and marketing hundreds of thousands of bushels of apples. He became one of the foremost American authorities on apples, and under his leadership Virginia began to rival the state of Washington as the country's leading apple-producing state.[28]

Growing apples was a risky business and in many years Byrd took losses. Early frosts, hot summers, hail, and insects all conspired to turn apple growers' dreams into nightmares. Byrd experimented with sprays, heaters (for the frosts), scientific farming, and the largest cold storage facility in the nation. Cold storage allowed Byrd to control temperature and oxygen in such a way to preserve his apples and allow him to market them at the best times. Byrd always paid competitive wages because he needed conscientious workers to pick the apples carefully, package them properly, and grade them for market accurately.[29]

The Great Depression almost ruined Byrd's business. For example, by 1930 he was exporting 75 percent of his crop, especially to Britain and Germany. But international retaliation from the Smoot-Hawley tariff closed many of Byrd's markets and forced him to sell domestically. Americans preferred redder and sweeter apples, and Byrd had to alter his growing strategy to cater to strictly American tastes. Also, in August 1934, a swirling storm destroyed three-fourths of his crop in one of his major orchards. Yet he refused to exploit New Deal programs. He did take a loan from the RFC, but he passed up almost $200,000 in federal subsidies for his apples. "I should dislike very much to see any apples in which I have any interest whatever sold to the government," Byrd said. But to stay profitable, Byrd found himself paying some of his employees in kind—and taking losses in some years anyway. He had paid apple pickers $2.50 per day in the 1920s, but in 1933 and 1934, when hard times and bad weather wrecked his orchards, he had to cut wages to $1.00 for a ten-hour day.[30]

When Tugwell came to Virginia competing for labor with his various resettlement experiments, Byrd was annoyed. Tugwell could afford to pay more because he had a $250 million budget and never had to show a profit. Tugwell's whole background and mindset differed from Byrd's. Byrd went to work at age fifteen to learn business and thereby put food on the table. Tugwell went to college, and from there to graduate school, a Ph.D., and a career in the classroom. Byrd earned tens of thousands of dollars on good years, but lost money in years when locusts, mice, frosts, or hail beat him to his apples. Tugwell had a desk job in Washington, where he could dine with the president and spend tax dollars in ways he helped choose. If he tired of that, or if criticism from Byrd and his cohorts began to prevail, Tugwell, according to Harold L. Ickes, Roosevelt's secretary of the interior, had a guaranteed job as a professor waiting for him at Columbia University that paid a steady and reliable $9,000 per year—a salary that put him in the top 3 percent of American wage earners.[31]

The two men did not understand each other. Tugwell was skeptical of private property; Byrd had transformed his private property into orchards that grew millions of apples annually. Tugwell said that "profits persuade us to speculate," and that "profits must be limited and their uses controlled." Byrd wanted to earn profits selling his apples, and in doing so to make the Shenandoah Valley the most prosperous apple market in the nation. Byrd also wanted to pay competitive wages, and improve the quality, texture, and taste of American apples; Tugwell wanted to pay above-market wages, and experiment with new modes of production. No wonder Byrd voted against confirming Tugwell as undersecretary of agriculture: "He had no proper conception of the principles of this government," Byrd observed. As for the Resettlement Administration, it was "a permanent monument to waste and extravagance such as has never been known in a civilized country." Byrd demanded that Henry Wallace end the unprofitable RA and quit hiring his laborers away with high wages for losing enterprises.[32]

Tugwell went to Roosevelt for protection and comfort from Byrd and his fellow critics in the Senate who were trying to cut the RA budget and discredit Tugwell publicly for his experimental communities. The president had his own grievances against Senator Byrd, a Democrat, for opposing so many New Deal programs. Roosevelt's response was interesting. He told Tugwell, "I know what's the matter with Harry Byrd. He's afraid you'll force him to pay more than ten cents an hour for his apple pickers." That comment was relayed to columnist Drew Pearson, who published it and put Byrd on the defensive. Since then, historians have cited and used it either to support Tugwell or to show Roosevelt's compassion for the poor.[33]

How should we analyze Roosevelt's well-publicized criticism of Byrd? First, Roosevelt's statement carries with it an ethical imperative—Byrd "ought to pay more" to his apple growers. Byrd could have responded to this by saying, "I was paying a lot more to my apple pickers, $2.50 a day in fact, until a government program, the Smoot-Hawley tariff, destroyed my export market and forced me to market different kinds of apples for the smaller group of American consumers. Now another government program, the Resettlement Administration, comes to my community and draws off some of my best apple pickers into a program that runs large losses with taxpayer dollars." If the removal of apple pickers had ever caused Byrd to show losses, the government would have lost his income tax revenue, which of course helped run the New Deal programs.

That point is a serious one. The Great Depression, and the high tariff that followed, closed off sales to Byrd. On top of that, storms or hail severely damaged Byrd's apple production in both 1930 and 1934. He was desperately trying to earn enough to keep his business from collapsing during these years. Unlike Tugwell, Byrd had no federal subsidy with which to pay high wages, and if he had done so with his own meager to nonexistent profits, the resulting red ink on his business ledgers might have forced him to sell some of his orchards, or possibly even go out of business. If that had happened then the whole apple economy of the Shenandoah Valley could have been in jeopardy of shutdowns and massive unemployment. Who in Virginia would then have earned the profits to generate the tax dollars to keep Roosevelt's New Deal programs going?

Roosevelt's moral judgment about the wages Byrd paid clearly put the Virginia senator on the defensive. But how did the president spend his own money? Roosevelt, too, ran a farm at Hyde Park, but unlike Byrd, Roosevelt's farm lost money every year—and he even deducted his losses on his income tax. Those deductions gave the government less revenue to operate the many federal programs the president supported.

Another point of interest is that when Roosevelt was spending his own money, he was sometimes very stingy. For example, when Roosevelt traveled by train from Washington to Hyde Park, he always wanted a private car for himself and his staff. Servicing this private car, which might include providing dozens of meals, newspapers, and various amenities for the president and his staff, would require great diligence and attention to detail. But for round-trip service on Roosevelt's private car, he tipped the porter a mere five dollars. The reporters, on their car nearby, combined to tip eight to ten times more than the president did. Walter Trohan of the *Chicago Tribune* observed the unhappiness this created:

> FDR wasn't a heavy tipper at any time, but was less so aboard trains. He gave five dollars to the porter on his car for the round trip from Washington to Hyde Park, which included payment for what guests he might have in his car. In the press car we each gave two dollars for the trip, but there were about twenty of us all told. Sam [Mitchell, the porter] soon begged off the private car; the honor of serving the President faded for a man raising a family and sending a boy to college as well as paying for a home, when he could count on forty dollars in the press car as against five dollars in the private car.[34]

If Senator Byrd had been mischievous, he could have supported a minimum wage law to mandate that porters be paid twenty dollars for private car service on each round trip from Washington to Hyde Park. He could have paraphrased the president and told the press, "Roosevelt is afraid the Senate will force him to pay his porters more than five dollars for their service."

RELIEF AND THE WPA:
DID THEY REALLY HELP THE UNEMPLOYED?

As the Great Depression worsened, unemployment skyrocketed, and many began to ask, "How will the jobless get enough food to eat? What should be done about relief?"

Throughout American history, right from the start, charity had been a state and local function. Civic leaders, local clergy, and private citizens evaluated the legitimacy of people's need in their communities or counties; churches and other organizations could then provide food, shelter, and clothing to help victims of fires or women abandoned by drunken husbands. Most Americans believed that the face-to-face encounters of givers and receivers of charity benefited both groups. It created just the right amount of uplift and relief, and discouraged laziness and a poor work ethic.[1]

The Founders all saw relief as local and voluntary, and the Constitution gave no federal role for the government in providing charity. James Madison, in defending the Constitution, observed, "No man is allowed to be a judge in his own cause, because his interest would certainly bias his judgment and, not improbably, corrupt his integrity." In other words, if relief, and other areas, were made functions of the federal government, the process would become politicized and politicians and deadbeats could conspire to trade votes for food. As Madison asked, "What are the different classes of legislators but advocates and parties to the causes which they determine?"[2]

In the 1800s, voluntary organizations such as the Red Cross and the Salvation Army were formed to give food, shelter, clothing, and spiritual help to individuals and groups that faced crises. Sometimes, of course, Congress was tempted to play politics with relief. In 1887, for example, several counties in Texas faced a long drought and some farmers lost their crops. Texas politicians helped cajole Congress into granting $10,000 worth of free seeds for these distressed farmers in Texas. After the bill passed the Senate and House, President Grover Cleveland vetoed it. "I can find no warrant for such an appropriation in the Constitution," Cleveland said. Such aid would "destroy the partitions between proper subjects of Federal and local care and regulation." He added, "Federal aid, in such cases, encourages the expectations of paternal care on the part of the Government and weakens the sturdiness of our national character." As for Texas, Cleveland noted, "the friendliness and charity of our countrymen can always be relied upon to relieve their fellow citizens in misfortune."[3]

Cleveland was prophetic. Voluntary contributions flowed into Texas from all over the nation, finally exceeding $100,000, more than ten times the amount Congress had tried to take from the taxpayers.[4] The Founders' view of charity, which was not always consistently applied, was vindicated by Cleveland's veto and the nation's generosity.

The constitutional view of relief that Cleveland upheld was strongly challenged during the Great Depression. Unemployment under Hoover soared to three, then six, then over ten million people. How would they get food for themselves and their families? Roosevelt, and even Hoover to a lesser extent, argued that the constitutional tradition needed breaking: use federal tax dollars to feed the poor. Hoover resisted at first. For one thing, if people wanted to deviate from the Constitution, then don't just ignore it. Campaign for a constitutional amendment. Of course, Hoover did not grasp at the time the damage caused by the Smoot-Hawley Tariff Act and the high interest rates at the Federal Reserve. Changes in those areas might have sparked more investment, more foreign trade, and more job creation. In any case, Hoover was not inclined to tinker with the tariff or the Federal Reserve Board. Instead, he was heartened by the impressive work of private charities in handling the overwhelming number of requests for help. As late as the fall of 1931, and even into 1932, Americans raised over $100 million for charity, especially relief, through community chest drives, benefit performances by movie theater owners, and exhibition games by sports teams.[5]

Finally, by the summer of 1932, the pressure on Congress and President Hoover to federalize relief became overwhelming. Many states opposed this move; even under strains, they were capably providing local relief. Many charities, such as the Red Cross, had long opposed federal intervention in feeding the poor. They correctly perceived that if government relief occurred, sources of support for private charities would dry up. Rich Americans, for example, such as Oscar Mayer in Chicago and Will Kellogg in Michigan, had been personally active in feeding the hungry, but Hoover and Congress in 1932 sharply hiked the income tax; therefore, these men, and others like them, were able to retain less cash to distribute food to hungry Americans. With almost 16 million unemployed in the summer of 1932, the political sentiment to federalize relief became overpowering, and Congress and the president decided to break America's long tradition of private relief.[6]

The law that brought the federal government into the relief business was the Emergency Relief and Construction Act of 1932 (ERA). Under this act, Congress made $300 million available to states whose governors and public officials requested help. Technically, this money was to be a loan, but most believed, as Senator Robert Wagner of New York predicted, "that the repayment would never take place, so that in effect, that $300,000,000, if we look at it realistically, was a gift to the states."[7] Most governors seem to have accepted Senator Wagner's public invitation: they began a frantic scramble, as suggested in Table 1, to get as much of the $300 million as they could.

TABLE 1.

Listing of Those Eight States Receiving the Most Money and Those Eight States Receiving the Least Money under the Emergency Relief and Construction Act of 1932, as Amended

State	Amount Received, August 4, 1932, to August 11, 1933
Illinois	$55,443,721
Pennsylvania	34,929,875
New York	26,600,000
Michigan	21,808,199
Ohio	19,257,205
Wisconsin	12,395,362
California	10,081,631
West Virginia	9,655,218
Maine	252,895
Maryland	176,380
Massachusetts	0
Connecticut	0
Vermont	0
Delaware	0
Nebraska	0
Wyoming	0

Sources: Edward A. Williams, *Federal Aid for Relief* (New York: Columbia University Press, 1939), 50–51; Josephine C. Brown, *Public Relief, 1929–1939* (New York: Octagon Books, 1971 [1940]), 125–34.

Granted, some states had more people and greater problems than other states. But the formula of allowing states to request funds if they would submit evidence of needs invited abuse. All states had high unemployment and all governors could show ample evidence of many thousands of ill-fed citizens. Many governors, therefore, rushed to claim as much cash as they could. Every federal dollar they could get was a dollar the state government, or its private citizens, did not have to raise out of their own pockets. That helps explain the frequent imbalance between the population of a state and the amount of federal aid it received.

The most flagrant example of abuse in federal relief was Illinois, which was able to secure over $55 million—or almost 20 percent—of the entire $300 million. That figure, as seen in Table 1, was more than twice as many tax dollars as New York, the most populous state, received; in fact, Illinois's sum was more than the combined amount received by over half of the states in the union; it even contradicted a rule set up under the Emergency Relief and Construction Act that prohibited any one state from grabbing more than 15 percent of the total pot. But when the act became law, the officials in Illinois seized their opportunities quickly. They manipulated a change in the rules and captured the most money.[8]

Interestingly, Massachusetts, a state almost comparable to Illinois in population, neither asked for nor received any of the federal money. Boston and many other parts of the state had serious need for relief, but Governor Joseph Ely and other state officials still believed that relief should be a local and state function. They constantly worked to raise local money for local needs. A statewide unemployment drive, for example, raised over $3 million. The Boston Civic Symphony repeatedly gave concerts to benefit the jobless. Boston College and Holy Cross played an exhibition football game for charity in 1931. A benefit wrestling match at the Boston Garden supplied $5,000 for local needs. City officials helped Mayor James M. Curley of Boston raise a remarkable $2.5 million from city employees; even the city's schoolteachers donated 2 percent of their salaries for six months in 1931 to feed the poor. Historian Charles Trout, who studied Boston's amazing efforts to meet local needs, wrote that "no major city assisted so high a percentage of its jobless" as Boston did in the early 1930s.[9]

Five other states, mostly in New England, joined Massachusetts. They raised money locally and took none of the $300 million offered under the emergency act. In effect, what that meant was that Massachusetts not only paid for all of its own relief, but for part of Illinois's as well. That is a critical point. The $300 million was largely raised by taxes on businesses and personal income, and by excises on cars, cigarettes, and movie tickets. Most adults in Massachusetts were forced to contribute some of this federal tax revenue, but many also paid local and state taxes to feed the unemployed in Massachusetts. They were thus taxed twice. In effect, then, the federalizing of relief shifted funds from the frugal and thrifty states like Massachusetts, Nebraska, and Maryland, to the inefficient and manipulative states like Illinois, Pennsylvania, and West Virginia.[10]

The next year, President Roosevelt continued federal relief. He signed bills that sharply increased funding available to states. Almost all governors and many mayors again began lobbying to receive large chunks from Roosevelt's new Federal Emergency Relief Administration (FERA).[11]

This historic shift to using federal dollars for local relief profoundly changed the American work ethic. Before the Hoover-Roosevelt presidencies, state and city leaders had incentives to be frugal with charities. They took care of their own, and in emergencies they sometimes received assistance from national charities such as the Red Cross or the Salvation Army. During the New Deal years, states had new incentives to look to Washington to solve their relief needs. In fact, they had incentives to do a poor job raising local funds, and then exaggerate their needs. That way they could secure more cash for their states, and disperse the costs of raising the taxes to cover these funds to other states.

These new political realities were not lost on Massachusetts politicians. Governor Ely, who asked for no federal funds in 1932, was replaced in 1934 by Curley, who eagerly pleaded tales of woe to Washington to bring federal money to Massachusetts. By 1935, Massachusetts had solicited and received over $114 million in federal funds for relief.[12]

Under the Emergency Relief and Construction Act of 1932, rules were broken that allowed Illinois to capture almost 20 percent of all available funds. In the FERA, created in 1933 from the Federal Emergency Relief Act, key rules were also broken. States were supposed to provide matching funds to receive federal money. But Harry Hopkins, director of FERA, had discretionary power to allow some governors to supply little or no matching state money. Again there were incentives for governors to exaggerate needs and downplay their ability to supply matching money. Such a system tended to make liars out of everyone involved. Governors and mayors would shed abundant tears telling Hopkins and Roosevelt of their financial hardships; Hopkins and Roosevelt then listened and pretended to dispense FERA money solely on the basis of need, not on political considerations.[13]

Professors Jim Couch and William Shughart studied New Deal relief in detail and concluded that poor states often had to contribute more state funding for their relief than did richer states. Tennessee, for example, had to contribute 33 percent of its total funding for relief, but richer Pennsylvania only had to supply 10 percent of its total funding. The key political point here is that Tennessee, as part of the solid South, was a safe Democrat state. Pennsylvania, however, went for Hoover in 1932, and Roosevelt wanted to lure it into the Democrat fold in 1936. Joseph Ely, the former governor of Massachusetts, watched this new trend with dismay. "Whatever the justification for relief," Ely said, "the fact remains that the way in which it has been used makes it the greatest political asset on the practical side of party politics ever held by any administration."[14]

Another problem with federal relief was that it encouraged those who could not find work to give up trying. Relief was no longer received from local charities, where local officials could be hands-on in assessing real need. Relief came now from Washington, and if some people abused the system, it cost local citizens very little to let it continue. Governor Ely was sad to see such a change of attitude, even in his state of Massachusetts. "To be on relief for a few months was a boon to be extended by a great government to a patient people. But to be told that you are to be on relief for the rest of your days . . . is to destroy the hope and, therefore, the morale of the people." He observed that "millions of men and women . . . have come to believe almost that there is no hope for them except upon a government pay roll."[15]

Roosevelt, who observed these unintended consequences of relief, was embarrassed and, to his credit, took action. In his 1935 State of the Union address, he said, "The lessons of history, confirmed by the evidence immediately before me, show conclusively that continued dependence upon relief induces a spiritual and moral disintegration fundamentally destructive to the national fiber. To dole out relief in this way is to administer a narcotic, a subtle destroyer of the human spirit. It is inimical to the dictates of a sound policy."

Roosevelt's solution was to promote work relief. In 1935, therefore, he dropped FERA and reformulated relief under the Works Progress Administration (WPA), which would emphasize working for relief, not just receiving direct aid. Some work relief was started under FERA, and the related Civilian Works Administration (CWA), but much more would continue under the new WPA. Under the WPA, Roosevelt wanted to encourage those on relief to work on newly created government jobs "to preserve . . . their self-respect, their self reliance and courage and determination." The WPA was funded under the Emergency Relief Appropriation Act of 1935, which dispensed over $4.8 billion, the largest appropriation of its kind in U.S. history.[16]

The switch from direct relief (FERA) to work relief (WPA)

would seem to be an advance. After all, doing a job brings dignity, purpose, and a sense of improving the world around you. However, many WPA jobs were make-work projects that accomplished little. Critics called the WPA "We Piddle Around" and the word *boondoggle* was often applied to WPA projects. Defenders of the WPA point to the many roads built, the 2,500 hospitals, the 5,900 school buildings, and the 1,000 airports (or landing strips) as part of a strong legacy for the program. Some of these projects were well done and the construction was completed in an efficient manner. That is a valid point. Other projects merely duplicated existing facilities and were so poorly constructed they had to be rebuilt almost immediately.[17]

Of the make-work projects, reporter Frank Kent of the *Baltimore Sun* studied the WPA in action and wrote, "Boondoggling on a gigantic scale is about to begin. Millions are to be spent giving piano lessons to the children of those on relief. Millions more will pay 7,000 men to write a guide book of America. A disgusted Congressman was here the other day telling of discovering seven men in an automobile going around his district counting caterpillars."[18]

Economist Henry Hazlitt, who wrote for *Newsweek* and the *New York Times* during the 1930s, argued that the WPA destroyed as many jobs as it created. "Every dollar of government spending must be raised through a dollar of taxation," Hazlitt emphasized. If the WPA builds a $10 million bridge, for example, "the bridge has to be paid for out of taxes. . . . Therefore," Hazlitt observed, "for every public job created by the bridge project a private job has been destroyed somewhere else. We can see the men employed on the bridge. We can watch them at work. The employment argument of the government spenders becomes vivid, and probably for most people convincing. But there are other things that we do not see, because, alas, they have never been permitted to come into existence. They are the jobs destroyed by the $10 million taken from the taxpayers. All that has happened, at best, is that there has been a *diversion* of jobs because of the project."[19]

Hazlitt had an interesting point. In 1931, the year before federal relief, the United States had a top tax rate of 24 percent and a starting rate, after exemptions, of 0.5 percent. In 1935 and 1936, the WPA spent billions of dollars on bridges, roads, airports, and school buildings, but the new tax rate, after exemptions, started at 5 percent and skyrocketed to 79 percent on top incomes. The country also saw a host of new excise taxes passed in the interim. That tax money could have been invested in the very projects (or maybe better ones) than the WPA was undertaking.[20]

If the capital for jobs was merely being diverted from the pockets of taxpayers to the staff at the WPA, then one might ask, why start the WPA? Here again, Hazlitt is helpful. "The government spenders have the better of the argument with all those who cannot see beyond the immediate range of their physical eyes. They can see the bridge. But if they have taught themselves to look for indirect as well as direct consequences they can once more see in the eye of imagination the possibilities that have never been allowed to come into existence. They can see the unbuilt homes, the unmade cars and washing machines, the unmade dresses and coats, perhaps the ungrown and unsold foodstuffs." These homes, cars, and washing machines were unbuilt, of course, because taxpayers sent their money to Washington for the WPA rather than buying their families a new car or a new coat. "We can think of these nonexistent objects once, perhaps, but we cannot keep them before our minds as we can the bridge that we pass every working day. What has happened is merely that one thing has been created instead of others."[21]

The inefficiency and uselessness of many WPA projects was a serious problem, but a greater problem was the increased politicization of relief under the WPA. In the new rules, President Roosevelt was allowed much discretion in allocating and distributing this WPA money. He would have a strong voice in choosing particular projects, and determining which states would receive what. The first problem with this approach is that it made relief a game of political manipulation. The problems that plagued the

FERA would sharply increase under WPA because more money was at stake. Governors worried that their states would not get their "fair share" of federal tax booty, and so they came to Washington, hats in hand, to curry favor with Roosevelt, Harry Hopkins, who became the WPA director, and other New Deal administrators. Frank Kent watched this corrupt process firsthand, and viewed it as almost inevitable. "Every city and state needs its portion of this incredibly great sum," Kent observed. "They all want as much as they can get. Failure to secure its proportion places a state at great disadvantage. It means heavier local taxation. . . ." Thus mayors and governors "are obliged to woo Mr. Roosevelt. They must have the money and he has it to give. . . ."[22]

Although Roosevelt and Hopkins said they would not use WPA and other relief organizations to play politics, the evidence suggests again and again that that is exactly what they allowed to happen. In private, Hopkins would sometimes present his proposals for WPA spending in blatantly political terms. At a luncheon with key Democrat leaders, for example, on April 12, 1938, Hopkins suggested a renewed public works program. According to Treasury Secretary Henry Morgenthau, who was present, Hopkins "previously in outlining the spending program had stressed its political advantages. . . . The issue of whether hungry people ought to be fed was one which everybody would understand and it would have its effects in the fall elections."[23]

Some Democrats were more politically calculating with WPA funds than others. V. G. Coplen, the Democrat county chairman of Indiana, explained his opinion clearly: "What I think will help is to change the WPA management from top to bottom. Put men in there who are . . . in favor of using these Democratic projects to make votes for the Democratic Party." James Doherty, a New Hampshire Democrat, agreed. "It is my personal belief that to the victor belongs the spoils and that Democrats should be holding most of these [WPA] positions so that we might strengthen our fences for the 1940 election." Governor Arthur Seligman of New

Mexico established a common pattern for relief right from the start when he systematically recorded the political affiliation of all applicants for federal relief and CCC work in New Mexico.[24]

Not all governors were as cunning as Seligman, but the evidence indicates that politics often was the key variable in distributing WPA jobs. Gavin Wright, an economic historian, did a state-by-state analysis of New Deal spending. He noted that safe Democrat states, especially those in the South, received fewer WPA dollars than richer battleground states in the North and West. Since southern states had more poverty than northern states, that meant that WPA jobs often went to the states that needed them the least.[25]

An example of this shift of WPA funds from poorer to richer states is in the wages paid from North to South. The WPA hourly pay scale for skilled workers ranged from 31 cents an hour in Alabama, Kentucky, Tennessee, and Virginia, to $2.25 an hour in New Jersey. New Jersey, unlike those southern states, was a swing state, and Mayor Frank Hague of Jersey City had been the key for Roosevelt narrowly carrying the state in 1932. As president, therefore, Roosevelt allowed all WPA jobs in New Jersey to be cleared through Hague. According to Lyle Dorsett, who has studied the Hague machine in detail, "Concrete evidence shows that from the outset of the New Deal, Frank Hague was in complete control of all patronage in the state." And Roosevelt poured patronage into New Jersey in the form of massive public works (Hague owned a construction company), which included almost 100,000 WPA jobs annually during the 1930s and the highest rate of pay in the nation for these skilled jobs. One minor drawback to the high pay was that WPA workers in New Jersey had to "tithe" 3 percent of their salaries to the Democrat Party at election time. One WPA director in New Jersey—a corrupt but candid man—answered his office phone, "Democratic headquarters!"[26]

Hopkins received mail regularly from people all over the nation who were denied federal jobs, or fired from them, because of their political views. Many of these letters are available in files for each state and housed in the National Archives. The title of these files is "WPA—Political Coercion." The hefty New Jersey file is very illuminating. One WPA worker complained about a mass-mailed postcard he received that stated, "You are either on the WPA or employed in some government department and by virtue thereof you owe a duty to the [Democrat] Party to do your part in making the canvass. Failure to do your active share will be reported to our county chairman, and you may find your position in jeopardy." [27]

Others made similar complaints. Robert Hall, a WPA worker in Camden, wrote, "Mr. Hopkins, I wish to thank you for giving me the job. A party asked me to donate two dollars toward election campaign, so I am asking your advice if this would be lawful." [28] Clinton Hoffman in Audubon, New Jersey, wrote, "WPA workers are forced to pay from $2.00 (for labor[er]s) and $50.00 (for foremen) to carry on the Democratic campaign." [29] A similar complaint occurred in Clementon, New Jersey: "At Atco they collected two dollars from the WPA workers for the campaign," observed Mrs. William F. Reid. "The WPA [workers] had to vote for him (Freeholder Emil McCall) or lose their jobs." [30] Alicia Medilo of Elizabeth, New Jersey, observed, "For the last 3 months, all peepul [sic] wanting work are told to go to Democrat headquarters no matter what your politics are; 3 big shots talk to you and tell you what you must vote to be put on relief or to get a job." [31] No wonder that freshman congressman Frank Towey of New Jersey announced at a Democrat rally in Newark, "In this county there are 18,000 on WPA. With an average of 3 in a family you have 54,000 potential Democratic votes. Can anyone beat that if it is properly mobilized?" [32]

Republicans in New Jersey were out of luck. Sadie M. Kearney wrote Hopkins, "The papers quote you as saying, 'There are no politics in the W. P. A.' We most certainly disagree with you. . . ." Her Republican father was turned down for work at the WPA in New Jersey, "but it seems he is on the wrong side of the fence: 'A Republican.' Even a Democrat time keeper in the Paterson City Hall said, 'He won't get any thing because he's a Republican.' "[33]

Not every state was as corrupt as New Jersey, but many were, especially those battleground states that were the key to future Democrat victories. In Pennsylvania, for example, journalist Lorena Hickok investigated the first years when relief was federalized. She reported, "Our chief trouble in Pennsylvania is due to politics. From the township to Harrisburg, the state is honeycombed with politicians all fighting for the privilege of distributing patronage." No wonder Governor Ely of Massachusetts observed that "relief agencies" had become "glorified political machines."[34]

In the scramble to win federal tax dollars, the New England states seem to have been the slowest to join the rush. Massachusetts, for example, in spite of Governor Ely, began to receive some federal relief in 1933, but waited until he stepped down in 1934 before rushing requests to Washington. "I have never asked the federal administration for anything," Ely said, but his successor, James M. Curley, was barely in office before he bombarded President Roosevelt with a request for relief of $600 million—more than FERA had given to any other state. The president did grant Curley a smaller amount, and by June 1935, 20 percent of the people of Massachusetts were on relief.[35]

In Connecticut, Governor Wilbur Cross, like Ely next door, accepted no dollars for relief under the original 1932 appropriation. Once Cross saw the new political system under the New Deal, however, he decided to pursue federal dollars. "I recall the excitement occasioned by the first federal grant" from Harry Hopkins for $858,526 in relief, he confessed. "This was but the beginning of monthly grants. . . ." Once the federal faucet had been turned on, Cross decided to increase the flow and run again for governor.[36]

Republicans, however, challenged Cross and the new system of relief. They argued against "the use within Connecticut of Federal funds to purchase a surrender of the rights reserved to this state."

Cross defended the new federal system vigorously. "Am I to understand," he said, "that if you Republicans come into power you intend to dam up this flow of Federal funds and to start a flow of your own by an enormous increase in state and local taxation? . . ." Then Cross, who was a former professor of literature at Yale, became as Dostoyevsky's Grand Inquisitor: "Have you considered," he asked, "that the citizens of Connecticut are paying Federal income taxes which nearly match the grants and loans of the national government? In the long run it will be an even break, whether or not you like the manner of it."[37] Given the large slice of revenue that went to support the mushrooming bureaucracy in Washington, D.C., Cross was optimistic to assume that Connecticut—or any other state—could break even.

In Massachusetts, Governor Ely could not play the new political game; in Connecticut Governor Cross decided he could—and once he got started he discovered that he could play it very skillfully. His treasure hunt included WPA funds for small local projects and the Public Works Administration (PWA) for larger, more expensive highways, bridges, and skyscrapers. Perhaps Connecticut really could break even with the federal government. Cross later wrote a book in which he openly boasted that "during 1938 Federal grants came with a rush. In April, WPA funds amounting to $1,341,000 were received." Then in July he "negotiat[ed] with Washington for $9 million more in PWA funds." That federal torrent, he boasted, allowed him to more than double the money Connecticut would be able to spend on state building programs. What's more, the governor also reported that he had won a "special grant" from Washington of $3 million to build a bridge and two parkways, one of which "was to bear my name." His political tenure as governor extended through four elections and began to rival his earlier academic tenure as professor.[38]

Governor Cross had a remarkable political odyssey. In 1932, he stood with Governor Ely. Massachusetts and Connecticut were two of the six states that asked for and received no federal aid for relief. To save money in Connecticut, in fact, Governor Cross cut his own salary 14 percent, and he tried to get the state legislators to do the same with theirs. He spent his days glumly searching his state budget for expenses to trim and jobs to cut. By 1938, however, he was merrily guiding a parade of federal grants into his state, and having one of the highways through which they would come named after him. Most other politicians approached the WPA more or less like Governor Cross.[39]

One of the very few who did not was Oklahoma senator Thomas Gore, who was first elected to the Senate in 1907, the year Oklahoma became a state. Gore had a populist streak in him, but he always recognized the protections to individual liberty that came from limited government. In the 1930s, therefore, he strongly opposed the federal government going into the relief business. Interestingly, Gore was made totally blind by two childhood accidents. He still managed to become a lawyer, and as a senator, he had to have family members or staff assistants read bills, books, and newspapers to him. Yet he claimed to see clearly through the political chicanery that would occur if the federal government entered the relief business. No depression, Gore argued, "can be ended by gifts, gratuities, doles, and alms handed out by the Federal Treasury, and extorted from taxpayers that are bleeding at every pore." On the issue of relief, especially, Gore argued that state and city officials "have immediate contact" with hardship cases and can best "superintend the dispensation of charity." Soon after the ERA brought federal relief into existence, Gore said, "The day on which we began to make these loans by the Federal Government to States, counties, and cities was a more evil day in the history of the Republic than the day on which the Confederacy fired upon Fort Sumter."[40]

In 1935, Gore helped lead the charge in Congress against funding the WPA with $4.8 billion. After he spoke against the bill, thousands of people in southeast Oklahoma held a mass meeting to denounce Gore. They sent him a telegram demanding that he cast his vote for the WPA and, by implication, start bringing more federal dollars into Oklahoma. Gore responded with a telegram of his own. Your action, he wrote, "shows how the dole spoils the soul. Your telegram intimates that your votes are for sale. Much as I value votes I am not in the market. I cannot consent to buy votes with the people's money. I owe a debt to the taxpayer as well as to the unemployed." Shortly after dictating these words, the blind Senator was led to the Senate floor to cast a lonely vote against the WPA.[41]

The thousands of protestors had their revenge against Gore on election day. The next year, when Gore tried to win renomination from the Democrat Party, he not only lost, he came in a distant fourth in the primary. Of the top two finishers, one campaigned on the slogan "Bring the New Deal to Oklahoma," and the other's slogan was "A Farm for Every Farmer and a Home for Every Family." Gore would never again win election to political office in Oklahoma. His career was over.[42]

That political development was not lost on Oklahoma's other senator, Elmer Thomas. He was up for reelection in 1938, two years later, and he loudly endorsed the WPA. In fact, during his campaign, right before the primary, the state's WPA workers received a large wage increase. Senator Thomas took credit for the pay hike, which was apparently part of a common pattern in New Deal politics. Economist Gavin Wright, who carefully studied WPA spending state by state, concluded, "WPA employment reached peaks in the fall of election years. In states like Florida and Kentucky—where the New Deal's big fight was in the primary elections—the rise of WPA employment was hurried along in order to synchronize with the primaries." When Thomas took credit for the large pay raise, his opponents bombarded him with criticism. Much to Thomas's delight, President Roosevelt came to Oklahoma to endorse Thomas. Unlike Gore, Thomas not only won the primary but won easy reelection in November as well.[43] The tale of two senators, Gore and Thomas, is a story of how the WPA changed American politics.

7

MORE PUBLIC PROGRAMS THAT FELL SHORT:
THE AIR MAIL ACT, FERA CAMPS, AND TVA

Capitalism had failed, in Roosevelt's view of the world, and that opened the door for new experiments in government ownership and government direction of the economy. Private enterprise would become public enterprise. For example, the delivery of air mail, the employment of veterans, and the building of dams and the creating of electric power were new areas for federal control under FDR. Two of these new government enterprises, unfortunately, had death rates.

DEATH BY AIR MAIL

Air mail service began in 1918, and the first such flights were made by the U.S. Army Air Corps. Private airlines, however, were improving so rapidly that soon after 1918 the government bid out contracts to major airlines to deliver the U.S. mail. By 1930, with almost all airlines losing money, Postmaster General Walter Brown decided to award a few large airlines most of the mail routes. That decision was contrary to the law, which mandated competitive bids from the airlines. Brown, however, did not believe that some of the low bidders, especially the former crop dusters, could safely, efficiently, and profitably deliver the mail. No airline could make a profit on passenger traffic alone, and Brown preferred to see three to five experienced airlines deliver the mail safely and show profits rather than having dozens of companies with varying experience and aircraft providing uneven service over the twenty-seven federal air mail routes. For example, some of the interested airlines had no experience with night flying and had no equipment to navigate through fog and rain.[1]

Brown may have been wrong in his approach. Perhaps the air mail system should even have been privatized. The existing system of large federal contracts and self-seeking companies was an invitation to collusion and possible fraud. As long as the Post Office Department was federally operated, however, Brown decided to scrap the competitive bids and give most of the air mail business to the largest companies with the best-trained pilots and the fewest accidents.[2]

In 1933, with Roosevelt elected president, Senator Hugo Black of Alabama launched a Senate investigation of the whole federal air mail business. In testimony, he discovered the absence of competitive bids, evidence of bribery, and the large subsidies given to the major airlines. Black urged Roosevelt to cancel the mail contracts and reopen them for competitive bids.[3]

Roosevelt became so enthusiastic for action that he wanted to cancel the contracts right away and, until new bids could be taken, let the U.S. Army Air Corps fly the mail. However, James Farley, the postmaster general, wanted to wait a few months and transfer the contracts directly to the new companies that won the bidding. Roosevelt prevailed. To pursue his request, one of Farley's assistants called Benjamin Foulois, the head of the Army Air Corps, who gave his opinion that he thought his fliers could do a capable job delivering the mail. According to Farley, "the President favored giving the service [the Army] an opportunity to distinguish itself." On February 9, 1934, Roosevelt publicly announced that all air mail contracts would be annulled in ten days; the U.S. Army Air Corps would fly the mail for several months until new bids could be taken.[4]

At one level, Roosevelt's canceling of the mail contracts was odd. These airlines had, in effect, done what the president was encouraging all business to do under the NRA: organize, set standards, set prices, and raise wages. Under the NRA, Roosevelt had restricted business competition and made legal the very thing he was condemning the airlines for doing.

As we have seen, when Firestone and Goodyear, for example, set high tire prices, they prevented Carl Pharis of Newark, Ohio, from securing business by charging customers less. When the tailors wrote into their NRA code a rate of 40 cents for pressing pants, they prevailed, and Jacob Maged of New York City went to jail for charging eager customers a nickel less.

But when the large airlines set standards for technical competence and pilot training—and then set high rates for their mail delivery service—Roosevelt denounced them, rescinded their contracts, and turned mail delivery over to pilots with much less training. If the airlines had been clever enough in 1933 to anticipate Roosevelt's attack, they could perhaps have written an NRA code for mail delivery that would have protected themselves—and ultimately saved many lives. Instead, the major carriers with the mail contracts had to furlough many employees and try to reduce their sudden loss of business.

Even without the comparison with the NRA, Roosevelt was vulnerable on two charges: he voided legally binding contracts, and he was risking the lives of the Army pilots. On the first point, the popular aviator Charles Lindbergh, who was employed by TWA, denounced Roosevelt for breech of contract "without just trial."

The *Magazine of Wall Street* concurred and asked this question: "if private industry is to be thus summarily punished without even a fair hearing, what industry can confidently enter into contracts with its Government?" On the second point, veteran pilot Eddie Rickenbacker predicted disaster for the less qualified Army pilots. To reporters in New York, Rickenbacker said, "The thing that bothers me is what is going to happen to these young Army pilots on a [foggy winter] day like this. Their ships are not equipped with blind-flying instruments. . . ."[5]

Rickenbacker did not wait long to be proven a prophet. On the first day the Army carried the mail, three pilots were killed in two separate crashes. One plane hit a mountain in Utah and another crashed in Idaho after encountering fog. "That's legalized murder," Rickenbacker told inquisitive reporters.

But Roosevelt persisted in his program. Crashes occurred almost daily, and at the end of the Army's first week of flying, six pilots had been killed, five severely injured, and eight planes had been destroyed. Roosevelt began feeling the sting of public rebuke, but he persisted and ordered the Army to make fewer flights in the harsh winter weather.[6]

Rickenbacker was so angry that he went on NBC Radio to denounce the continuing Army flights. But as he prepared to deliver a second radio address, he received a phone call from William B. Miller of NBC, who said "orders had come from Washington to cut me off the air if I said anything controversial." Thus Rickenbacker was held somewhat in check. Lindbergh had also been complaining, but he was partly negated by Stephen Early, Roosevelt's press secretary, who accused Lindbergh of merely seeking publicity when he criticized the president.[7]

Meanwhile Benjamin Lipsner, superintendent of the Aerial Mail Service, had been trying to contact the president. On March 8, he finally did so and pleaded with him to "stop those air mail deaths." Roosevelt did agree to limit Army air mail service, but the next day four more Army pilots crashed and were killed.

As the criticism of the president increased, Roosevelt wrote Harvard professor Felix Frankfurter: "The scattered forces of the opposition seized on the loss of life among the Army fliers to come together and make a concerted drive. For the last three weeks we have been under very heavy bombardment." He complained that "the aviation companies have been shrieking to high heaven, using Chambers of Commerce and every small community with a flying field to demand the return of their contracts."[8]

After twelve deaths, Roosevelt decided he had had enough. He called in the airlines to negotiate: Roosevelt was suffering politically and the airlines were suffering financially. They struck a deal to turn their mutual suffering into recovery. Under the Air Mail Act of 1934, FDR returned the air mail business to them and in turn they agreed to more competitive bidding, new rules on maximum loads, and the separating of authority of the manufacturers of airplanes from those who flew them as a business. The airlines also had to change their names because Roosevelt insisted that no company doing business under the old contracts could have new business. Thus Eastern Air Transport became Eastern Air Lines, and United Aircraft and Transport became United Air Lines. Lindbergh called Roosevelt's solution "reminiscent of something to be found in Alice in Wonderland." Eddie Rickenbacker, who became president of Eastern Air Lines, said, "As it stands today, Eastern Air Lines is held up by government subsidy. I believe it can become a free-enterprise industry, and I will pledge all my efforts and energies to making it self-sufficient."[9]

DEATH BY PUBLIC WORKS

Twelve Army pilots were not the only fatalities from New Deal projects. At least 256 military veterans died in FERA camps in the Florida Keys, where they were sent in hurricane season with poor provisions and no plan of retreat or rescue.

The hurricane tragedy had its origin in a seemingly shrewd political decision by FDR. Unemployed veterans had been difficult to deal with. Ever since World War I, they had campaigned in Congress for a special "bonus" for their service. In 1924, they secured an agreement from Congress to pay a bonus to war veterans in twenty-one years. The veterans, however, wanted their money much sooner. In 1932, they put pressure on President Hoover by traveling to Washington, camping near the White House, and publicizing their demands for immediate payment for their wartime service. In a political blunder, Hoover decided to restore order among the rowdy veterans by sending Douglas MacArthur to confront them with cavalry, infantry, and six tanks. MacArthur decided to fire on them and disperse their camp—and photos blanketed the country showing the fleeing vets under fire from their own government. It was an election year, and when Roosevelt, then the Democrat candidate, saw the pictures and news reports he reportedly told Felix Frankfurter, "Well, Felix, this will elect me."[10]

Once in office, Roosevelt was determined not to repeat Hoover's mistake. Protesting veterans were not allowed to camp in Washington, D.C. They were directed to Fort Hunt, Virginia, where they received offers to work in Civilian Conservation Corps (CCC) and FERA camps for a dollar a day plus food and shelter. Thousands of veterans accepted this offer and Roosevelt sent them far away from Washington to camps in South Carolina and Florida. In December 1934, over four hundred veterans were specifically transferred to the Florida Keys, where they were told to build bridges and roads that would help connect the ninety-mile chain of islands from Miami to Key West.

Roosevelt's plan to export the contentious vets to Florida was clever, but Harry Hopkins and FERA officials in Washington tended to ignore the veterans once they were out of the capital. In Florida, Fred Ghent, the director in charge of the three camps of four hundred veterans, had trouble first in getting supplies for the camps and second in enlisting help preparing for hurricanes. On the first point, the veterans were housed on lowland, almost at sea level, in tents and flimsy barracks with poor food, inadequate supplies, and no water for bathing. On the second point, they were given no serious shelter to protect them from a hurricane, or even high tides.

In April, three months before hurricane season, Ghent became concerned about the possibility of hurricanes. He wrote FERA in Washington that "this area is subject to hurricanes" and "it is our duty . . . to furnish a safe refuge during a storm."[11] Specifically, he requested the building of a solid, two-story warehouse and also the making of arrangements with the Florida East Coast Railway to transport the men out of the Keys if a hurricane warning should occur. Ghent never received a response from Washington, and in the absence of instructions, he took no action.

Trouble began in late August with weather reports of possible hurricanes coming toward Florida. On Sunday, September 1, at 10:00 A.M., a weather bulletin reached Key West warning of hurricane danger. Residents of Key West, twenty miles west of the camps, boarded their houses. The owner of the Hotel Matecumbe, who was within one mile of the veterans' camps, boarded his hotel as well. Ghent was in Miami. On Monday, September 2, he finally sent the Florida East Coast Railway to the veterans' camps. The railroad was in receivership, and many crewmen were not available because it was a holiday weekend. That day a severe hurricane hit the Keys and knocked the train off the tracks before it ever reached the FERA camps.

When the full force of the hurricane hit the veterans' camps, the carnage began. Firsthand accounts among the few survivors reveal part of the horror: "There was a big wall of water—15 feet high—20, maybe," reported one veteran. "It swept over those shacks and messed them up like they were match boxes." Another reported, "I heard William Clark holler that the roof [of the canteen] was coming down. We all started away in the same direction and the roof came down on us. It must have hit every one of us. After the roof fell all I could hear was the grunting and groaning of the boys. I never saw any of them after that." After hours of the swirling hurricane, one survivor said, "bodies were lying all over the roadway and lumber piled on them and some of them had holes in their heads." In the aftermath one survivor said, "I saw bodies with tree stumps smashed through their chests—heads blown off—twisted arms and legs torn off by flying timber that cut like big knives." When the body parts were finally reassembled, the total count was 256 veterans dead. As *Time* magazine reported, "it was slaughter worse than war." [12]

When the news of the deadly hurricane reached Washington, many newspapers began criticizing the president and FERA. Harry Hopkins, the FERA chief, denied responsibility. "I don't think anyone reading the weather reports—and I have been reading them—would necessarily have evacuated these people." Hopkins's assistant, Aubrey Williams, called the tragedy an "act of God." The *Washington Post*, however, disagreed. "In spite of Relief Administrator Hopkins' denial that his organization was negligent in failing to evacuate the veterans on the Florida Keys, there is considerable evidence to support Governor [David] Sholtz's conclusion that 'gross carelessness somewhere' was responsible." D. W. Kennamer, whom the Veterans Administration assigned to investigate the deaths, concluded that "the only extenuating circumstance" for the failure to evacuate the veterans was Mr. Ghent's regret "that his letters to the National Emergency Relief Administration in Washington regarding this matter were unanswered." [13]

In the search for responsibility, novelist Ernest Hemingway wrote an essay, "Who Murdered the Vets?" He asked, "Who sent nearly a thousand war veterans . . . to live in frame shacks on the Florida Keys in hurricane months?" He also asked, "Why were the men not evacuated on Sunday, or, at latest, Monday morning, when . . . evacuation was their only possible protection?" Neither President Roosevelt, Harry Hopkins, nor any other federal official answered these questions. [14]

TVA

The greatest public works project of the 1930s was the Tennessee Valley Authority. The TVA consisted of a series of dams and hydroelectric plants that provided cheap electricity and fertilizer for residents of the Tennessee Valley.

The TVA started in World War I as a federally built nitrate plant in Muscle Shoals, Alabama. It made little contribution to the war, and President Harding wanted to privatize it in 1921 after he became president. Henry Ford even offered to buy it, but Senator George Norris of Nebraska wanted the Muscle Shoals plants to be the genesis of a large federal system of electricity in America. He mustered the votes in Congress to stop Ford from buying the TVA, but couldn't persuade Presidents Coolidge or Hoover to back public ownership.[15]

When Roosevelt became president in 1933, Norris at last found an ally and TVA became a huge federal project. Roosevelt was very delighted with the photogenic dams, the large generators, and the fabulous arcs of steel and concrete. Historian William Leuchtenburg declared, "TVA was the most spectacularly successful of New Deal agencies. . . ."[16]

But the TVA created problems in two ways. First, the concentrating of benefits among the 2 percent of the population living in the Tennessee Valley had to be done by taxing away wealth from the other 98 percent. As economist Henry Hazlitt noted, "We must make an effort of the imagination to see the private power plants, the private homes, the typewriters and [after 1950] the television sets that were never allowed to come into existence because of the money that was taken from people all over the country to build the photogenic Norris Dam."[17]

More than this, as William Chandler has documented in his book *The Myth of TVA*, the state of Tennessee in the fifty years after the 1930s actually lagged behind nearby states in economic development. To prove his point, Chandler has systematically compared income levels of Tennessee with Georgia, where the TVA is absent. Tennessee and Georgia started with roughly the same per capita incomes in 1933, but in the next two decades Georgia began inching ahead. Furthermore, as Chandler reveals, "Among the nine states of the southeastern United States, there has been essentially an inverse relationship between income per capita and the extent to which the state was served by TVA."[18]

Why would the states without the subsidized electricity perform better than the states with it? Chandler concludes that subsidized power gave many people in Tennessee (and Kentucky and Alabama as well) incentives to stay on small farms, not to change their way of life. In Georgia, North Carolina, and Virginia, by contrast, more people were willing to move and start businesses in the city—cheap electricity and fertilizers were not holding them to the farms. What's more, with the non-TVA states industrializing faster, that created larger incomes and a larger market for electricity in the cities. Thus even the sale of electrical products was greater in the non-TVA states. Finally, the TVA flooded hundreds of thousands of acres in Tennessee, Kentucky, and Alabama. Those acres, when flooded, had to be removed from the tax rolls, and that reduced economic development.[19]

Historian Jim Powell suggests we should not be surprised by this outcome. The Soviet Union in the 1930s borrowed engineers from TVA to build huge hydroelectric plants in Dnieprostroi, for example, but without market incentives Soviet agriculture was inefficient. Sometimes, as in the case of TVA, the presence of a subsidy distracts the recipient from doing something else that might lead to better results. Thus, with the TVA we have the irony of 98 percent of the country subsidizing electric power for the other 2 percent, and the result is that the 2 percent started lagging behind and did not perform as well as the 98 percent who gave them the tax dollars.[20]

FINANCIAL INTERFERENCE:
MANIPULATION OF GOLD AND SILVER MARKETS,
TARIFFS, STOCKS, AND BANKS

The New Deal, especially in the arena of finance, was rarely the result of consistent planning. As Roosevelt conceded, "We seldom know, six weeks in advance, what we are going to do." Some historians profess to see a first New Deal from 1933 to 1934 and a second New Deal in 1935 and 1936, but Roosevelt, Frankfurter, and other New Dealers admitted that most programs were experimental—trial and error. "It is common sense," Roosevelt said, "to take a method and try it: If it fails, admit it frankly and try another. But above all, try something." The prices of gold and silver, the regulation of stocks and banks, and the manipulation of tariffs were all fresh experiments in New Deal finance.

GOLD AND SILVER

During the New Deal, Roosevelt, for different reasons, manipulated prices for both gold and silver. In both cases, the results were a weakened currency, diminished property rights, and a sharp rise in interest group politics.

In the case of gold, Roosevelt found the country's gold standard to be hindering his political goal of promoting inflation. After four years of deflation (in which the Fed kept interest rates high) Roosevelt faced angry farmers and even businessmen who wanted higher prices, even artificially higher prices, to diminish the impact of debts they owed. Under the gold standard, the federal government for a third of a century had been buying or selling gold at $20.67 an ounce. That was a check against inflation. If Roosevelt issued massive amounts of paper dollars to satisfy different voting blocs he had a problem: Americans could quickly redeem these plentiful dollars for gold and the treasury would either run out of gold or have to devalue the dollar. If, however, Roosevelt took the country off the gold standard then he could control the money supply more easily and inflate the currency more freely. In fairness to Roosevelt, taking the United States off the gold standard also had the positive effect of stopping the outflow of gold to foreign countries.[1]

In Roosevelt's first week in office he closed the nation's banks, and while they were closed, he cited a passage in the Trading with the Enemy Act (1917) that allowed him to forbid the export of gold in financial transactions. Then, after Congress passed the Emergency Banking Act in 1933, Roosevelt insisted that Americans exchange their gold for paper money. That also meant that future contracts, even government contracts, payable in gold were now void. The next month Roosevelt issued an executive order, under penalty of a fine or a prison term, forcing Americans to surrender all their gold to the U.S. government in return for paper dollars. Gold had to be removed if Roosevelt was to be free to inflate the currency.[2]

In Roosevelt's next step he began buying gold both from gold mining companies in America and from foreigners. He had come to believe that if he purchased large quantities of gold, and raised its price, then farm prices would rise as well. Roosevelt believed this theory because two Cornell University professors, George Warren and Frank Pearson, proclaimed it to be true in their recent book, *Prices*.[3]

Warren and Pearson argued that a historical relationship existed between the price of gold and the price of farm commodities—they rose and fell together. The professors even displayed charts and graphs to promote their idea. Roosevelt became fascinated with Warren, consulted with him regularly, and gave him an office in the Department of Commerce. Most other economists emphatically rejected Warren's theory—Keynes called it "puerile"—but Roosevelt embraced it and had the government, through the Treasury Department and the Reconstruction Finance Corporation, bidding for gold on world markets at ever-increasing prices. In fact, Roosevelt and Henry Morgenthau, then his future secretary of the treasury, set the price of gold each morning while Roosevelt had breakfast in bed.[4]

On November 3, for example, Morgenthau suggested to Roosevelt a 19 to 22 cent rise in price and Roosevelt responded that he wanted 21 cents. Why? "It is a lucky number," Roosevelt said laughing, "because it's three times seven." Morgenthau later wrote in his diary, "If anybody ever knew how we really set the gold price through a combination of lucky numbers, etc., I think they would be frightened."[5]

Roosevelt's "lucky numbers" may have hiked the world price of gold, but they did nothing for farm prices. Those numbers for farmers remained unlucky—and in fact commodity prices fell during the very time Roosevelt was bidding up gold on the world market. Warren's whole theory proved to be false, and even William Leuchtenburg, a historian very sympathetic to Roosevelt, concluded, "Gold buying was one of the most ill-considered moves Roosevelt ever made." In January 1934, during Roosevelt's State of the Union message, he switched arguments and began defending the confiscation of gold as necessary to stabilize the dollar. But during the previous year, the gold purchases had made the dollar so unstable that John Maynard Keynes likened the fluctuating dollar to watching "a gold standard on the booze." On January 30, Congress gave the president the Gold Reserve Act, which allowed Roosevelt to fix the gold price at $35 an ounce. Since the federal government now had 190 million ounces of gold, most of which was bought at prices far below $35 an ounce, the president had manipulated a fine profit from his confiscation policy.[6]

Roosevelt was under strong attack from those who had government contracts payable in gold. Many others wanted their property rights in gold protected, and the result was three Supreme Court cases—the Gold Cases—that challenged Roosevelt's interference. The president's lawyers argued that the Constitution did give Congress the right to coin money and regulate its value; therefore, Roosevelt had, at least in part, a constitutional defense. After the Supreme Court heard the Gold Cases, Roosevelt became nervous he might lose, and have to return the gold at a huge financial loss. To create a climate of public opinion more favorable to him, he had his attorney general, Homer Cummings, announce publicly that a reversal of Roosevelt's gold policy would create "chaos" for America.[7] After this, Roosevelt met with Cummings and Morgenthau to reveal a plan. According to Morgenthau,

The President argued with me that he wanted me to keep things on an unsettled basis until the Supreme Court handed down its decision. He said that he wanted this for judicial and political reasons. He said the only way that the man in a taxicab can become interested in the gold case is if we kept the story on the front page. He said I want bonds to move up and down and [chaos in] Foreign Exchange. He said if we keep things in a constant turmoil if the case should go against us the man on the street will say for God's sake, Mr. President, do something about it and, he said, if I do everybody in the country will heave a sigh of relief and say thank God.

Morgenthau argued against this strategy of deliberately manipulating the bond market. "Mr. President," he pleaded, "you know how difficult it is to get this country out of a depression and if we let the financial markets of this country become frightened for the next month it may take us eight months to recover the lost ground." According to Morgenthau, Roosevelt "continued to press me very very hard, arguing all the time for the political effect."[8]

Morgenthau, in this case, prevailed. The next evening Roosevelt had seemingly abandoned his plan for chaos and even suggested to him that the whole plan was a bit of a joke. Morgenthau was relieved, but Roosevelt may have by that time sensed he would win the case, and in fact he did so, by a narrow 5–4 majority.[9]

Once Roosevelt began raising the price of gold, the pressures to do the same for silver became overpowering. Silver was mined in seven states and the senators from those states were aggressive and influential in Congress. As a special interest group, the "silver bloc" wanted its subsidy. The world price for silver during 1933 was around 40 to 45 cents an ounce. That price was a sharp rise from the previous year, but the silver producers wanted more. Senator Elmer Thomas's amendment to the AAA gave the president wide powers in buying silver and setting its price. Then, in December 1933, the president began his subsidy to the silver bloc—he promised to buy the nation's annual output of silver at a sharply increased price of 64.5 cents an ounce.[10]

Even this was not enough. The silver bloc joined forces with those who believed that massive purchases of silver would promote inflation. In 1934, Congress passed the Silver Purchase Act, which authorized the Treasury Department to buy silver until it reached one-third of the nation's monetary reserve, or until the world price hit $1.29 an ounce. Roosevelt did veto this second bill, but did not make his veto a high priority, and Congress overrode it. Silver miners were quick to exploit this subsidy. American production of silver skyrocketed from 33 million ounces in 1933 to 70 million ounces by 1940.[11]

Harold Ickes, secretary of the interior, watched the silver purchases with puzzlement. He asked two questions, and made a penetrating observation: "Why should we be buying silver way above the market [price]? And if we do this for silver, why shouldn't we buy other products for what the producers want instead of paying what they are worth? I think this is bad policy. It points to the enrichment of Senator [Key] Pittman, of Nevada, and other Senators, Representatives, and investors in our silver mines."

Interest group politics has always been important in American history, but when the constitutional safeguards in Article 1, Section 8 were weakened during the 1930s, those politics flourished. The case of silver is an excellent example. If the United States had not subsidized the price of silver and instead had just paid every one of the 5,000 or so silver miners in the country an annual salary of $10,000 a year (over $100,000 a year in current dollars) each year for fifteen years, the country would have saved about half of the $1,500,000,000 it spent in the end to prop up the price of silver from 1934 to 1948. What hurt the taxpayer, however, helped the president in that he easily carried the seven silver states in his runs for reelection to the presidency.[12]

RECIPROCAL TRADE AND THE SECURITIES AND EXCHANGE ACT

Not all of Roosevelt's programs were economic disasters. Some were helpful to the economy, even if the results were often mixed. As we have seen, the Great Depression was triggered by the actions of the Federal Reserve in lowering interest rates and in the passing of the highest tariff in American history, the Smoot-Hawley tariff. Roosevelt appointed to the Federal Reserve economists who were not committed to lower interest rates. In 1934, he also supported the Reciprocal Trade Agreement Act, which gave him the power to negotiate tariffs downward on a country-by-country basis. From

1934 to 1939, the president and Secretary of State Cordell Hull signed agreements with twenty nations to lower tariff duties. Since those twenty nations constituted 60 percent of American trade, the flow of goods back and forth across the Atlantic was a welcome relief from the high retaliatory tariffs on American goods all over Europe during the early 1930s. "Since 1934," a League of Nations study noted, "the most important attempt to liberalise trade has been that undertaken by the United States of America in the prosecution of its programme of trade agreements." The trade between the United States and the British Empire alone accounted for about one-third of all trade in the world in 1938. Much credit for this goes to Roosevelt.

On the negative side, the president could and did use his tariff powers to threaten particular businessmen and industries in the United States and subtly coerce their cooperation with him, or risk having him reduce their level of protection. Also, the reciprocal agreement law gave Roosevelt executive powers not envisioned by the Founders to negotiate tariffs on his terms with foreign countries. Still, the reduced tariff rates and the changed Fed policy on interest rates were a plus for American economic development.[13]

Roosevelt made other constructive moves. When he took office, many banks had closed and others faced runs that threatened to deplete their cash reserves. Roosevelt declared a national "banking holiday" and closed them for a week while he tried to promote confidence in the nation's economy. Also useful was the Banking Act of 1933 (also known as the Glass-Steagall Act), which insured depositors' savings up to $2,500. With federal protection, many savers felt more secure and less willing to withdraw their savings. Bank failures sharply declined. On the negative side, the Banking Act of 1933 did harm to the banking business. Commercial and investment banking now had to be separated, and branch banking was forbidden. The problem was that the larger banks were the ones more diversified and they had already combined commercial and investment banking. These larger banks were more stable than, say, small-town banks, which were not diversified and more easily subject to collapse. Ninety percent of bank failures in the Great Depression were those of small-town banks, but the Banking Act gave advantages to continuing that risky method of banking. When many of those small banks later collapsed, it would be the taxpayers (through the Federal Deposit Insurance Corporation or FDIC) picking up the tab.[14]

Also worthy of commendation is the Securities and Exchange Act (1934), which increased the safety requirements for stock-trading companies. To the extent that weak and risky companies were forced to improve their standards, this law helped American investors. Roosevelt deserved credit for this effort. On the negative side, the new Securities and Exchange Commission (SEC) increased red tape and penalties to the point that legitimate investors were scared off. New business starts declined. As Raymond Moley concluded, "the market for new securities was virtually frozen during the year that followed. Bankers and lawyers were unwilling to advise investors to risk entanglement with a law that might be enforced with Draconian severity."[15]

A look at some of the public works completed under the New Deal shows some value for the tax dollars spent. From the Triborough Bridge in New York to the River Walk in San Antonio to the rebuilt sewer system in Oakland, we can see improvements in the nation's infrastructure. The millions of trees planted by the Civilian Conservation Corps, and the thousands of roads, post offices, and municipal buildings completed by the WPA did add value to their states and communities. Given that Roosevelt accumulated more federal debt in the first five years of his presidency than all thirty-one presidents before him, he should have indeed shown some improvement in the nation's infrastructure.

Finally, Roosevelt's upbeat attitude and his optimistic speeches did encourage many Americans during the Great Depression. His first inaugural address, for example, followed by his temporary closing of the banks, did calm the monetary fears of many Americans. After the banks reopened, few had runs on their deposits. Roosevelt's contagious smile, his hearty laugh, and his smooth tenor voice all helped reassure many Americans that their country would somehow return to prosperous days.

9

SAFETY NET OR QUAGMIRE? MINIMUM WAGE, SOCIAL SECURITY, AND LABOR RELATIONS

FDR was a reformer in the sense that he wanted to rearrange American economic life permanently. Centralize power, FDR argued, and reduce the influence of free choice to create new economic arrangements between employer and employee, and between young and old. Strong labor unions became part of the New Deal and Roosevelt especially promoted minimum wage laws and social security to guarantee certain levels of income to all American workers.

MINIMUM WAGE

The minimum wage and social security laws are two of the most durable parts of the New Deal today. Roosevelt was in favor of both early in his administration. In fact, he called minimum wage, or "Wages and Hours" as it was then termed, indispensable to his arsenal of programs. It was "must" legislation, but did not become law until the Fair Labor Standards Act was passed in 1938.

The idea of a "minimum wage," which would guarantee a certain level of pay to most workers, was not new with Roosevelt. Congress, in fact, passed a minimum wage law for women in Washington, D.C., in 1918. Women, according to that law, had to be paid at least $71.50 a month for their labor. The Supreme Court, however, in *Adkins v. Children's Hospital* (1923), declared that law unconstitutional because it violated "liberty of contract." Justice Sutherland, who wrote the majority opinion, said, "freedom of contract is . . . the general rule and restraint the exception." The Minimum Wage Act of 1918, Sutherland stressed, was simply "a price-fixing law." "It forbids two parties . . . to freely contract with one another in respect of the price for which one shall render service to the other in a purely private employment where both are willing, perhaps anxious, to agree. . . ."[1]

Observers noted that more than liberty of contract was at stake with minimum wage. It also caused unemployment—unemployment of the very people the law was crafted to protect. Twenty-one-year-old Willie Lyons, for example, was at the center of the *Adkins* case. She had worked as an elevator operator at the Congress Hall Hotel in Washington, D.C., for $35 a month plus two meals per day. The new minimum wage was $71.50 a month, and the Congress Hall Hotel could not legally continue to use her service for any pay less than that, even though she was willing to stay for $35 plus meals. The law therefore denied her the ability to earn the market value for her work. Since the value of her service to the Congress Hall Hotel was not $71.50, her employers had to let Lyons go. They hired a man to replace her at $35 a month. Thus a law designed to increase the wages of women had the effect of throwing women out of work. If the law had applied to men as well as women, then the Congress Hall Hotel would have had incentives to buy self-operating elevators and cut out all jobs for all elevator operators, men and women alike.[2]

Given the propensity of minimum wage to create unemployment, it is perhaps surprising that Roosevelt backed it so vigorously. He first had success in having minimum wage sections built into most NRA codes—businessmen themselves designed minimum wages for their industry, but did so knowing that prices for their products were fixed at high levels and that competitors who charged less could, if convicted, go to jail. When the NRA was struck down in 1935, Roosevelt began promoting a federal minimum wage law. Many congressmen opposed it for constitutional reasons and others because they were alarmed at the prospect of increasing unemployment during a depression.[3]

A new alliance of New England Democrats and Republicans, however, came to Roosevelt's rescue and in 1938 passed America's first minimum wage: 25 cents an hour, rising to 40 cents an hour over the next seven years. The driving force behind the bill was not the working poor, like Willie Lyons, but the highly paid textile workers of New England, who were eager to use the force of government to protect their jobs.

During the 1920s and 1930s, the American textile industry had begun to shift from New England to the South, where the cost of living was lower and where southern workers produced a high-quality product for lower wages. Politicians in Massachusetts, led by Republican U.S. senator Henry Cabot Lodge, Jr., and House Minority Leader Joseph Martin, battled in Congress for a law that would force southern textile mills to raise wages and thereby lose their competitive edge. Democrat governor Charles Hurley demanded that Congress pass a law to hike southern wages so that "Massachusetts [would] have equal competition with other sections of the country, thus affording labor and industry of Massachusetts some degree of assurance that our present industries will not move out of the state."[4]

Southerners were well aware of what Massachusetts was doing, and they scuttled all minimum wage laws before Congress during 1937 and well into 1938. In doing so, they handed President Roosevelt his first major defeat in Congress on any piece of New Deal legislation. "Northern industries are trying to stop the progress of the South," Representative Sam McReynolds (D-Tenn.) observed, "and they feel if they can pass this [minimum wage] bill it will really be a tariff against Southern goods."

Southern congressmen joined those economists who argued that Congress couldn't make a man worth a certain amount by making it illegal to pay him any less. Instead, the man would end up being unemployed. They said that people whose skills and experience were worth less than whatever Congress decreed as the minimum wage would be priced out of the labor market, and the Great Depression would persist.

The desperate plight of unskilled workers trying to hold on to their jobs especially disturbed Representative Carl Mapes (R-Mich.). "The enactment of this [minimum wage] legislation," Mapes concluded, "will further increase unemployment, not reduce it. It is bound to increase unemployment unless all human experience is reversed." Mapes predicted that the law would most harm workers who had limited skills and were desperately trying to secure a foothold on the first step of the job ladder. Mapes cited the case of a local minimum wage law passed in early 1938 in Washington, D.C. Immediately after its passage, the *Washington Post* lamented, scores of maids and unskilled workers were laid off by local hotels.

In fairness to Roosevelt, self-interest was not the only force behind minimum wage. Roosevelt, and others as well, were alarmed by poverty, and they wanted to see the working poor have more to eat and spend. But the actions of minimum wage, critics argued, often led to many southern workers losing their jobs, and thereby losing a chance to use that job to climb higher on the economic ladder.

SOCIAL SECURITY

The idea of a government-insurance plan did not originate in the New Deal. If we switch the discussion to pensions, the U.S. government had paid pensions to disabled veterans and their widows for many years after the Civil War. And of course some American corporations, particularly railroads, offered private pension plans to employees. Part of what stirred Roosevelt's interest in the related issue of a government-insurance plan was the crusade by California physician Francis Townsend, who stirred support throughout the country for his plan to have the government give $200 a month to all retirees over age sixty.

Roosevelt rejected Townsend's idea and developed his own federal retirement plan, which he called social security. In this plan, employees paid a maximum of $30 a year—1 percent on each dollar of earned income up to $3,000. Employers had to match this payment and send it all to Washington. At age sixty-two, the employees were eligible for checks of $22.54 per month. The percentages and benefits were subject to change by Congress. The government did not set aside the social security revenue after the early 1940s; instead social security became a pay-as-you-go system with percentages and benefits determined by Congress. The mandatory payroll tax began in 1937 and the payouts began in 1940; after that, Congress has steadily increased the benefits doled out and also the percentages of income to be paid by employee and employer.[5]

Roosevelt's social security plan created an array of problems. First, it retarded recovery from the Great Depression by contributing to unemployment. From 1937 to 1940, employers and employees were docked for social security, and that money was out of private hands and lying fallow in the treasury. Lloyd Peck of the Laundryowners National Association concluded, "The burden of this proposal for employers to carry, through a payroll tax, will act as a definite curb on business expansion, and will likely eliminate many businesses now on the verge of bankruptcy."[6]

Second, social security was unsound financially. Unlike life insurance policies, workers had to live to age sixty-two to collect anything. Life expectancy in 1930, the year of the most recent census, was almost sixty years, which meant that most people of that time would lose money from their paycheck every month for thirty to forty years, and neither they nor their children would ever receive a return on it. In the case of black Americans, who had only a forty-eight-year life expectancy in 1930, most contributed to pensions that would go disproportionately to whites. What's more, the payroll tax was regressive—Henry Ford and Andrew Mellon paid in the same amount as their employees who earned $3,000 a year.[7]

While some Americans were soaked by social security, others, especially the first retirees, rolled in benefits after making only minimal payments. Ida Fuller, for example, a legal secretary in Ludlow, Vermont, paid a total of $24.75 into social security from 1937 to 1940, when she retired at age sixty-five. Her first monthly social security check of $22.54 almost matched her entire contribution. At her death in 1975, she had received $22,888.92 from social security, a payout of roughly $1,000 for each dollar she paid in.[8]

When an accountant quizzed Roosevelt about the economic problems with social security, especially its tendency to create unemployment, he responded, "I guess you're right on the economics, but those taxes were never a problem of economics. They are politics all the way through." Roosevelt explained that "with those taxes in there, no damn politician can ever scrap my social security program." That's why, as Roosevelt admitted, it's "politics all the way through." Most politicians, following Roosevelt's lead, have taken delight in raising social security payouts and using that gift to plead for votes from the elderly at election time.[9]

In the original debate in the Senate on social security, Senator Bennett Champ Clark of Missouri wondered if private pensions for retirement might outperform the government pensions proposed in the social security bill. He introduced the Clark Amendment, which would have allowed private employers to opt out of social security.[10]

The key provision in the Clark Amendment was that employers had to at least match the government's social security program in benefits to the employee and in premiums extracted from the employee. The employer also had to agree to place the premiums with an insurance company—or an approved alternative—and to give all employees the right to choose the government-run program instead of the private alternative.[11]

When the Clark Amendment was debated before the Senate in 1935, the advocates of a government monopoly were on the defensive. One of them, Senator Robert La Follette, Jr., of Wisconsin complained, "If we shall adopt this amendment, the government having determined to set up a federal system of old-age [insurance], will provide in its own bill creating that system, for competition, which in the end may destroy the federal system." La Follette was perceptive. If private insurance or mutual funds were allowed to compete with the government, no one might choose the government plan. The Senate decided that workers ought to have a choice and voted 51-35 to make the Clark Amendment part of the social security law.

President Roosevelt was furious at the Senate, and threatened to veto the social security bill if it came to him with the Clark Amendment attached. When the House passed a social security bill without the Clark Amendment, Roosevelt and his supporters used a parliamentary tactic to gain victory. The House-Senate conference committee met to work out a compromise bill, and naturally the Clark Amendment was the main point of debate. The committee decided to submit a final bill to Roosevelt with the government monopoly intact. But they agreed to appoint a special joint legislative committee to study the Clark Amendment and report to Congress the next year on how best to provide for competition. But after the government monopoly was instituted, the promised meeting in 1936 was never held. Given that many private pension plans over the last sixty years have returned around 8 percent a year, and that social security benefits have averaged less than a 2 percent return, Senator Clark's alternative showed much wisdom, but he couldn't overcome Roosevelt's political skill.

LABOR RELATIONS

Employer-employee arrangements drastically changed during the New Deal. Before the Great Depression, "liberty of contract" tended to be the rule. "Whatever may be the advantages of 'collective bargaining,' it is not bargaining at all, in any just sense, unless it is voluntary on both sides," wrote Justice Mahlon Pitney of the Supreme Court in 1917. "The same liberty which enables men to form unions, and through the union to enter into agreements with employers willing to agree, entitles other men to remain independent of the union and other employers to employ no man who owes any allegiance or obligation to the union."[12]

President Roosevelt wanted to tilt the balance of power more in favor of unions. The year he was elected president he had help from two of his friends, Senator George Norris of Nebraska and Representative Fiorello La Guardia of New York. Their Norris–La Guardia Anti-Injunction Act, passed in 1932, made it harder for employers to stop union organizing. Yellow-dog contracts, which required employees to agree not to join a union, were made unenforceable by law, and federal courts could issue no injunctions in labor disputes except in cases of fraud or violence.[13]

When Roosevelt became president, his NRA gave further help to union organizing. According to the NRA, in the writing of industrial codes, workers had "the right to organize and bargain collectively through representatives of their own choosing, and shall be free from interference, restraint, or coercion of employers of labor." Workers were free to have a variety of unions, including company unions, represent them. The NRA did not necessarily require that a single union be the exclusive bargaining representative for all workers in an industry.[14]

Even before the NRA was struck down by the Supreme Court, Senator Robert Wagner of New York, with Roosevelt's later tacit approval, began formulating a law that would strengthen the power of unions. The National Labor Relations Act, or the Wagner Act as it was sometimes called, proposed to sharply alter the industrial workforce. The key part of the bill had a list of "unfair labor practices." Employers were not allowed to stop any union from organizing. They could not fire anyone because he or she was a union member, and they had to agree to bargain collectively with union representatives. If 30 percent of employees in an industry wanted a union, they could have a vote and whichever union they might select would represent all workers. Every worker had to accept the union as its bargaining agent with his employer. Furthermore, if that union declared a strike, the strike could not be legally stopped, and the employer was not encouraged to hire replacements, or to refuse to let striking workers back on the job after the strike was over.[15]

Roosevelt initially hesitated to support this Wagner Act, but eventually he promoted it and, after it passed through Congress, he signed it into law in 1935. In late 1936, after he had been safely reelected, the nation was rocked by strikes—more than at any time in U.S. history. The most publicized strike was that of Walter Reuther and his United Auto Workers (UAW) against General Motors (GM). From December 30, 1936, to February 11, 1937, the UAW shut down the huge GM plant at Flint, Michigan. The UAW men conducted a sit-down strike. They took control of GM property, refused to leave or to allow any work to be done there, and fired bullets at any strikebreakers or policemen who tried to move them off GM's property. Key issues of property rights were at stake and the UAW, with this sit-down strike, was trying to stretch the new Wagner Act to the limits. Neither Governor Frank Murphy of Michigan nor President Roosevelt was willing to support evicting the strikers from GM property.[16]

Alfred Sloan, president of GM, was alarmed at the lack of cars his company was producing; he urged the enforcing of the laws to get his property back. Frances Perkins, secretary of labor, suggested that Sloan come to Washington and negotiate with John L. Lewis there. Sloan declined: "We cannot see our way clear to accept the invitation to negotiate further with the Union while its representatives continue to hold our plant unlawfully." According to polls, most Americans seemed to side with Sloan. Columnist Westbrook Pegler said the "illegal seizure of property" seemed to have the country "thoroughly bulldozed." Roosevelt, however, chastised Sloan and GM. "I told them," the president said, "I was not only disappointed in the refusal of Mr. Sloan to come down here, but I regarded it as a very unfortunate decision on his part."[17]

Sloan, with no state or federal support to recover his property, capitulated to the UAW leaders on February 11, 1937. That victory for the UAW was a visible demonstration of the new world of labor relations. The rest of GM, U.S. Steel, Ford Motor Company, and other major corporations all fully unionized before World War II.[18]

The Wagner Act certainly weighted the scales toward labor. The United States had thousands of strikes and work stoppages as unionization proceeded rapidly in the 1930s and 1940s. Wages, of course, increased for many workers in the newly unionized industries. But from a standpoint of the Great Depression and overall employment, the new labor relations had problems as well. Since much higher wages were the cost of doing business for many corporations, they hired fewer workers and trimmed down their labor forces when possible—especially by mechanization, which occurred rapidly in the coal industry, for example. Unions often discriminated against blacks, so they rarely benefited from new labor laws. And American exports were sometimes less competitive on world markets. That also diminished sales and new hiring, which prolonged the Great Depression.[19]

10

NO FREE RIDE:
THE BURDEN OF EXCISE, INCOME, AND CORPORATE TAXES

Franklin Roosevelt depended more heavily on excise taxes for revenue than any president before him. Whereas a tariff is a tax on imports, an excise is a tax on commodities manufactured within a country. It is a use tax and has been applied historically in the United States to so-called vices, starting with the whiskey tax in the 1790s. Most economists label excise taxes as regressive because they hit lower-income groups proportionally more heavily than richer groups. This was especially true with the excise taxes collected by the Roosevelt administration.[1]

Before the Great Depression, excise taxes in the United States were usually limited to tobacco and alcohol. In 1929, for example, the year Hoover took office, over 80 percent of all excise revenue came from tobacco, especially the six cents per pack tax on cigarettes. In 1932, however, Hoover, with support from Democrat congressmen, introduced a host of new excise duties. They were touted as a one-year emergency to offset the decline in revenue from the Depression. These new excises included duties on cars, movie tickets, radios, phonographs, telephone calls (long distance), telegrams, cosmetics, cameras, bank checks, stock transfers, yachts, jewelry, furs, and a new one cent per gallon tax on gasoline. These taxes went way beyond the former vice taxes. They tended to hit ordinary commodities—even necessities—used by middle- and lower-income groups as well as by the rich. True, the new duties on yachts, jewelry, and furs were clearly luxury taxes, but the levies on cars, gas, radios, and movie tickets hit most Americans each day. They were truly regressive taxes, and when they became law they became the first federal taxes that most Americans paid. The income tax, in contrast, with its high personal exemptions, only covered about the top 3 percent of Americans. The promise that these new excises were only temporary taxes helped them slip through Congress during an election year.[2]

The new taxes did indeed almost double excise revenue for Hoover in 1932. When Roosevelt took office the next year he had several choices. First, he could urge Congress to continue the new "emergency" excises. That would mean a more permanent shift toward regressive taxes for federal revenue. Or the government could lower the personal exemption on the income tax and expand it to include the top one-third or one-half of Americans. If Roosevelt was concerned about the regressive direction of the tax structure, another possibility would have been to eliminate the excise on gas or movie tickets, which especially hit lower incomes, and raise the tax on, say, furs and yachts—or introduce new excises on other luxuries.

Roosevelt chose to keep the "emergency" excises of 1932 and renew most of them each year during the 1930s. For one thing, many of these taxes were hard for many millions of Americans to elude because they were put on necessities, or at least on very desirable and cheap commodities. Mark Leff, who has written an excellent book on New Deal taxation, makes this point clearly. Under the New Deal, Leff observes, "the drawback of regressivity had become an asset. Excise taxes targeted consumers. The imposition of a gas tax, for example, upon an overproducing industry was predicated on an inelastic consumer demand that would maintain gas purchases despite price hikes." Also, the taxes were "painless" in that the consumer was tapped for only a few cents on his purchase, and often didn't even notice it—or if he did he might blame the increase on business, not on government. For example, the six-cent tax per pack of cigarettes was part of the total price each buyer paid at the counter. When the customer paid, for example, fifteen cents for a pack of cigarettes, he had no way of knowing that 40 percent of his purchase price was tax. The same is true with buying gas at the pump or tickets at a movie theater. In both cases, the tax had been incorporated into the total purchase price.[3]

Congressman Francis Maloney (D-Conn.) made an interesting point when he observed that "if the individual or the family were sent a bill for $10 and were told it was for cigarette taxes, there would be a tax rebellion." But if a husband and his wife each smoked a pack a day, they would pay $43.80 in taxes a year, which in the 1930s was close to 5 percent of a typical family's income. Henry Simons, a University of Chicago economist, was alarmed by how regressive so many of Roosevelt's excise taxes were. "The plain fact," Simons said, "to one not confused by moralist distinctions between necessities and luxuries, is simply that taxes like the tobacco taxes are the most effective means available for draining government revenues out from the very bottom of the income scale."[4]

Roosevelt sometimes said he didn't like raising revenue by excise taxes, but he did so anyway. Roosevelt, his secretary of treasury, Henry Morgenthau, and others who worked with finances in his administration clearly knew that these taxes siphoned revenue disproportionately from middle- and lower-income families. In 1936, for example, Herman Oliphant, general counsel for the Treasury Department, collected masses of data on "tax incidence," the science of who is hit hardest by which taxes. In his report to Morgenthau, Oliphant described the New Deal tax structure and concluded that with excise duties "the bulk of such taxes falls upon the lower income groups of our population." He further told Morgenthau that fully 55 percent of all federal revenue in 1935 came from these consumption taxes.[5] Table 1 helps show the transformation from a revenue structure based on the income tax, which hit high income earners, to one based on excise taxes, which hit lower income earners.

TABLE 1.

Year	Total Income Tax Revenue	Total Excise Tax Revenue
1929	$1.096 billion	$540 million
1935	$527 million	$1.364 billion

Source: U.S. Bureau of the Census, *Historical Statistics of the United States: Colonial Times to 1970* (Washington, D.C.: U.S. Government Printing Office, 1975), II, 1107.

If we study excise taxes during the New Deal years we see that Roosevelt steadily increased the impact of particularly regressive taxes. For starters, in Roosevelt's first year, the gas tax increased from 1.0 to 1.5 cents per gallon. Then came the revived tax on alcoholic beverages. Roosevelt helped remove prohibition as a national law, in part because of the new revenue stream that he predicted would flow into the federal treasury from beer, wine, and hard liquor. Many observers, brewers in particular, complained that alcoholic beverages were "a poor man's drink" and that a whiskey tax weighed "heavier on the poor than on the rich." Nonetheless, by 1936, the federal revenue from taxes on alcohol had slightly surpassed the tobacco tax as the major excise revenue tax in the United States. In 1938, the New Deal Congress raised the whiskey tax from $2.00 to $2.25 per gallon.[6]

Two new taxes Roosevelt imposed were both regressive. First was the social security tax, which started as a 1 percent levy on employer and employee to fund a national system. Since only the first $3,000 of income was subject to taxation, the burden fell hardest on lower-income families. A Treasury Department analysis in 1936 confirmed that the social security tax "will be borne mostly by the lower income groups." Second was the processing tax on food and clothing that was part of how the AAA would be funded. Since the processors—flour millers, textile companies, and so on—passed this tax on to consumers, it therefore hit the poorest the hardest. One critic said it was foolish to "pay farmers, with public money—in part, hungry people's money—to grow less food." Even Henry Wallace conceded that "the most serious objection to the processing tax" was "that the greatest burden falls on the poorer people."[7]

Interestingly, those few alterations that Roosevelt made in the excise tax structure made it even more regressive. For example, during the New Deal years, the president and Congress eliminated the luxury excises on yachts, furs, and jewelry. But after extensive debate, they did not remove the cosmetics tax on cold cream and face powder. All five female members of Congress campaigned vigorously against the cosmetics tax, but to no avail. Historian Mark Leff concluded that because the cosmetics tax (and other similar regressive taxes) created so much revenue, congressmen were reluctant to let that money go. The yacht tax and the fur tax, in contrast, generated less revenue and were, therefore, more easily lobbied by the relevant industries and the users of these products, both of which could afford strong campaigns to get the taxes removed.[8]

Roosevelt did not relish the tax system becoming more regressive, but he did little to stop it because he wanted the revenue. He said little publicly about excise taxes, but in a major budget message of January 5, 1939, he summarized his reasons for promoting all excise taxes for yet another year. "I am recommending the reenactment of the excise taxes which will expire in June and July of this year," Roosevelt said, "not because I regard them as ideal components of our tax structure, but because their collection has been perfected, our economy is adjusted to them, and we cannot afford at this time to sacrifice the revenue they represent."[9]

Table 2 helps indicate the importance of excises taxes in funding New Deal programs during the 1930s. In the first four years of Roosevelt's presidency, revenue from excise taxes exceeded that of income and corporate taxes combined. When we think of the various New Deal programs, we need to visualize their funding either largely or heavily coming from nickels and dimes paid weekly by tens of millions of smokers, car drivers, telephone callers, moviegoers, and cosmetics users all over the nation. On the spending side, with the TVA, the Silver Purchase Act, or the WPA, for example, we need to see farmers in Tennessee, silver mine owners in Nevada, and road builders for Governor Wilbur Cross in Connecticut receiving salaries paid in part by a textile worker in North Carolina who smoked cigarettes, a house painter in Ohio who found work and then celebrated by taking his family that weekend to a movie, or maybe a single mother in Philadelphia who found a job and bought gasoline to drive to work.

TABLE 2.

Percentage of Revenue to the U.S. Government from Income Taxes, Corporation Income Taxes, and Excise Taxes Only

Year	Income Taxes	Corporation Income Taxes	Excise Taxes
1929	38	43	19
1930	39	42	19
1931	35	43	22
1932	28	42	30
1933	22	25	53
1934	20	19	61
1935	21	23	55
1936	23	25	52
1937	28	28	45
1938	30	31	40
1939	26	29	45
1940	24	29	47

Source: U.S. Bureau of the Census, *Historical Statistics of the United States: Colonial Times to 1970* (Washington, D.C.: U.S. Government Printing Office, 1975), II, 1107.

With excise taxes as the largest component of federal revenue each year of the New Deal, that meant that income tax revenue, which had been so significant in the 1920s, paid for only a small portion of the New Deal. Interestingly, Roosevelt tried very hard to extract more tax revenue from wealthy Americans. Taxing the rich was one of his stated ambitions. In 1935, in fact, he vigorously promoted a bill that hiked the top marginal tax rate to 79 percent, the highest in U.S. history. That meant that past a certain amount, almost four of every five dollars earned had to be paid to the federal treasury. Roosevelt heartily approved of that tactic, but it brought in very little revenue. That tactic had also been tried during and after World War I and it did not work well then, either. If we look at the 1920s, when President Coolidge and Treasury Secretary Andrew Mellon were in office, that will give us good background to understanding why the "soak the rich" tactics of the 1930s failed.[10]

Andrew Mellon, a Pittsburgh industrialist and banker, helped found Alcoa and Gulf Oil. He was an expert financier, and by the 1920s he was reputed to be the third wealthiest man in the country, trailing only Henry Ford and John D. Rockefeller, Sr. In 1921, President Harding asked the sixty-five-year-old Mellon to be secretary of the treasury; the national debt had surpassed $20 billion and unemployment had reached 11.7 percent, one of the highest rates in U.S. history. Harding invited Mellon to tinker with tax rates to encourage investment without incurring more debt. Mellon studied the problem carefully; his solution was what is today called "supply-side economics," the idea of cutting taxes to stimulate investment. High income tax rates, Mellon argued, "inevitably put pressure upon the taxpayer to withdraw this capital from productive business and invest it in tax-exempt securities. . . . The result is that the sources of taxation are drying up, wealth is failing to carry its share of the tax burden; and capital is being diverted into channels which yield neither revenue to the Government nor profit to the people."[11]

Mellon wrote a popular book, *Taxation: The People's Business*, in which he developed his ideas. "It seems difficult for some to understand," he wrote, "that high rates of taxation do not necessarily mean large revenue to the Government, and that more revenue may often be obtained by lower rates." Mellon illustrated this principle with an example from his world of business. He compared the government setting tax rates on incomes to a businessman setting prices on product. "If a price is fixed too high, sales drop off and with them profits." Mellon asked: "Does anyone question that Mr. Ford has made more money by reducing the price of his car [from $3,000 to $380] and increasing his sales than he would have made by maintaining a high price and a greater profit per car, but selling less cars?" [12]

Mellon, of course, recognized that there was a limit to how far you could cut tax rates and still increase revenue. "The problem of the government," he said, "is to fix rates which will bring in a maximum amount of revenue to the Treasury and at the same time bear not too heavily on the taxpayer or on business enterprises." Mellon believed that 25 percent was about as much as rich people would pay in taxes before they rushed to the tax shelters, which included foreign investments, collectibles (for example, art or stamps), and tax-exempt bonds. [13]

As secretary of the treasury, Mellon promoted, and Harding and Coolidge backed, a plan that eventually cut taxes on large incomes from 73 to 24 percent and on smaller incomes from 4 to ½ of 1 percent. These tax cuts helped produce an outpouring of economic development—from air conditioning to refrigerators to zippers, Scotch tape to radios and talking movies. Investors took more risks when they were allowed to keep more of their gains. President Coolidge, during his six years in office, averaged only 3.3 percent unemployment and 1 percent inflation—the lowest misery index of any president in the twentieth century. [14]

Furthermore, Mellon was also vindicated in his astonishing predictions that cutting tax rates across the board would generate more revenue. In the early 1920s, when the highest tax rate was 73 percent, the total income tax revenue to the U.S. government was a little over $700 million. In 1928 and 1929, when the top tax rate was slashed to 25 and 24 percent, the total revenue topped the $1 billion mark.[15] Also remarkable, as Table 3 indicates, is that the burden of paying these taxes fell increasingly on the wealthy.

TABLE 3.

Percentage of Total Personal Income Tax Paid by Different Net Income Groups

Income Group	1920	1925	1929
Under $5,000	15.4	1.9	0.4
$5,000–$10,000	9.1	2.6	0.9
$10,000–$25,000	16.0	10.1	5.2
$25,000–$100,000	29.6	36.6	27.4
Over $100,000	29.9	48.8	65.2

Source: Benjamin G. Rader, "Federal Taxation in the 1920s: A Re-examination," *Historian* 33 (May 1971), 433.

What's more, in every year of the 1920s, the United States had a budget surplus. No wonder Mellon was nicknamed by his devotees as "the best secretary of the treasury since Alexander Hamilton."

Roosevelt's philosophy of government, driven partly by his belief in underconsumption theory, contrasted sharply with Mellon's. The president was mired in the Great Depression, and in part he used deficit spending to "prime the pump." He also believed in high taxation to generate the revenue for government planners to build industry, cut back farm crops, and federalize relief. Roosevelt believed the Great Depression was partly caused by poor investments and stock manipulations by rich people. They paid their employees too little and worked them long hours for selfish reasons, not because of market forces—supply and demand, world prices, and stiff competition.

Roosevelt liked the NRA and the WPA in part because they often enforced higher wages and fewer hours of work. Roosevelt liked high tax rates on the rich because that increased the power of government to work in the public interest. Market forces, he believed, not tariffs or other government interventions, had caused the Great Depression. It would be far better, Roosevelt thought, to redistribute the wealth and give poor people the chance to buy more consumer and industrial goods to help push an economic recovery. Mellon's very presence as a popular former treasury secretary was an affront and a constant reminder to many Americans of "the good old days" when tax rates were low, jobs were plentiful, and government was unobtrusive.[16]

Roosevelt had other reasons as well for wanting high tax rates on the rich. First, such a move would equalize wealth, which Roosevelt thought was especially important during such a time of economic hardship. Homer Cummings, Roosevelt's attorney general, expressed this view well when he said, "I cannot understand why it is immoral to stop people from becoming rich."

Second, Roosevelt was irritated at businessmen for not starting or expanding their businesses, which would ease unemployment, and then gladly paying more in taxes, which would help fund the president's New Deal. When many businessmen criticized him for raising personal income and corporate taxes, Roosevelt took offense and increasingly viewed businessmen, many of them at least, as bitter enemies. He saw himself in a political struggle in which he wanted to tax them as much as they wanted to oust him from the White House.[17]

Roosevelt often publicized this struggle because he said he would win more votes than he would lose by doing so. His "class war" or "war against business," as it was sometimes called, developed in two phases.[18] First was the buildup to the 1936 presidential election, and in this phase Roosevelt was constantly on the offensive. The second phase was during Roosevelt's second term as president, and in this phase he was often on the defensive.

The Revenue Act of 1935 was a major thrust of phase one. That act provided for a more progressive tax on corporate earnings, a 70 percent tax rate on large estates, a gift tax, and a new 79 percent tax rate on personal income over $5 million. In supporting these new taxes, Roosevelt maintained that big business was using its power to monopolize industry and hoard wealth; it was refusing to take risks or create new jobs. Wealth was too concentrated, Roosevelt insisted; it was stagnant, and was not helping with recovery. Furthermore, he argued, such unfortunate accumulations of wealth perpetuated "great and undesirable concentration of control in a relatively few individuals over the employment and welfare of many, many others." High rates on large incomes and estates, Roosevelt argued, would break up large private and corporate fortunes and level the playing field for all businessmen.[19]

Many businessmen responded angrily. Many large corporate executives were either losing money or barely making ends meet in their businesses already. They complained that they were still having to cut back production and lay off employees during seasonal lulls. What incentives, they wondered, did they have to take risks and hire more workers? After these new tax hikes, their costs of doing business were now higher; how could they plan for expansion when the president's tax men were on hand to gobble up most of the new profits they might figure out a way to earn?[20]

Forbes magazine protested that "a fundamental motive of the New Deal is to wage war against bigness in business." The magazine noted, "Many employers and executives who heretofore have cooperated with the President and urged other men of affairs to do so, now confess that he has deliberately slapped them in the face; and they agree that the only course to follow is to oppose openly every recommendation made by the Administration calculated to injure recovery." The National Association of Manufacturers, at its annual meeting in 1935, issued a statement that it "was out to end the New Deal." The DuPonts and other businessmen had already formed the Liberty League to oppose Roosevelt in the 1936 election.[21]

Roosevelt encouraged this fight and tore into business in his

State of the Union message in January 1936. He condemned the "selfish power" and the old "resplendent economic autocracy" that was fighting his "new instruments of public power." Roosevelt added, "In the hands of a people's Government this power is wholesome and proper. But in the hands of political puppets of an economic autocracy such power would provide shackles for the liberties of the people."[22]

Roosevelt's next step was to impose yet another tax on business—this one a tax on all undistributed corporate profits. The intent of this law was to force corporations to distribute profits as dividends and salaries, which the government could then tax. Many corporations, however, preferred to leave profits within the company to expand the business, buy new machinery, and save for research and development. Under the new undistributed profits tax, corporations would now be assessed on all profits held back for expansion or for reserve.[23]

Roosevelt argued that this new tax "made it harder for big corporations to retain the huge undistributed profits with which they gobble up small business." But many small businessmen sharply disagreed. In fact, for small, profitable companies, Roosevelt's tax was a special burden because it prevented them from buying the equipment to expand and compete with larger enterprises. *Fortune* magazine conducted a poll of business executives and found almost 90 percent of them eager to repeal the undistributed profits tax, or at least modify it.[24]

Businessmen may have been nearly unanimous in criticizing this new tax on profits, but Roosevelt believed it was a vote-getter in November, and throughout the election year he hammered away at "economic royalists" and "malefactors of great wealth."[25]

Some of Roosevelt's advisors became uneasy about the possibly damaging economic effects of these attacks on business. One of these men was Columbia professor Raymond Moley of the Brains Trust, who wrote, or helped write, several of the president's major speeches. Moley had been a staunch supporter of the NRA and, in a long meeting with the president, he tried to soften the president's hostility to businessmen by remarking that he had "every reason to believe that many reasonable business men were anxious to cooperate in some way in the restoration of the NRA idea, if not in its detail." As Moley confided in his journal, Roosevelt

> then launched into a violent attack upon business men generally, saying that he had talked to a great many business men, in fact to more business men than had any other President, and that they were generally stupid. He said that the trouble with them . . . was that they had no moral indignation for the sins of other business men. . . . He then turned from that to a violent attack upon the newspapers, saying that the newspapers had no moral indignation, . . . that all of these [newspapers—he "named a long list"] were guilty of falsifying news. . . . He said that nothing would help him more [in the 1936 election] than to have it known that the newspapers were all against him.

The subject then switched back to businessmen.

> He then launched into a denunciation of bankers and business men and said that every time they made an attack on him, as they did in the Chamber of Commerce of the U.S., he gained votes and that the result of carrying on his sort of warfare was to bring the people to his support. I said that was quite true, and that he clearly had the election in hand, but that inasmuch as our system involved the newspapers on the one hand and business on the other, I did not see how ultimately the welfare of the country would be served by totally discrediting business to the people, unless we planned to go into a different form of economic life. He made no particular comment on this, and the inference can clearly be drawn that he was thinking merely in terms of the political advantage to him in creating the impression through the country that he was being unjustly attacked by business men.[26]

Moley was alarmed by the president's attitude that attacking business was useful for securing votes, but the two of them changed the conversation to speechwriting and the president asked Moley, his trusted advisor, "to start to prepare the acceptance speech" before the Democratic convention, and Moley agreed to do so. They parted on good terms, but Moley wrote this evaluation of their meeting:

> I was impressed as never before by the utter lack of logic of the man, the scantiness of his precise knowledge of things that he was talking about, by the gross inaccuracies in his statements, by the almost pathological lack of sequence in his discussion, by the complete rectitude that he felt as to his own conduct, by the immense and growing egotism that came from his office, by his willingness to continue the excoriation of the press and business in order to get votes for himself, by his indifference to what effect the long-continued pursuit of these ends would have upon the civilization in which he was playing a part. In other words, the political habits of his mind were working full steam with the added influence of a swollen ego. My deliberate impression is that he is dangerous in the extreme, and I view the next four years with no inconsiderable apprehension.[27]

Moley became even more disenchanted with the president when he chose to ignore Moley's ideas for the acceptance speech, and instead go on the attack against business. In that speech, Roosevelt told the assembled Democrats that his crusade against "economic tyranny" was like the Founders' struggle against "royalists who held special privileges from the crown." These "economic royalists," who were threatening America, were a small band of "privileged princes" who were "thirsting for power." They had "created a new despotism" that "had concentrated into their own hands an almost complete control over other people's property, other people's money, other people's labor—other people's lives." Against this "economic tyranny" Roosevelt stood strong. "The election of 1932 was the people's mandate to end it. Under that mandate it is being ended."[28]

During the 1936 campaign, Roosevelt portrayed himself as the friend of the people, challenging those "economic royalists." It culminated on October 31 at New York's Madison Square Garden, where Roosevelt challenged "business and financial monopoly" and other selfish forces directly: "Government by organized money is just as dangerous as Government by organized mob," Roosevelt said.

> Never before in all our history have these forces been so united against one candidate as they stand today. They are unanimous in their hate for me—and I welcome their hatred. I should like to have it said of my first Administration that in it the forces of selfishness and of lust for power met their match. I should like to have it said of my second Administration that in it these forces met their master.[29]

For Roosevelt, on the plus side of the presidential election was an overwhelming victory that he received at the polls. It vindicated his tax strategy, his attacks on economic royalty, and his tactic of using federal money to advance his political interests. The negative side is that Roosevelt committed himself to promoting recovery and balancing the budget. He would be accountable for the American economy after the election.[30]

With victory in hand, Roosevelt crafted the Revenue Act of 1937, which closed some of the loopholes businessmen were using to protect their incomes and their corporations from high taxation. That revenue bill, for example, restricted the definition of personal holding companies, made it harder to set up multiple trusts, and ended the option of incorporating a yacht. Roosevelt tried to tighten the noose. But his ongoing attacks against "economic royalists" and now "tax avoiders" were losing their grip on public opinion.

Unemployment, however, by December had edged up to 18.9 percent—some analysts were calling it a depression within a depression. The *New York Herald Tribune* observed, "For more than four years President Roosevelt has labored continuously, with all the extraordinary eloquence and political skill of which he is master, to divide the country into two warring factions." Gallup polls and other indicators, however, were shifting away from the president and toward businessmen.[31]

Donald W. Baker, a small retailer in Battle Creek, Michigan, expressed the sentiments of many small businessmen when he wrote the president:

> There are hundreds of thousands of men just like me. . . . These people, Mr. Roosevelt, object to the stirring up of class hatred. It is the last thing we could ever want in this country! . . . To make the people of the country class conscious is to stir up hatred which will defeat that progress. . . .
>
> Do all you can to encourage harmony among the people of the country and to stifle hatred. Tell business men that the Government will co-operate with them to bring about a more stable and more prosperous economy under which the living conditions of *all* our people will be raised.[32]

Roosevelt was stung by these criticisms, some of which began to come from longtime political allies. Investor and Democrat strategist Bernard Baruch urged Roosevelt to cut taxes and encourage business to expand. Adolf Berle, a professor, Brains Truster, and assistant secretary of state, said in 1937, "I wish I could convert anybody in Washington to the theory that you cannot run a government based on business and have a perpetual warfare with business at the same time." With the seasonal cutbacks in WPA employment (1937 was not an election year), Henry Wallace suggested to Roosevelt that he "ought to call some of us together and see if we can't think up some suggestions to encourage private business enterprise so that they can go ahead and take up the slack which would be left due to the government ceasing spending." But no such meetings took place. Instead Congress acted to improve the climate of investment; it reduced the undistributed profits tax in 1937 and 1938, and eliminated it completely in 1939 against Roosevelt's wishes.[33]

Baruch, Berle, and Wallace all stayed with the administration, but Moley, with great sadness, broke with Roosevelt. As one of the original Brains Trusters, Moley knew Roosevelt very well, but came to believe he "is dangerous in the extreme," and the two men had a falling out. That left the president more dependent than ever on Morgenthau, who became increasingly nervous during 1937. In November, with unemployment at 17.1 percent, he told Roosevelt he thought the economy might be headed for another crash. The combination of labor unrest, more federal deficits, a jump in unemployment, and the backlash from Roosevelt's efforts to add justices to the Supreme Court all were sapping the nation's morale.[34]

In the midst of these defeats, and the rising unemployment, Roosevelt became more explicit in describing a conspiracy of businessmen trying to undermine his administration. They were still avoiding taxes and refusing to invest in economic development. Morgenthau received first news of this conspiracy in a phone call to Roosevelt in November 1937.

> I called the President last night at 6:15 and told him that I was now convinced that we were headed into another depression and that I thought he had to do something about it. I said I would like to call in a number of people over Saturday and Sunday and discuss whether we should do something about gold. From then on the President got very excited, very dictatorial and very disagreeable.
>
> He quoted at great length a man whom he described as a "wise old bird" who had told him that there were 2,000 men in this country who had made up their minds that they would hold a pistol to the President's head and make certain demands of him, otherwise

they would continue to depress business. He quoted a lot of other generalities.

I said, "A great [deal] depends on who this person is" and, like a crack from a whip, he said, "It is not necessary for you to know who that person is, ["] which, after thinking it over, led me to believe that the "wise old bird" was himself whom he was quoting.[35]

Four days later, when Morgenthau had lunch with the president, Roosevelt again—in mellower terms—described the ominous threat of these mysterious 2,000 men. "Now I don't say that 2,000 men have all got together and agreed to block us but I do say that 2,000 men have come to about the same conclusion," Roosevelt insisted.[36]

Interestingly, as the depression within a depression persisted, Roosevelt thought the conspiracy was still there, but that the conspirators had diminished in numbers. At a cabinet meeting in February 1939, with unemployment at 19.3 percent, Roosevelt said that fifty rich men had formed a kind of cabal to raise money to discredit the president. Morgenthau summarized that cabinet meeting and noted that Vice President John Nance Garner, who had been critical of the president, was annoyed at FDR's allegation. "The Vice-President," according to Morgenthau, "got on a tirade about what he [FDR] said about fifty rich men who had put $5,000,000 into a pot to discredit this Administration and that something should be done about them. . . ."[37]

By 1939, more of the president's men were urging a loosening of restrictions on business to help it recover. Harry Hopkins, the biggest spender in the whole Roosevelt administration, had become secretary of commerce and even he, after rounds of talks with investors, joined the recovery bandwagon. Morgenthau was so anxious to stanch the economic bleeding that he had signs printed up that read, "Does it contribute to recovery?"[38] He kept one on his desk and announced that he wanted that question to influence his thinking on all policy suggestions coming through the Treasury

Department. He even offered a recovery sign to Roosevelt, but was turned down. For the first time, according to Morgenthau, even cabinet meetings became contentious as a few of Roosevelt's advisors urged him to think of ways to persuade people to start businesses, or expand existing ones. Still the president would not budge.[39]

Finally, in March 1939, with unemployment at 19.3 percent, Morgenthau knew he had to confront the president about his economic views. A Gallup poll released that month revealed that 67 percent of Americans believed that the Roosevelt administration's attitude toward business was delaying recovery. Morgenthau may have been too nervous to face the president alone, because he brought along John Hanes, his undersecretary of the treasury. Morgenthau and Hanes had prepared a list of suggested changes— "repeal the capital stock and excess profits taxes," for example, and give corporations a greater chance to deduct and carry over net losses.

Morgenthau then included what he must have known would be the hardest sell of them all: reduce the top federal income tax rate from 79 to 64 percent. To Morgenthau, 64 percent was still high—a millionaire would still have to earn over $2.5 million per year once he reached the top bracket before he would be allowed to keep $1 million per year. Such a concession was not large, but Morgenthau thought it would send businessmen the right message that they should take risks because they would be able to keep more of their money.[40]

At the meeting, Roosevelt criticized the tax cut immediately. He also became hostile and, according to Morgenthau, said, "I think that sign you have up on your desk 'Does it contribute to recovery' is very stupid, and he showed considerable displeasure when he said it. He did not say it with a smile. I said, 'I am sorry. I disagree with you.'" On Morgenthau's tax cut idea, Roosevelt labeled it "the Mellon plan of taxation." Morgenthau and Hanes pointed out that under Mellon, 25 percent was a top rate and that even with a small cut, the proposed top rate would still be a punitive 64 percent—the 4 percent standard tax plus a 60 percent surtax. "We are not returning to the Mellon era," they told Roosevelt, but businessmen needed incentives to invest.[41]

Interestingly, Roosevelt seemed to agree with this point. "Now, for instance," Roosevelt said, "Barney Baruch has been saying right along that you have got to reduce the top taxes and that if you do that people will take chances." Morgenthau responded that "under the present circumstances" he agreed with Baruch. Roosevelt then asked, "Well, you are willing to pay usury in order to get recovery?" and Morgenthau responded, "Yes, sir," but the president did not agree.[42]

Three points are worth noting about this exchange. First, to Roosevelt, a small tax cut was a return to the Mellon era, and therefore unacceptable. Second, Roosevelt seemed to agree, however, that lowering tax rates would spur business recovery and reduce the 19 percent unemployment. Third, he did not seem to think that aiding business, or "paying usury," as he worded it, was worth it even if it helped recovery. Did Roosevelt prefer a national state of depression to a national recovery—if giving incentives (such as a tax cut) to businessmen was the method of securing the national recovery?

Roosevelt's startling comments illuminated for Morgenthau another exchange he had with Roosevelt during this meeting. After Roosevelt announced his displeasure with Morgenthau's recovery sign, the president

> then proceeded to give Hanes and me a long lecture that while he would concede that this [tax incentives for business] would be helpful for the rest of this year and possibly into 1940, as a result of what he called a complete turn-about position [i.e., tax incentives] on the part of the Treasury as to where we were two years ago, that this would put a man in as President who, as he called it, would be controlled by a man on horseback, the way Mussolini and Hitler

are. This lecture went on and on, he saying that this [Morgenthau's tax suggestions] was going backwards and that this simply would mean that we would have a Fascist President.[43]

Roosevelt's idea that cutting taxes would probably help recovery, but would then lead to a fascist president in the next election was clearly troubling to Morgenthau.

When he got through I said, "I disagree with you; I felt that if we had recovery in 1940 that that would enhance our chances greatly of having the next President a liberal president and that further-more the situation was a very tight one in the world and that recovery in the United States was terrifically important at this time in deciding the fate of what kind of Governments we would have in the rest of the world." He said he did not agree with me. He did not think the domestic situation played such an important part in the world[,] one[,] and he also disagreed that a prosperous 1940 would give us a liberal President after 1940. He said, "You come to me on my farm in Hyde Park in 1941 and say there has been a catastrophe and somebody like General [Oswald] Mosley has called out the troops and you will call on me to come to the aid of the country and," he said, "I will tell you this thing has been brought about by this sort of thing you are talking to me about today."[44]

Morgenthau was clearly surprised by Roosevelt's point of view. Morgenthau reasoned that if we have tax cuts, and if the tax cuts help lead to recovery, then that will (1) improve both the United States and the position of democratic governments in world affairs and (2) also increase the chance that a liberal president like Roosevelt would be elected in 1940. Roosevelt, however, according to Morgenthau, said that he "would concede that [tax incentives] would be helpful for the rest of this year and possibly into 1940," but that the gains from that, which would be a "turn-about position," would actually encourage the electing of a fascist like Oswald Mosley, British member of Parliament, as president of the United States in 1940. Roosevelt didn't mention any particular person, or group of people, so we can't be sure who he thought this fascist, or these incipient fascists, were. Possibly he believed that this fascist-behind-the-scene was in some way led by, or part of, the two thousand men who were "going to hold a pistol to the president's head and make certain demands," or to the "fifty rich men who had put $5,000,000 in a pot to discredit this Administration." Whatever the case, at the end of this remarkable conversation, Roosevelt insisted that Morgenthau and Hanes promise not to "mention what we have talked about here to a living soul."[45]

Morgenthau had some slight encouragement from this meeting in that Roosevelt did not completely dismiss the proposed tax incentives. But in less than two months, Roosevelt was again on the hunt. He asked Morgenthau for a list of the thousand richest people in America. The president seemed to want them investigated because he thought they were avoiding the payment of taxes. He was particularly annoyed at tax-exempt bonds as possible loopholes, and told Morgenthau about a conversation he allegedly had with a rich man who confessed outright to the president that he was stashing $1 million in tax-exempt bonds to avoid paying more in income taxes.[46]

The ongoing depression, and Roosevelt's response to it, greatly distressed Morgenthau. By April 1939, unemployment reached 20.7 percent and Morgenthau was desperate. He began to confide in veteran congressmen Robert Doughton and Jere Cooper of the House Ways and Means Committee. Doughton especially, as chairman of the committee, had irritated Roosevelt because he was trying to repeal the president's undistributed profits tax and favored giving incentives to business to invest. Roosevelt probably never knew it, but Morgenthau met with Doughton and Cooper in private and unloaded his frustrations:

Now, gentlemen, we have tried spending money. We are spending more than we have ever spent before and it does not work. And I have just one interest, and if I am wrong, as far as I am concerned, somebody else can have my job. I want to see this country prosperous. I want to see people get a job. I want to see people get enough to eat. We have never made good on our promises. . . . I say after eight years of this Administration we have just as much unemployment as when we started. . . . And an enormous debt to boot! We are just sitting here and fiddling and I am just wearing myself out and getting sick. Because why? I can't see any daylight.[47]

Morgenthau had massive public support for his efforts to help business recover. According to a March 1939 Gallup poll, only 9 percent of the population thought Roosevelt had been too friendly to business, and 52 percent said he had not "been friendly enough." Forty percent of the respondents said the hostility toward business had delayed recovery. In a *Fortune* poll in September 1940, over 77 percent of the executives surveyed opposed "Roosevelt's policies designed to achieve . . . recovery."[48]

If we put Roosevelt's tax policies in context what we find is that regressive excise taxes were the major source of funding for many of his New Deal programs. "We cannot afford at this time to sacrifice the revenue [these excise taxes] represent," Roosevelt said as late as 1939. Such revenue from tens of millions of lower- and middle-income earners was needed because wealthier Americans were shifting their earnings to avoid the president's near confiscatory income tax rates. Even Roosevelt himself, however, privately conceded to Morgenthau in 1939 that tax cuts would probably stimulate investment and prosperity, which would allow rich Americans to earn more and thus pay more in taxes—just as happened in the 1920s. But Roosevelt refused to cut taxes or encourage businesses because, as he told Morgenthau, it might lead to the election of a fascist as president in 1940.[49]

As a postcript, Roosevelt continued his attacks on business

until World War II. Even after he was safely in the White House for a third term, and the internal fascist threat was thereby seemingly removed, he still wanted to raise the income tax on rich people. In July 1941, as he planned his third term, he suggested to his budget director a proposal for a 99.5 percent tax rate on all income over $100,000. When the budget director was clearly startled by such a request, Roosevelt responded, "Why not? None of us is ever going to make $100,000 a year."[50]

11

THE IRS:
FDR'S PERSONAL WEAPON

"My father," Elliott Roosevelt observed of his famous parent, "may have been the originator of the concept of employing the IRS as a weapon of political retribution." Not until Franklin D. Roosevelt's presidency had the federal government taken so much individual income. In 1935, when Roosevelt hiked the top marginal income tax rate to 79 percent and the top marginal estate tax rate to 70 percent, millionaires searched for deductions and loopholes to protect their private property. During the 1930s, FDR began experimenting with the Bureau of Internal Revenue (later renamed the Internal Revenue Service, or IRS), which had earlier been placed under the Treasury Department, as a means of attacking political enemies and generating more revenue for his New Deal programs.[1]

The first person to incur Roosevelt's wrath, and thereby receive a long, sustained investigation by the IRS, was Huey Long. As a flamboyant and clever politician—some would say demagogue—

Long became governor of Louisiana in 1928 and built a successful political machine in the state. He promised free textbooks, cheap health care, and other benefits to the voters of Louisiana, and he fulfilled some of his promises by levying high corporate taxes. Long and his political cohorts also took kickbacks from oil companies, highway builders, and other service providers. Long built up a strong enough cash base to sustain his minions in office in Louisiana after he was elected to the U.S. Senate in 1930.[2]

In Washington, Long became the sharpest thorn in Roosevelt's side. Long supported the president at first, but gradually came to criticize almost all of his New Deal programs as inadequate or misdirected. He castigated the AAA and argued for inflation, not for paying farmers not to produce. Of the NRA, Long said, "Every fault of socialism is found in this bill, without one of its virtues." He also ridiculed Roosevelt's New Deal administrators as charlatans and incompetents. He regularly baited Democrat Joe Robinson, the Senate majority leader, and made it hard for Roosevelt to get his bills passed.[3]

Roosevelt, after denouncing Long as (along with Douglas MacArthur) one of the two most dangerous men in the country, searched his arsenal for weapons to deploy against the Louisiana senator. At first, Roosevelt tried to check Long by denying him federal patronage. The president made Louisiana unique by appointing a director from outside the state to come in and administer federal relief programs. Roosevelt also sent federal patronage to Long's political enemies, led by ex-governor John Parker. The order came down from Roosevelt: "Don't put anybody in and don't help anybody that is working for Huey Long or his crowd: That is a hundred percent!"[4]

Long responded by having the state turn down federal funds. Harold Ickes, director of the Public Works Administration (PWA), then criticized Long publicly for refusing to take about half the federal money allocated to the state for highway construction. Refusing to accept federal funds was unprecedented, Ickes said, and would cripple economic development in Louisiana. Long simply denounced the men appointed to use such money as crooks. "Pay them my further respects up there in Washington," Long told reporters. "Tell them they can go to hell."[5]

T. Harry Williams, who wrote an exhaustive biography of Long, thoroughly researched the patronage dispute between Roosevelt and Long. Williams concluded:

> He [Long] was not greatly concerned about the practical effect of his loss of the patronage: the number of federal jobs involved was relatively small, and the number of state jobs at his disposal was more than sufficient to enable him to sustain his power. But it was humiliating to him that his enemies should control the [federal] patronage and then boast about it. It would encourage them to continue their opposition to him. . . .[6]

Long's solution was to recruit a national base of supporters, perhaps for a future presidential run himself. In February 1934, Long, in a national radio speech, announced his Share Our Wealth (SOW) clubs with the slogan "Every Man a King." He promoted a steeply progressive income tax to guarantee every family a "homestead" and a minimum annual income. Long's crusade generated sixty thousand letters weekly, mostly from fans eager to start SOW clubs in their communities. As Long encouraged the national membership in his clubs, Roosevelt tested Long's potential presidential support for 1936. Postmaster General James Farley, Roosevelt's accurate pollster, estimated Long's national strength at between four million and six million votes by 1936—perhaps 15 percent—easily large enough to swing an election to the Republicans.[7]

Farley's estimates were confirmed when Long traveled around the nation to promote SOW clubs and explore a presidential run. The Carolinas, for example, became a testing ground for Long. "South Carolina is the strongest state for Roosevelt," Long observed. "If I can sell myself here, I can sell myself anywhere." In

March 1936, Long toured South Carolina. Governor Olin Johnston tried to ignore Long, especially because Roosevelt had telephoned him earlier threatening to cut off all federal patronage if he helped the Louisiana senator. Even after Johnston's snub, Long spoke on the University of South Carolina campus, at the capitol, and throughout the state. He attracted huge crowds, and 140,000 voters in South Carolina signed cards vowing support for Long if he would run for president.[8]

Long's budding national support was a major threat to the president's reelection. If Long ran for president as a third-party candidate, he might siphon enough votes from the Democrats to elect a Republican.[9] Also, Long's ability to hold Louisiana without federal patronage could spur other rebels to challenge Roosevelt's allies, who were distributing patronage in other states. Much was at stake, and Roosevelt's team turned to the IRS to investigate Long and give the president an advantage.

We can't tell for sure when Roosevelt decided to use the IRS against Long, but we do know this: Henry Morgenthau, Roosevelt's longtime friend, became secretary of the treasury in January 1934. Three days after his Senate confirmation, Morgenthau called in Elmer Irey, head of the special intelligence division of the IRS. "Why have you stopped investigating Huey Long, Mr. Irey?" Morgenthau asked. Irey explained that any investigation of Long was on hold. "Get all your agents back on the Louisiana job," Morgenthau then ordered. "Start the investigation of Huey Long. . . ." Morgenthau further asked Irey to report to him once a week. Irey did so for almost a year. When he failed to schedule an appointment one week—for lack of new information—Morgenthau made a phone call to him and said, "You haven't been to see me in eight days." Irey sent dozens of agents into Louisiana, and one of them even infiltrated the Long organization. In the course of the investigation, Irey also spoke with Roosevelt face-to-face, and they worked together to get the right lawyer to prosecute Long and his cohorts.[10]

Roosevelt's (or Morgenthau's) decision to use the IRS against Long was a logical move. Long was not independently wealthy. Yet he somehow had enough money to hold the loyalty of his state even though his opponents were endowed with federal funds. How could this be? Roosevelt logically concluded that graft and kick-backs from state contracts were enough to keep Long in power. Here, however, Long had a dilemma. Most state officials and con-tractors had to pay the Long machine to keep their jobs and their state contracts. If Long refused to report these kickbacks on his tax return, the IRS could prosecute him for tax evasion. If, however, Long did itemize this cash, and did report it as income, then Roosevelt could publicize Long's abuse of politics to extort wealth and preserve power. Those who gave the kickbacks to Long would also be publicly embarrassed.

Long naturally resented the swooping down of the IRS into Louisiana. On the floor of the Senate, he protested the "hordes" of agents, 250 at least, on his trail and that of his friends. "They did not try to put any covering over this thing," Long said. They just boasted that he and his friends "were all going away." At one level, Irey had an agent infiltrate the Long organization; at another level, Irey learned what he could from Long's enemies. Among these were the Jahnke brothers, highway contractors whose information on Long was useful to Irey. But since the Jahnke brothers were unable to get state contracts from Long, they were near bankruptcy. Irey, therefore, secured for them a federal loan from the Reconstruction Finance Corporation to keep them in business, thus giving them more incentive to help the IRS catch Long.[11]

By 1935, the IRS began indicting lower-level and more vulner-able members of Long's team. State representative Joseph Fisher was successfully prosecuted for tax evasion in April 1935. Then Long was assassinated in September and his machine fell into dis-array. In October, Abraham Shushan, a Long stalwart, was acquit-ted of tax evasion. Others eventually settled with the IRS in civil court. "It was widely reported at the time," tax expert David Burnham concluded, "that the cases had been dropped in return for a pledge from Long's heirs to support Roosevelt in his bid for a second term." Most of the remnants of the Long machine, led by Huey's brother Earl, did, in fact cooperate with Roosevelt, and the president won almost 90 percent of Louisiana's vote in 1936—a larger percentage than he got in either neighboring Texas or Arkansas. After the election, Irey was able to secure more prosecutions for tax evasion, mail fraud, and misuse of WPA labor for personal use—but no more would Louisiana politicians thunder against Roosevelt and the New Deal.[12]

Roosevelt marveled at the potential of the IRS for removing political opponents. Newspaper publisher William Randolph Hearst also found himself under investigation when he began opposing Roosevelt's political programs. Such a situation was awkward for Elliott Roosevelt, the president's son, whom Hearst had astutely hired as aviation editor for his newspaper, the *Los Angeles Express*. According to Elliott, "At about the same time that he [FDR] sent federal investigators into Louisiana to prove the financial shenanigans of Huey Long and company, father had the Internal Revenue Service conduct a similar scrutiny of every corner and crevice of Hearst's empire...."[13] Hearst, however, did not depend on patronage and kickbacks to make his money and extend his influence. The nature of his business differed from that of Long's, and Hearst's books were in order.

So were those of Father Charles Coughlin, the popular radio priest from Detroit, who began meeting with Huey Long in 1935 and joined him in denouncing Roosevelt. The IRS sent reports on Coughlin's finances to the president, who also put James Farley, the postmaster general, to work on Coughlin's mail—how much was he getting and how successful was his financing? Roosevelt learned much about Coughlin's financing, but could not find evidence to put him in jail. Thus Coughlin joined Long and Hearst in regularly denouncing Roosevelt. Sometimes those three critics were able to join forces to defeat Roosevelt on key political issues. The president, for example, wanted the United States to join the World Court, part of the League of Nations. He was furious when Hearst in his papers, Coughlin on the radio, and Long on the Senate floor helped generate enough opposition to the World Court to defeat Roosevelt's plan.[14]

As Elliott Roosevelt admitted, "Other men's tax returns continued to fascinate Father in the [nineteen] thirties." Boake Carter, for example, was a radio commentator who criticized Roosevelt for his attempt to pack the Supreme Court and for "meddling" in the Far East and risking a war with Japan. Roosevelt—according to his son—had an IRS investigation of Carter and also asked Frances Perkins, the secretary of labor, if she would check Carter's status as an alien and see if he could be deported.[15]

Another target of the president was Hamilton Fish, the Republican congressman from Roosevelt's home district in New York. When Fish began to oppose Roosevelt on program after program, Roosevelt at first tried to oust Fish at the ballot box. Hyde Park was Roosevelt's territory and FDR hated the idea of Fish representing the president and his neighbors in Congress. When Fish kept winning reelection, sometimes by large margins, Roosevelt brought in the men at the IRS. They alleged that Fish owed $5,000 in back taxes and demanded payment. Fish challenged this ruling in court. "The case dragged on for several years," Fish observed, "costing the government many thousands of dollars as it attempted to make me pay the money, which if I had agreed, would have besmirched my reputation." Eventually, the IRS lost its case completely, and even had to concede a tax refund to Fish of $80. In 1942, the IRS launched a multiyear audit of Fish and that also failed. Finally, during World War II, Roosevelt asked J. Edgar Hoover at the FBI to investigate Fish on a charge that he was engaging in "subversive activities." That effort also fizzled, but Roosevelt finally got his way when his friends in New York gerrymandered Fish's congressional district, and he lost his seat in the 1944 elections.[16]

Fish was an exception to the rule that Roosevelt had less success using the IRS against media opponents than political opponents—especially those like Long who needed an influx of questionable financial contributions to operate.

Just as Long was vulnerable in Louisiana, so were all the city bosses in America, who, by the 1930s, needed federal patronage to win elections and generate operating funds. How these bosses fared with the law often depended on whether they had value to the president. In New Jersey, for example, Enoch "Nucky" Johnson was the political boss of Atlantic City during the 1920s and 1930s. He made his money from bootlegging, gambling, protection, and kickbacks. Johnson's tax returns always included a large income under a vague category called "other contributions." The gamblers and racketeers in wide-open Atlantic City liked Nucky, who provided security and stability, and they were willing to lie and even go to jail to protect him.[17]

Unfortunately for Nucky Johnson, however, when he chose his political affiliation in the early 1900s, he happened to select the Republican Party. The United States had no income tax then, and Johnson focused on local, not national, politics. Before 1933, local profits held much more potential for city bosses than federal. Atlantic County went Republican in 1932, but Democrat in 1936 by a small margin. Johnson seems to have been indifferent to Roosevelt—and when Johnson was ultimately convicted of tax fraud in 1941, Roosevelt seems to have cared little one way or another. Johnson neither hurt him nor helped him, so FDR simply watched from the sidelines as the IRS audited and then convicted Johnson.[18]

The story of Frank Hague, the political boss in Jersey City, had a very different plot development and ending. Hague, born of Irish parents, grew up in a rough neighborhood in Jersey City. He was expelled from school in the sixth grade, and as a teenager worked as a blacksmith and even a boxer. Politics was a way out of the slums for Hague, and he joined the Democrat political machine and worked his way up from constable to city commissioner to mayor. By 1932, the fifty-six-year-old Hague was undisputed boss of Jersey City. He initially backed Al Smith for president in 1932, but quickly shifted to Roosevelt after the Democrat convention; Hague promised the swing state of New Jersey to Roosevelt and gave the future president a spectacular parade with one hundred thousand people present in Sea Girt, New Jersey, the largest crowd Roosevelt saw anywhere during the entire campaign.[19]

On election day, Hague's support proved to be indispensable. Roosevelt carried New Jersey by fewer than 28,900 votes out of over 1.6 million cast. The major urban counties all went Republican, but not Hague's Hudson County. He delivered that county to FDR by over 117,000 votes, nearly a three-to-one margin.[20]

Once in the White House, Roosevelt funneled all federal patronage in the state through Hague and none through the governor or the two U.S. senators. When a man from Newark wrote to the governor of New Jersey asking for a job, the governor responded, "I do not have the power to appoint to these Federal positions. They are made upon the recommendation of the local organizations to Mayor Hague. . . . I would suggest that you also get in touch with the mayor." Roosevelt's men James Farley and Harry Hopkins helped the mayor strengthen his hold on the state. Hopkins began the federal flow by giving Hague $500,000 per month for relief in 1933 and 1934; in the five years after that Hopkins directed the WPA to pour an incredible $50 million into Jersey City. Harold Ickes and the PWA gave $17 million to Hague's city—some of which helped Hague build the third largest hospital in the world. Those who could not, or would not, pay their medical bills could get them reduced or removed by seeing Hague's district political leaders. Roosevelt came down to Jersey City in October 1936, right before the presidential election, to dedicate Hague's hospital and receive the boss's official blessing. On election day, Hague delivered an even larger county vote for Roosevelt—almost four to one—and New Jersey's sixteen electoral votes again went to the president.[21]

Hague used his patronage shrewdly and controlled his city with an iron hand. "I am the law," Hague often boasted. Political opponents had no patronage jobs and sometimes found themselves in jail for their critical remarks. Hague openly flouted civil liberties and his enemies labeled him the "Hudson County Hitler." One outside reporter depicted Hague as "Dictator—American Style" and another called him "King Hanky Panky." Even with the torrent of federal funds cascading into New Jersey, and charges of corruption rampant, the IRS never made a serious investigation of Hague. Nucky Johnson, with a smaller city and only local funds to swindle, went to prison, but Hague never did.[22]

The IRS had overpowering reason to go after Hague on WPA corruption alone. Harry Hopkins had piles of evidence, including sworn affidavits, that Hague was manipulating elections, politicizing the dispensing of jobs, and forcing jobholders to pay 3 percent of their salaries to the Hague machine at election time. Many letters and statements describing this corruption are available in the WPA "Political Coercion" files, which are housed in the National Archives. Hopkins not only did nothing to stop Hague but actually seemed to encourage him.[23]

Roosevelt was embarrassed by Hague and never included him in his inner circle, but Hague was needed if New Jersey were to remain in the president's column. Roosevelt was firm on that and proved it when James Farley discovered that Hague had a crony at the post office who was opening and reading all mail to and from major political opponents. Tampering with the U.S. mail was a federal offense, and some of Huey Long's henchmen had gone to jail for misusing the post office. Farley, in fact, came to Roosevelt for instructions on how to prosecute Hague. The president, however, stopped Farley in his tracks: "Forget prosecution. You go tell Frank to knock it off. We can't have this kind of thing going on. But keep this quiet. We need Hague's support if we want New Jersey."[24]

Historian Lyle Dorsett, who has studied the evidence carefully, reported the following example of how Hague misused federal funds:

After a plea from Hague, Harry Hopkins decided to stretch the letter of the law and use WPA funds which were earmarked for labor to buy seats and plumbing for Jersey City's new baseball stadium. Hague knew he was asking Hopkins to put his neck out, but assured him it was for a good cause, inasmuch as the facility was to be named Roosevelt Stadium and the president was going to be present for the grand opening.[25]

Hague was not the only politician who needed the president's help to stay out of jail. Roosevelt would use his powers to help others who were useful to him. Lyndon Johnson, for example, was a young congressman from Texas in the 1930s. He always backed Roosevelt enthusiastically—especially in 1937 when others abandoned Roosevelt after he tried to pack the Supreme Court. Johnson, in running for a special election to Congress that year, argued that the New Deal was a seamless web and that to support Court packing was an essential test of loyalty to the president and his agenda.[26]

Roosevelt came to like Johnson, especially when he proved himself useful in controlling Texas politics. Whenever Roosevelt needed help from Sam Rayburn, the House majority leader (and later Speaker of the House), Johnson was there as an intermediary. When Vice President John Nance Garner of Texas mounted a presidential campaign in 1940, Johnson secretly undermined Garner in the state and helped swing support to Roosevelt. In return Roosevelt channeled much federal patronage into Texas through Johnson.

Just as the president used a mayor in New Jersey as his key political connection, so he used a junior congressman in Texas to dispense patronage. Thomas Corcoran, a close friend and advisor to FDR, once observed that Lyndon Johnson "got more projects, and more money for his district, than anyone else. He was the best kind of Congressman for his district that *ever* was." Those who received Johnson's patronage in turn made Johnson a millionaire and financed his political ambitions to the U.S. Senate. Brown & Root, Inc., a huge Texas contracting firm, built dams and other projects with federal dollars. In turn, they donated heavily to Johnson's two Senate campaigns in the 1940s. Campaign contributions were not tax deductible, but Brown & Root did so anyway and with such carelessness that they triggered an IRS audit. Even Morgenthau was annoyed. The IRS investigated Brown & Root and determined that they owed over $1.5 million in back taxes and penalties. They were also vulnerable to a jail sentence.[27]

Johnson himself became an IRS target for failing to properly report income from his campaigns. On January 13, 1944, just as six IRS agents were winding up their eighteen-month investigation of Johnson, President Roosevelt held an emergency meeting with Johnson. That day, the president contacted Elmer Irey and began the process of halting the investigation. Brown & Root settled quietly—with no publicity—for a mere $372,000 in back taxes and no jail time. Johnson was not harmed at all. He had proven himself too valuable to the president to lose.[28]

Roosevelt, however, would not protect political allies from the IRS if they were insufficiently useful to him. An interesting example is "Big Tom" Pendergast, the Democrat boss in Kansas City, Missouri. Pendergast was an early supporter of Roosevelt for president in 1932, and on election day he helped deliver Missouri to Roosevelt. Jackson County, Pendergast's stronghold, went for FDR by more than a two-to-one margin—which must have taken some arm-twisting because that county had voted Republican in the previous three presidential races. In return, Roosevelt had Hopkins filter federal patronage in Missouri through "Big Tom."[29]

Pendergast used his new friend in a high place to consolidate further his power in Missouri. For example, he had his own construction company and, like Hague, he used his power to gain wealth, distribute jobs, and win elections. In 1934, Pendergast's choice for U.S. Senate was a failed haberdasher named Harry Truman. After Truman won his election handily, a constituent wrote asking him for a WPA job. Truman responded, "If you will send us endorsements from the Kansas City Democratic Organization, I shall be glad to do what I can for you." That response spoke volumes about where the political influence in Missouri was located and which party held it. Pendergast's choice for governor in 1936 was Lloyd Stark, and "Big Tom" coerced WPA workers all over the state to vote for Stark or lose their jobs. The same applied for Roosevelt's reelection campaign, and the president carried Missouri easily, with Jackson County leading the way with a three-to-one margin for Roosevelt.[30]

Pendergast's exuberance to deliver a large vote for Roosevelt proved to be his undoing. After the election, some observers noticed that Pendergast's first ward had cast more ballots than it had eligible voters. And some of the precincts in the ward had unanimous voting for Roosevelt—even though some voters there swore they had voted for Alf Landon, the Republican candidate. A police captain accused of intimidating voters responded, "I wouldn't hurt none of them women, but I consider it a patriotic duty to see that votes are cast the way the ward leader wants 'em cast. After all, I'm employed by the city." Maurice Milligan, the district attorney, prosecuted more than two hundred election judges, precinct captains, and partisan clerks—all of whom had legal defenses financed by Pendergast. Seventy-eight went to jail. Governor Stark, in the meantime, became nervous and took a calculated risk. He switched sides, joined forces with Milligan, and helped bring in the FBI and the IRS to investigate Pendergast. Would the president intervene?[31]

Roosevelt no doubt appreciated the large Democratic vote mustered by Pendergast, but the bad publicity that followed gave ammunition to those critical of the president and his New Deal. Roosevelt therefore pondered the idea of switching his patronage to Governor Stark. When 259 of Pendergast's men were convicted of vote fraud, and then when Stark's candidate defeated Pendergast's candidate for a key statewide election in 1938, Roosevelt dropped Pendergast and gave more of Missouri's patronage to Governor Stark. Roosevelt sat back as the IRS fined and imprisoned Pendergast for tax evasion. Unlike Hague in New Jersey and Johnson in Texas, Pendergast was not indispensable to Roosevelt and thus did not receive his help in calling off the IRS.[32]

By Roosevelt's second term, he was accustomed to using—or at least to contemplating using—the IRS for political help. Major crises such as the Court-packing plan especially stimulated the Roosevelt administration into using the IRS to stymie political enemies. Senator Burton Wheeler of Montana, who helped mobilize votes against Court packing, complained loudly to Secretary Morgenthau of rumors that the IRS had been investigating him. Morgenthau promised Wheeler freedom from a tax investigation. Morgenthau later received a memo from a colleague in the Treasury Department that Thomas Corcoran had come to the Department of Justice with "a request for information concerning the income tax returns of the Justices of the Supreme Court." Morgenthau refused to allow Corcoran to have those returns, and Roosevelt apparently never insisted that that decision be overridden.[33]

Wealthy Americans were a natural target for Roosevelt and the IRS. For one thing, rich people had the money that Roosevelt wanted to fund the WPA and other programs. His highly progressive tax rate secured some of this cash, but people with wealth quickly sought tax loopholes. The complexity of earning money, and then trying to shelter it legally, made rich Americans an obvious target for generating federal revenue. Another related consideration is that rich people were a nucleus of energy blowing against the New Deal. No one likes to pay taxes, and many wealthy Americans resented paying over half of their annual earnings for federal programs that they loathed. Working from January to July or August for Roosevelt and the rest of the year for themselves became a dreary prospect to face, and they complained loudly.

Roosevelt's first target among the rich was Andrew Mellon, the Pittsburgh industrialist and banker. As mentioned earlier, Mellon helped found Alcoa and Gulf Oil, and he was on the board of directors of about sixty companies. By the 1920s, he was reputed to be the third wealthiest man/in the country, trailing only Ford and Rockefeller. His wealth alone made him a tempting candidate for an IRS audit, but his political actions during the 1920s made him an irresistible target. Mellon, after all, was Morgenthau's predecessor in the Treasury Department.[34]

Roosevelt's philosophy of government contrasted sharply with Mellon's. The president was mired in the Great Depression, and he believed that the way to combat it was through high taxation, government planning, farm quotas, and massive spending for relief. Roosevelt, as we have seen, believed in underconsumption, that the Great Depression was partly caused by poor investments and stock manipulations by rich people. Mellon's very presence as a popular former treasury secretary served as a constant reminder to many Americans of "the good old days" when tax rates were low, jobs were plentiful, and government was unobtrusive. In Roosevelt's first term, Mellon—almost as much as Huey Long—became the object of a massive and unrelenting IRS investigation.

Roosevelt initiated the tax investigation through Homer Cummings, the attorney general, and Henry Morgenthau, the secretary of the treasury. The audit and the eventual trial of Mellon for tax fraud were precarious right from the start. "The Roosevelt administration made me go after Andy Mellon," said Elmer Irey, head of Morgenthau's Intelligence Unit at the IRS.

Irey knew the situation and firmly believed Mellon's tax returns were in order. Actually the Roosevelt administration had first tried an FBI investigation on Mellon; that failed, so the IRS was the next step. According to Irey, "Bob Jackson [future attorney general] was made chief counsel of the Internal Revenue Department and he said to me: 'I need help on that Mellon thing. The F. B. I. investigation was no good. You run one on him.'" When Irey hesitated, he received a phone call from his boss, Henry Morgenthau. "Irey," Morgenthau announced, "you can't be 99⅔ percent on that job. Investigate Mellon. I order it." Irey pleaded with Morgenthau that Mellon was innocent, but Morgenthau ended the conversation by saying, "I'm directing you to go ahead, Irey." Irey reluctantly began the audit, but more than ten years later he was still upset that he had to launch a futile and wasteful IRS audit of an innocent man.[35]

Since Morgenthau and Roosevelt were longtime friends, and since the two of them met privately on a regular basis, we can assume Roosevelt directed Morgenthau to launch the tax audit of Mellon. At the very least Roosevelt tacitly approved. Certainly Morgenthau was a willing accomplice. "You can't be too tough in this trial to suit me," Morgenthau told the government's prosecutor, Robert Jackson. Morgenthau added, "I consider that Mellon is not on trial but [d]emocracy and the privileged rich and I want to see who will win."[36]

In fact, Mellon won. A Pittsburgh grand jury, heavily composed of working-class laborers, heard the evidence and refused to indict Mellon. Then the Board of Tax Appeals voted unanimously that Mellon "did not file a false and fraudulent return with the purpose of evading taxes." The board did claim some technical errors in Mellon's tax returns. Mellon decided to settle for $486,000—less than one-sixth of the original indictment—and get the "political prosecution," as he called it, behind him.

Mellon was pleased, but he always expected to win the lengthy trial. "For several months," Mellon observed, "a campaign of character-wrecking and abuse against me and other large taxpayers [banker Thomas Lamont, for example] has been carried on in the press and over the radio." Columnist Walter Lippmann called the trial "an act of profound injustice," and said the chances that a tax expert like Mellon had cheated on his income taxes—especially when he was preparing to donate his large art collection to start the National Gallery of Art—were "not one in a million." The tax case was trumped up, Lippmann concluded, and was "one of those stunts that politicians stoop to every now and then, thinking that they can gain some advantage by it for their party." The Roosevelt administration may have lost a case it never had a chance to win, but it did send a message that lining up with the Republicans could be embarrassing, and might be costly.[37]

Moses "Moe" Annenberg, who was almost as wealthy and almost as Republican as Mellon, also drew an IRS audit—with thirty-five agents working for two and a half years to prosecute him. Unlike Mellon, who was born into Pittsburgh's elite, Annenberg was a poor German immigrant who came to America at age eight. He showed skill selling newspapers for the Hearst chain and worked his way up to be circulation manager of the whole Hearst newspaper empire. He wanted to create a business of his own and his most successful venture was in the horse-racing industry. He was an investor, not a gambler, and he sold racing forms (to describe the horses), wall sheets (to post the racing results), and the wire service, which was used to obtain immediate results of the races. He developed the largest horse-racing network in the country, and made many millions of dollars from that enterprise alone. He also invested effectively in real estate and the stock market.[38]

But Annenberg continued to like the newspaper business, and in Roosevelt's first term he bought the *Philadelphia Inquirer*. Annenberg quickly became immersed in Republican politics, writing against the New Deal in general and competing against the *Philadelphia Record* in particular. J. David Stern was the editor of the *Record* and Stern enjoyed playing chess with Morgenthau and high-stakes politics with Roosevelt—who appreciated Stern's successful efforts to elect more Democrats in Pennsylvania. Annenberg's conservative politics and his entrepreneurial spirit made him an effective Republican competitor in the newspaper and political wars.

Annenberg's aggressive advertising and news reporting helped the *Inquirer* sharply increase its subscriptions and sales at the expense of Stern's *Record*. The *Inquirer*'s success meant that more Pennsylvania readers were absorbing Annenberg's pungent editorials against the New Deal in general and Roosevelt in particular. "The War Against Business Goes On" and "No Room for Fascism in a Democracy" were typical of his headlines. The content was also hard-hitting. "Never before has class hatred been elevated to the status of an unctuous virtue," wrote Annenberg in one editorial. "Government, by swinging its mailed fist at business, has not brought lasting recovery," Annenberg argued in another editorial. The *Inquirer* also insisted, "Under its [government's] stern restrictions and oppressive taxes, millions of employables have failed to obtain work," and Annenberg further blasted "WPA boondoggles and shovel leaners." Roosevelt's State of the Union message in 1938, Annenberg wrote, "indicates not the slightest retreat from a program and an economic philosophy which have signally failed, in five years of drastic and costly experiments, to establish the United States on a sound recovery footing."[39]

What made things so awful for Stern, Roosevelt, and the Pennsylvania Democrats was that Annenberg was selling his ideas effectively, making money for the *Inquirer*, and helping lead the Republicans to a stunning victory in the 1938 midterm elections. His handpicked candidate for governor, Arthur James, was an obscure superior court judge, but he thrashed incumbent governor George Earle. The situation for the Democrats was desperate; much New Deal money had poured into Pennsylvania. Moreover, Earle left office under a cloud of suspicion for taking political kickbacks. Stern was losing money at the *Record* and he turned to the government for help; in desperation, for example, he was able to get the Federal Trade Commission to prosecute Annenberg for selling advertising at rates too low. Then Roosevelt helped Stern secure a $1 million federal loan from the RFC to keep him in the fight.

The Roosevelt administration had a better idea: an IRS investigation of Moe Annenberg. Unlike Mellon, who as secretary of the treasury knew tax law inside out, Annenberg was careless and paid little attention to his taxes. His accountant filled out the forms and Annenberg signed them with no questions or probing. His corporate earnings—from news, horse racing, and dozens of other interests—were complicated. It may well have been that Annenberg was secretly trying to hide some of his revenue. Viewpoints differ on that issue. Whatever the case, after Morgenthau's massive investigation it became clear that Annenberg would owe the government about $8 million. He offered to pay all back taxes and fines that he owed, whatever the amount, but the Roosevelt administration wanted back taxes *and* Moe Annenberg locked up in jail. As Elmer Irey told Morgenthau, "They are not going to have the opportunity to pay the tax [and avoid prison]." When Morgenthau and Roosevelt discussed the matter over lunch on April 11, 1939, Morgenthau asked Roosevelt if he could do something for the president. "Yes," Roosevelt said. "I want Moe Annenberg for dinner." Morgenthau responded, "You're going to have him for breakfast—fried."[40]

That attitude, according to Annenberg biographer Christopher Ogden, led to Annenberg's $8 million fine and three-year prison sentence. "The key to the Annenberg case for Morgenthau," Ogden observed, "was not simply penalizing Moses with a fine, which no matter how high, he was certain that the wealthy publisher could pay. The goal was removing Moses from the scene so that he could cause no further political trouble." With Annenberg going to jail in 1940, the *Philadelphia Inquirer* became less strident; Roosevelt had an easier time carrying Pennsylvania to win reelection; and the treasury had $8 million more to spend on New Deal programs.[41]

Auditing Mellon and sending Annenberg to prison fulfilled Roosevelt's larger goal of scaring rich Americans into sending the government more of their money. If, for example, the law as of 1935 said that people with large incomes should pay a 79 percent marginal tax rate to the government, then Roosevelt wanted to see 79 cents out of each of their last dollars earned. Roosevelt was furious when he discovered that wealthy Americans were finding ways to take large deductions, and keep most of what they earned instead of sending it to Washington. With tax shelters protecting the income of rich Americans, only John D. Rockefeller, Jr., was actually reporting taxable income in the 79 percent bracket.

Roosevelt tended to lump "tax evasion" and "tax avoidance" together. Tax evasion was breaking the law. But tax avoidance was using legal means—"loopholes" and various tax-deductible investments—to shelter income and thereby keep more of it. Alfred P. Sloan, the president of General Motors, expressed the issue this way: "No conscientious citizen desires to avoid payment of his just share of the country's burden. I do not seek to avoid mine. . . . While no one should desire to avoid payment of his share . . . neither should anyone be expected to pay more than is lawfully required."[42] In other words, if a taxpayer can find legitimate tax deductions, he should take them.

Alexander Forbes, a Harvard classmate and a cousin of Roosevelt's, went one step further. He argued that some of the chief tax deductions, especially charitable giving, did more good than if the money had been used for federal programs. Forbes was professor of physiology at the Harvard Medical School. "Look," he wrote in a letter to Roosevelt, "at the sorry spectacle presented by long rows of beneficiaries of the 'boondoggle,' leaning on their shovels by the hour, at futile projects, and contrast it with the great universities, museums, and research laboratories which have come from the wise and generous giving of such as [J. P.] Morgan, and then consider which is the major constructive force in building a stable civilization."[43]

Roosevelt was indignant with Forbes's reasoning. "My dear cousin and old classmate," he responded. "That being your belief, I do not hesitate to brand you as one of the worst anarchists in the United States." The president argued that if Congress passed the law, Forbes and other rich men ought to obey it, not sneak around it. When J. P. Morgan publicly defended avoiding taxes by strictly legal means, Roosevelt was similarly angry with him. "Ask yourself," the president wrote a New York lawyer, "what Christ would say about the American Bench and Bar were he to return today?"[44]

By 1937, Roosevelt insisted that Morgenthau launch an assault. Close all loopholes, the president urged, publicly name the tax avoiders, and turn loose the IRS. "Henry," Roosevelt announced, "it has come time to attack, and you have got more material than anyone else in Washington to lead the attack." Roosevelt also suggested that Democratic leaders in Congress create a "subcommittee to investigate tax avoidance." Exposing tax avoiders, Roosevelt told Senator Pat Harrison of Mississippi and Congressman Robert Doughton of North Carolina, would also bring the Democrats "at least 10,000,000 [votes]." "Mr. President," Morgenthau inquired, "how did you arrive at the ten million figure?" "I don't know," Roosevelt said with a smile, "but it sounded good! . . . Everything's settled."[45] Thus Congress established the Joint Committee on Tax Evasion and Avoidance and gave it power to hold hearings, call witnesses, and secure tax returns from the treasury.

Oddly enough, one witness the committee could have called was Roosevelt himself. Roosevelt may have been the first president to use a major tax loophole to shelter personal income. Unlike other presidents, he wanted to build a large presidential library in Hyde Park to house his presidential papers and his vast memorabilia. For donating his books, naval prints, and other material to his own library, Roosevelt took a $9,900 (about $100,000 in today's currency) tax deduction. In a similar vein, in 1932, the year Roosevelt first ran for president, he took so many deductions on his income tax—including tax-exempt bonds, farm losses, and charitable gifts—that he only paid $31.31 (less than 0.2 percent) on more than $19,000 of earned income. And that was apart from his salary as governor, which was also tax-exempt. Roosevelt's decision to employ tax avoidance was, of course, completely legal—just as the IRS concluded it was legal for Andrew Mellon to deduct from his tax burden the value of the paintings he donated to start the National Gallery of Art in Washington, D.C.[46]

By taking such deductions, however, especially the library donations, Roosevelt ultimately agreed with his cousin Alexander Forbes, who argued that tax deductions for museums and research institutions were wiser than spending the tax dollars on the WPA.

In fact, given Roosevelt's criticism of Forbes and others, it is odd that he would take any tax deduction, however reasonable, for donations to his own presidential library. That potentially meant fewer tax dollars for his New Deal programs.[47]

Whatever the case, Roosevelt rewarded those who helped him spearhead IRS investigations. Robert Jackson, though he failed to convict Mellon, found favor with the president for trying. Jackson, after the Mellon case, was appointed to the president's cabinet as attorney general; in 1941, Roosevelt appointed him to the U.S. Supreme Court. The president also gave a Supreme Court appointment to Frank Murphy, who helped lead the charge against Annenberg. William Campbell, who helped prosecute Annenberg, won from the president an appointment as a federal judge two months after Annenberg went to prison.

PATRONAGE TRANSFORMED:
THE ELECTIONS OF 1934 AND 1936

Roosevelt seemingly dazzled the nation with his election victories. In his first midterm election, for example, he led his party to the most stunning triumph of any president in the twentieth century. Two years later, he won reelection with almost 99 percent of the nation's electoral votes, the largest of any contested presidential election in U.S. history. How do we explain such spectacular success? Some have focused on ideas, that Roosevelt's desire for an active federal government in making policy resonated with voters; others have pointed to the president himself, his charisma, his optimism, his popular fireside chats, and his energy to get the nation moving again by galvanizing voters during the crisis of depression. Both of these views have some merit, but they can't go far as convincing explanations. After all, Roosevelt's programs, by and large, did not work. They did not reduce unemployment and mostly had unintended consequences that made the Great Depression persist and even grow worse in the late 1930s. Also, much of Roosevelt's

optimism and presidential energy were dedicated to clearly unpopular causes: jailing those who disobeyed the NRA, hiking income
and excise taxes, packing the Supreme Court, and purging those
Democrats who tried to oppose his centralization of political
power.

If the New Deal didn't work, that is, if unemployment after six
years in the White House was greater than in any previous era of
U.S. history, and if FDR often initiated dangerous and unpopular
programs, how do we account for his astonishing success at the
polls?

The starting place to answer this question, I believe, is to look
at patronage. Such patronage includes not only the traditional jobs
in the government bureaucracy, but more broadly the newly created jobs in the federal programs of the New Deal. If we probe
deeply into Roosevelt's popularity, we almost always discover the
presence of patronage—the creating and the manipulating of federal jobs to strengthen his political support. "The party in power
should reward its own," insisted James Farley, chairman of the
Democratic National Committee and Roosevelt's postmaster general. "Patronage . . . is also of assistance for building the party machine for the next election." Farley practiced what he preached: the
Democrats, under Farley and Roosevelt, would use the federal jobs
primarily (1) to "reward" party members, and (2) for "assistance for
building the party machine for the next election."[1]

Under the New Deal, Roosevelt sponsored a flurry of new federal programs—including the AAA, FERA, CCC, and later the
mammoth WPA, which provided government jobs for millions of
American voters. Roosevelt and Farley distributed the jobs connected with these agencies (as Farley promised) in ways that best
served the Democrat Party. Emil Hurja, deputy director of the
Democratic National Committee and Farley's right-hand man, was
an expert pollster and he gathered data regularly on the political
effects of patronage. He sampled voters in every state and most
counties—"What were the specific reactions to Roosevelt's federal

spending?" Hurja asked, and "What swing states (or congressional districts) would benefit from special injections of federal dollars?"[2]

Roosevelt used patronage not only to help Democrats, but as a club with which to discipline wayward congressmen. In Roosevelt's first session of Congress, Hurja recorded all congressional votes; Roosevelt gave out "as few jobs as possible until the session was over." Then, when sympathetic congressmen could be more clearly identified, Roosevelt began distributing federal programs to his loyalists. As Ray Moley observed, "Patronage would be used, if not as a club, then as a steel-pointed pic."[3]

The first test of Roosevelt's system was the 1934 midterm election. Here Roosevelt seemed to be at a disadvantage because national unemployment was still 22 percent. The first wave of spending did little to reduce unemployment. Also, the party in power historically loses seats in midterm elections. The Republicans, who were down by a three-to-one margin in Congress—the worst in the party's history—anticipated a big gain. Even veteran reporters like Mark Sullivan predicted a Republican gain of thirty seats in the House.[4]

But Farley and Hurja had other ideas. First, Hurja identified over sixty key congressional districts and ran polls to see which Democrats had chances to win. Loyal New Dealer candidates found a stream of federal programs trickling—and sometimes pouring—into their districts. So much came into many districts that Hurja tried to help Democrat politicians keep track of it all in pleading their cases for reelection. Specifically, Hurja sent charts to Democrat candidates, showing "Federal appropriations segregated by department for your state. You can use this any way you like— in speeches, radio talks or newspaper interviews." That way, Democratic candidates could cite specific projects and take credit before the voters for bringing jobs into their districts.[5]

In West Virginia, for example, Hurja hoped to engineer a sweep of all six of the state's House seats. In one closely contested district, Hurja explained that "in three of these [ten counties] there is no chance of victory; in three others there is no chance of defeat. Of the remaining four, two are small and two are large. Concentrate on the two largest and the district will be won." Congressman George W. Johnson followed Hurja's advice and won his seat; in fact, all six of West Virginia's House seats became Democrat in 1934.[6]

The state of Maine provides an even more useful case study in the power of patronage. Maine was a Republican state and held its elections in September, not November. That gave the New Dealers a chance to focus early on Maine, find out what worked and what didn't, and then shift resources to the other states for the November contests. The interesting question was this: "Could an influx of federal programs into a strong Republican state persuade grateful voters there to change their political allegiance?"

The starting point for the Democrat campaign in Maine was Governor Louis Brann, who had narrowly won an upset victory in the Roosevelt landslide two years earlier. Brann published large ads in key newspapers along the lines suggested by Hurja and Farley. In the *Portland Press Herald*, for example, the day before the election, Brann had a large ad with his picture that said, "The knowledge and force of Governor Brann secured from the federal government $108,000,000 [for Maine,] providing employment for 44,000 people." In case voters missed the implication of these facts, Brann emphasized on the campaign trail, "The Roosevelt policies are such that a state must have friendly contacts with Washington to properly serve the interests of its people."[7]

Maine's Democrat congressman Edward C. Moran echoed Brann's claim that "Maine has received $108 million from New Deal agencies." He then described the fruits of this government largesse in towns where he campaigned. For example, Moran boasted that the key town of Bath was given large naval contracts from the federal government.[8]

The *Baltimore Sun* reported on how the influx of New Deal spending influenced politics in Eastport, Maine, a pivotal seaport in eastern Maine. In 1932, Governor Brann lost Eastport, 785 to

502. Then the courtship began. Federal money constructed a sea-wall, rebuilt a bridge, ditched the streets, completed some tennis courts, and built a basketball court at the local high school. The government took over canning factories and distributed 40,000 cases of canned fish, and then spent about $350,000 on local busi-nesses. For local relief work, the government paid workers above the standard minimum wage. What's more, with great fanfare, Harold Ickes, head of the PWA, toured Maine three weeks before the election and gave a speech in Eastport. Ickes's job was to tanta-lize the voters in the whole region by suggesting the PWA might fund a project to generate electric power in Eastport from water-power in the Bay of Fundy and Passamaquoddy Bay.[9]

The Republicans in Maine watched in horror as the Democrats saturated their state with federal tax dollars—four times the amount that New Hampshire was receiving, bragged one Demo-crat. Alfred K. Ames, the Republican candidate for governor, challenged Governor Brann's "enormous waste of public funds." "Economic ills cannot be cured by political cure-alls," he warned. "The enormous debt which is daily piling up will have to be paid and the end is not yet." The *Bangor Daily News* caught the spirit of the campaign and described "prancing gift horses from Washing-ton" to Maine. The editor concluded, "Democratic hopes of success in Maine seem to be based upon Al Smith's sagacious remark that 'Nobody shoots Santa Claus.'"[10]

On election day, Governor Brann won reelection as governor and carried Eastport 906-502. In other words, Governor Brann's vote in Eastport went from 39 to 65 percent from 1932 to 1934. The rest of Maine followed suit. Not only did Brann win reelection easily, but the Democrats captured two of Maine's three House seats in that normally Republican state. Off-year elections usually have a lower voter turnout than presidential elections. Not so in Maine. Eastport and the whole state of Maine increased voter turn-out by almost 10 percent over two years. With Maine as a model, New Dealers pumped $135 million of relief money during the last week of the campaign into every state with the possible exception of Maine.[11]

The implications of how the Democrats had triumphed in Republican Maine were discussed in detail after the September 10 election. The *Portland Press Herald* emphasized how Governor Brann "repeatedly told" voters of the more than $100 million in federal dollars marching into Maine. "It was the fear," the editor observed, "which Maine voters had that the state would lose its part of the federal money which is being so lavishly distributed." He added, "Many thousands of Maine citizens have been receiving some of this money, either directly or indirectly, and they do not want to have it 'choked off.'" The next day the editor added, "the average voter [in Maine] apparently is not yet in a mood to inquire where the money is coming from. . . . He is content with the immediate benefits."[12]

With Maine in the Democrat column in September, the editor of the *Daily Kennebec Journal* predicted that patronage, that "glowing promises of federal aid," would define the elections in the other states in the next two months. "Inevitably it will be the main, and should be the dominant issue at the November elections." Naturally the Republicans were startled by the turnabout in Maine, and the discovery of Democrat patronage. John D. M. Hamilton of Kansas, who later became the Republican national chairman, complained that "the suggestion that the voter must cast his ballot for Democratic candidates if he is to be permitted to share fairly in the future distribution of federal moneys is an interesting but brazen attempt to corrupt the voters of the nation through the use of their own money." Hamilton Fish, a Republican congressman from New York, complained that "funds distributed in Maine amounted to nearly $350 a vote for registered Democrats." He had hope, however, that because of "the paralysis of business" the Republicans would do much better nationwide in November.[13]

Republicans were especially distressed by the ongoing PWA surveys distributed by Harold Ickes, secretary of the interior. Ickes sent these surveys into major cities in key battleground states, asking officials to fill out surveys that might bring major federal projects—hospitals, stadiums, bridges, or seawalls—to their cities. Ickes, of course, never promised to bring those federal projects to the targeted cities, but the survey brought the message that under Democratic rule, such huge federal projects might be possible if that city cooperated with President Roosevelt and the Democrat Party. Raymond Clapper, a columnist normally sympathetic to FDR, deplored the Democrats' use of PWA surveys right before the election to tantalize voters. He observed, "Ordering of these surveys is going on almost daily. This has become standardized political technique to entice the grab-bag vote." He quoted one observer as saying, "They've got a whole lot of money to spend and they're running around looking for gigolos."[14]

But how would Republican candidates counter the influx of federal tax dollars? Nine Republican candidates for U.S. Senate met in Chicago three weeks after the Maine debacle to discuss strategy. "All conferees," a reporter noted, "laid stress on the golden flood of farm disbursements now starting to pour in as election day approaches." Senator Daniel Hastings (R-Del.), a leader of the group, said, "All appreciate the difficulty Republican candidates generally are confronted with and the large sums of money being used, at least indirectly, by the New Deal for campaign purposes." He predicted "that this indirect bribery of the voters will be overcome. I cannot believe the American people are willing to be sold that way."[15]

Farley and Hurja, the Democrat strategists, strongly disagreed with Senator Hastings. The election in Maine helped confirm their polling data: targeted and well-advertised federal subsidies produced votes on election day. Pennsylvania, a state carried by Hoover, was a pivotal battleground and the Senate election there matched incumbent Republican David Reed, a friend of Andrew Mellon's and a strong advocate of limited government, against Joseph Guffey, an early supporter of Roosevelt and the New Deal.

"The Democrats," the *New York Herald Tribune* observed, "are moving heaven and earth to elect Guffey and the whole Democratic ticket." Guffey, the editor recognized, "does not hesitate to use the enormous sums already poured into the state of Pennsylvania by the Federal government as a reason for voting for the Democrats." To support his point, the editor described some campaign literature distributed by Guffey. In less than two years under President Roosevelt, Guffey bragged, Pennsylvania received $678,074,195 in federal money.

In Hoover's whole presidency, by contrast, Pennsylvania only obtained $12,835,538 from the federal government. Furthermore, during 1933 and 1934, Pennsylvania had only paid into the federal treasury $297,942,173. "Compare this $297,942,173 contributed by Pennsylvania to the U. S. Treasury," said Guffey's campaign literature, "with the cash and credit of $678,074,195 contributed to Pennsylvania by the Roosevelt Democratic administration." Guffey was also helped by the PWA surveys that inundated Pennsylvania, and by the highly publicized $135 million in relief payments that were announced by the Roosevelt administration on October 31. As the *Chicago Tribune* noted, "Mr. Farley saw to it that the benefit checks went out for the most part just a few weeks before [the] election."[16]

On election day, Joseph Guffey joined many fellow Democrat challengers in gaining nine Senate seats for their party. No party in power had ever gained nine Senate seats before (nor would after) 1934 in U.S. history. The 1934 midterm elections were, in fact, an astounding success for the Democrats across the board. The gain of nine Senate seats was matched by a gain of nine House seats, which made the Democrat margin over the Republicans even more lopsided—319 to 103 in the House and 69 to 25 in the Senate. Those victories followed a 53-seat gain in 1930 and a 90-seat gain when Roosevelt was elected in 1932. That Roosevelt would be the only sitting president from 1904 to 1996 to win House seats in a midterm election—and that he would do so following party gains of 53 and 90 seats the two previous elections—and that the country still had 22 percent unemployment showed that America was in a new political universe, and that patronage politics would be a major part of this new political world.[17]

"As went Maine so now goes the nation," observed the *New York Herald Tribune.* "When such vast streams of Federal moneys are flowing over the land it is probably beyond human nature to give a sincere opinion on broader issues. It is Santa Claus with his pack that has been [e]ndorsed rather than any definite program of recovery or reform." Political observers all over the nation agreed. "The Democratic majorities in Congress are accounted for by the government billions," the *Chicago Tribune* concluded. "One doesn't shoot Santa Claus," complained Norman Thomas, the head of the Socialist Party in America. "The strength of the Democratic support is not based on particular satisfaction with the New Deal or confidence in it but simply on the fact that the federal government is administering a great quantity of relief money and that in some cases that administration is politically shrewder than it is socially wise. . . ."[18]

Of course, patronage politics has always been part of American history. The difference in 1934 was that Roosevelt, with the AAA, CCC, FERA, and PWA, had much more federal money available to distribute than all previous presidents combined. The magnitude of what he could accomplish politically dwarfed that of his thirty predecessors in the White House.

Also unique in the 1930s was Roosevelt's use of patronage to command the loyalty of Democrat congressmen for his more controversial New Deal programs. Before Roosevelt, most patronage originated and ended within each individual state. If state legislatures decided to build a bridge or a seawall, the governor and the legislature made decisions on what would be built and who would do the building. The economic power was worked out within each state because the Constitution limited the federal role to national economic matters. Under Roosevelt, however, the building of public works was federalized. So was farming (AAA), relief (FERA), and business development (NRA). That meant that Roosevelt and the loyalists among his New Dealers could dictate the terms of projects, and congressmen and governors would have to appease Roosevelt to keep the flow of funds coming. Farley and Hurja, with polling and networking, kept close tabs on all states and congressmen, on who was receiving what, and on how supportive they were of FDR. Hurja recommended that "political counselors"—men loyal to the president—go into various districts and "go over [voting and patronage] problems with them." Hurja concluded, "This sort of service to congressmen will be different from anything hitherto attempted in Washington, and will be the best kind of 'big stick' when it comes to legislation." It would, Hurja insisted, "obtain a high degree of cooperation [toward FDR]" from those congressmen receiving federal largesse.[19]

FDR seems to have agreed. With briefings from Farley and Hurja, Roosevelt called in various congressmen and startled them by displaying a keen grasp of their states and districts. "I have heard awestruck Congressmen," observed speechwriter Stanley High, ". . . admit after a conversation with the President that he knew more than they did about the state of mind of their constituents."[20]

Patronage became a crutch for the president, and he used it to help pass his favorite bills. In 1935, for example, Roosevelt wanted Congress to pass the Public Utilities Holding Company Act, which stiffly regulated electric and gas holding companies. The bill had a "death sentence" clause that, under certain conditions, could force a utility holding company to be dissolved. The "death sentence" clause was somewhat unpopular, and Roosevelt sent Corcoran and Hurja to work on Senator Alva Adams of Colorado to entice him to change his vote. Corcoran and Hurja discovered that Adams wanted an office of the Securities and Exchange Commission centered in Denver. When they offered Adams that office, he changed his vote, and Roosevelt won his battle for the death sentence by only one vote.[21]

Even with Roosevelt's masterful use of patronage, he still faced political problems because his programs were expensive and unemployment was still high. The AAA raised the price of food; the NRA raised the price of factory products; and paying for them was burdensome to taxpayers. During 1934, Hurja began to notice a slow, steady drop in Roosevelt's approval ratings. By 1935, the New Deal was under increasing fire, and the Supreme Court began declaring many New Deal programs—including the NRA and later the AAA—unconstitutional. In 1935, there were a few political contests, a couple of House vacancies for example, and Roosevelt began to suffer some defeats.[22]

The most interesting race was the contest in Rhode Island to succeed Democrat congressman Francis Condon, who resigned his seat to take a place on the state supreme court. In 1934, Condon had easily won, but after he resigned, Charles Risk, a Republican state legislator, competed for the seat by criticizing the New Deal—in particular the AAA processing tax. Rhode Island was a textile state and the mill workers saw markets lost and mills closed because of the processing taxes imposed on textile operators to pay for the AAA. "The administration at Washington," Risk said, "has demonstrated such a lack of sympathy for our people in this part of the country. . . ."[23]

On election day, August 6, 1935, Risk baffled Farley and won the seat with almost 60 percent of the total vote. The number of Democrat voters dropped in half from 1934 to 1935, and the *Providence Tribune* concluded, "the outstanding issue of the campaign was the support or repudiation of the recent aspects of the New Deal."[24]

Both of Rhode Island's U.S. senators saw the Republican win as a portentous blow to Roosevelt. Peter Gerry, the Democrat senator, called the Republican victory "evidence [of] a distinct trend against some of the Roosevelt policies." Republican Jesse Metcalf, the other senator, was elated: "The overwhelming defeat of the New Deal in the Rhode Island congressional election means that the people are now realizing that huge taxes, which must be collected to repay the squanderings of the administration, will force the closing of more industries." [25]

Three months later, the Republicans chalked up bigger victories—the state legislature in Roosevelt's home state of New York, the mayor's races in Cleveland and Philadelphia, and increased seats in the New Jersey legislature. Afterward, the stock market surged, and so did Republican optimism for the 1936 presidential election. Henry P. Fletcher, chairman of the Republican National Committee, crowed, "The boondogglers are on their way out." The *New York Times* editorialized that Farley "evidently believes that by promises of patronage and the bestowal of offices he has found the secret of victory in elections." That strategy, which had worked so well in 1934, seemed stale in 1935. S. Davis Wilson, the new, Republican mayor of Philadelphia, said the strong Republican vote "presages a united party for the election of a Republican president in 1936." [26]

The Republican victories in 1935 helped the party form a strategy for countering Roosevelt's steamroller. Yes, as the *New York Times* noted, the Democrats had the "promises of patronage" and "the bestowal of offices." [27] But all of this federal spending (1) hiked taxes, which had to be paid, and (2) raised the cost of living for all Americans, and (3) did not seem to be increasing employment significantly. In the 1936 presidential campaign, which group would be greater—the number of Americans who were benefiting, or hoping in the future to benefit, from New Deal programs or those Americans who resented the higher prices, new taxes, persistent unemployment, and centralizing of power in Washington?

As historian William Leuchtenburg has noted, in early 1936 Roosevelt's reelection was "very much in doubt." Hurja's polls had seen the president's favorable ratings fall from 69 to 50 percent from early 1934 to late 1935. Hurja was almost ready to write off Roosevelt's home state of New York, and he was not optimistic about Roosevelt's prospects in the industrial Midwest. In a January

1936 poll, the American Institute of Public Opinion contended that Roosevelt might win reelection if he could hold on to five states that were barely Democrat. As late as July 1936, two Gallup polls showed Alf Landon beating Roosevelt in the electoral college, and even increasing his victory margin as the month wore on.[28]

Even more startling was an August Gallup poll that asked, "Do you believe the acts and policies of the Roosevelt administration may lead to dictatorship?" That such a question would ever be asked of any American president was remarkable, but that 45 percent of Americans said "yes" was astonishing. High prices, record high taxes, persistent unemployment, and the centralizing of power were taking a toll on Roosevelt's presidency.[29]

The relief statistics would be especially troublesome to Roosevelt. Much of the success of his presidency would be tied to his promised decline in relief cases. After all, if any recovery was occurring, the numbers of Americans on relief should decline; but that is not what was happening. Roosevelt's friends were nervous because of the implications of high unemployment and limited recovery. Morgenthau confided in his diary, "If we keep on spending money at the rate we are and in such helter-skelter, hit and miss method, we cannot help but be riding for a fall. . . . It seems to me we are not making any headway and the number of unemployed is staying more or less static." Yet in March 1936 the *New York Times* confirmed Morgenthau's fears. It announced that Americans on relief had increased every year since Roosevelt took office—from 3.6 million in 1933 to 4.3 million in 1934 to 4.7 million in 1935. In part, of course, this occurred because many people were attracted to relief work—the wages were often competitive with factory work and the supervision and requirements were often much less.[30]

When the Roosevelt administration avoided discussing these statistics on relief, many reporters were annoyed. Frank Kent of the *Baltimore Sun* said, "the more money the Administration has spent on relief and public works, the more men there are on the relief rolls and fewer are the jobs. No contradiction of these facts is attempted. The way the Administration meets them is by ignoring them."[31]

But Roosevelt was not ignoring them. He was shrewdly using them to jump-start his reelection campaign. In 1935, Congress had allocated $4.8 billion for the newly created WPA to use for relief work, and much of that cash the president had personal discretion in distributing. What that meant was that state governors had to come hat in hand to Washington hoping to persuade the president to build roads, dams, bridges, and model cities in their states. These governors "want to keep on the good side of Santa Claus," Raymond Clapper noted. "This does not seem to be good government as it has been known, but it is right now the lasso which enables Mr. Roosevelt to hold the country in hand."[32]

During 1936, the New Dealers launched many federal projects and promised many others. PWA surveys, WPA projects, CCC camps—all of these and more became campaign tools that Roosevelt, Farley, and Hurja used for Roosevelt's reelection. Hurja did tracking polls and argued that funds should flow heavily only into those states closely contested by both parties. "Money, time and effort should not be wasted," Hurja said, "but applied in those states close to the fifty percent line and carrying the largest possible electoral vote at the least expense."[33] Melvin Holli, who has studied Hurja's career at great length, described Hurja's campaign strategy:

> With notepad in hand, Hurja would tell the Democratic high command, "We have this state for sure—waste no effort on it. We are certainly to lose that state. Ignore it." And then, "Now here is a doubtful state that may be lost or won." With Hurja's advice, Postmaster General Farley, who directed the flow of funds for the Democrats, would signal the announcement of new WPA projects and relief programs or designate speakers and campaign materials for those states that Hurja's notebook indicated were doubtful.[34]

Farley and Hurja even used WPA administrators and jobholders as campaign workers—in the 1936 campaign and in other elections. They went into key states to do polls, distribute questionnaires, and solicit support for Roosevelt. Sometimes those working in the WPA or other programs had to kick back part of their salaries to support Roosevelt, or other Democrat candidates. Pennsylvania was always a swing state and one county chairman sent out the following letter:

> Dear Madam:
>
> I am very much surprised that you have not responded to our previous letter requesting your contribution in the amount of $28.08 to Indiana County Democratic Campaign Committee, as I was sure that you appreciated your position to such an extent that you would make this contribution willingly and promptly. I must, however, now advise you that unless your contribution in the above amount is received promptly it will be necessary to place your name on the list of those who will not be given consideration for any other appointment after the termination of the emergency relief work, which as you know will terminate in the near future.[35]

In other states, the connection between WPA and the Democrats was more subtle but still very real. In South Dakota, a Democrat county chairman sent this note to the director of the WPA: "Please place this man on WPA on the special set-up you have that takes care of rush men as Welfare will not certify. Have looked into affair—has nine votes in family." In the four months before the 1936 election, 300,000 men were added to the WPA. In the month after the election, 300,000 were promptly removed from WPA work. As Thomas Dewey observed, "Three-hundred thousand men and their families moved on and off relief as pawns of New Deal politics."[36]

Some members of Roosevelt's cabinet were nervous about moving poor Americans on and off the WPA for political purposes.

When, after the election, Harry Hopkins told Morgenthau that he was ready to lay off hundreds of thousands of WPA workers, including 150,000 from the cities, Morgenthau shot back, "If you can find 150,000 people now on relief rolls who you say now are not in need of relief, how are you going to answer the charge that you must have known before November that these people were not in need of relief?"[37]

Roosevelt's attitude seemed to be to win the election now and answer questions about how he won it later. When, for example, Roosevelt heard that thousands of WPA workers were to be laid off October 1—the month before the election—he told Morgenthau, "I don't give a god-dam[n] where he gets the money from but not one person is to be laid off on the first of October." In part as a result, work relief expenditures increased sharply from the fall of 1935 to the fall of 1936—a 268 percent increase, according to a Treasury Department memorandum. The biggest increase was 3,663 percent in Pennsylvania—a swing state that Hoover had carried in 1932, and that Roosevelt specially targeted in 1936.[38]

For the farmers, Morgenthau described the plan to make sure Soil Conservation Service checks arrived in farm households before the election—four farm states were in the balance, Morgenthau believed. Earlier in February, Roosevelt dealt directly with Henry Wallace, his secretary of agriculture. Roosevelt demanded, "Henry, through July, August, September, October and up to the 5th of November I want cotton to sell at 12 cents [a pound]. I do not care how you do it. That is your problem. It can't go below 12 cents."[39]

Wallace always tended to obey Roosevelt's wishes, and his loyalty would later win him the vice presidency in the 1940 election. On the use of subsidies for votes, however, Wallace was embarrassed. Yet he rationalized, "Politicians of whatever party seem unable to rise above the temptation of using government expenditures as reasons for persuading voters...."[40]

Naturally, Roosevelt's use of federal programs to woo voters irritated Alf Landon, the Republican nominee: "If he [Roosevelt] did not have the $5 billion [of WPA money] his election would be very much in doubt. . . ." Landon criticized the politicizing of relief and in a New York campaign swing he promised to "keep politics out of relief." During the campaign, Landon had pamphlets and leaflets distributed. One had a picture of Farley on the telephone and was titled "Relief for Votes." It was subtitled "Will the American people accept the imputation that their votes can be bought with relief money?" Another leaflet said, "If We Don't Stop the New Deal the Nation Will Be Bankrupt."[41]

As the campaign wore on, and with the New Deal money spigots turned on high, Landon fell behind more and more. Landon won a majority of donations from businessmen, but that cash was dwarfed by Roosevelt's federal money machine. Roosevelt's patronage trumped Landon's protests of high prices, high taxes, failed programs, and executive usurpation of power. The spirit of this campaign was captured by Senator Hiram Johnson, a California Republican who was endorsing Roosevelt for reelection. By September 22, Johnson predicted a "clear" Roosevelt victory. He added, "Any man who could not be elected who goes on a train through the Middle West, takes out his checkbook, and says, 'I will allot a few million dollars to this particular place, and a few million dollars to some other'; and who carries with him the Agricultural Department, with checks for the farmers in untold amounts, and Mr. Hopkins, who doles out relief in unstinted quantities, should retire from politics. He starts with probably 8 million votes bought. The other side has to buy them one by one, and they cannot hope to match his money."[42]

Even black Americans, who had been loyal Republicans since the Civil War era, began to be enticed by federal largesse. In 1932, Roosevelt lost the black vote by a three-to-one margin. Then came the FERA, the WPA, the CCC, and especially the PWA, which targeted large building projects in black communities throughout America. Harold Ickes, who headed the PWA, created a director ship of Negro economics and hired many blacks, such as Dr. Robert C. Weaver. In 1966, Weaver became the first black cabinet head in U.S. history, but in 1936 he was a twenty-nine-year-old special assistant, who helped Ickes secure quotas for blacks on many PWA projects. During Roosevelt's first term, $13 million of PWA money went to black causes, especially schools and hospitals. On October 26, 1936, eight days before the election, Ickes gave a national radio speech from the campus of Howard University, a premier black school, dedicating a chemistry building that was constructed with $625,000 from the PWA. "Not only has the Public Works Administration made grants to Howard University," Ickes boasted, "it has also sought to increase the educational equipment available to Negroes in all sections of the nation from elementary schools to colleges." He then told his radio audience of $3.25 million more in PWA funds that had gone to "hospitals for Negroes" and "construction of low-rent housing projects" for blacks.[43]

Would Ickes's national advertisement of PWA spending help dislodge blacks from their Republican allegiance? On election day, Weaver received a telegram from Los Angeles that read "Tremendous swing for Roosevelt of Negro vote in southern California since the Secretary's broadcast at Howard University." Blacks elsewhere responded to Roosevelt's willingness to include them in some (but not all) of his New Deal programs. Naturally, the Republicans objected to such naked appeals for votes, especially through the relief programs. The New Dealers, Alf Landon charged, were using "relief rolls as modern reservations on which the great colored race is to be confined forever as a ward of the Federal Government."[44]

Landon's problem was even greater than countering the effects of carefully distributed tax dollars—great as that problem was. For one thing, he was a weak public speaker and Roosevelt, especially with his radio charisma, coaxed voters with his words. Second, Landon had the problem of trying to win votes by denouncing government programs, but he had to do so without alienating the increasingly large number of voters who had federal jobs, or hoped to have them. For example, Landon thundered against "public money for political purposes" before a cheering crowd at Madison Square Garden. He received even more cheers when he followed with "I am against the principles of the Agricultural Adjustment Act [and] . . . the concentration of power in the hands of the chief executive." But earlier in Iowa, according to the *Des Moines Register*, Landon "dumped 'laissez-faire' ideology clear out of the window." He promised to continue subsidies to farmers and even used the phrase "cash benefits" four times. According to reporter Thomas Stokes, "he virtually promised to open all spigots of the Treasury at Washington and pour out to the farmers to their satiety."[45]

Landon had a dilemma, and it has been a Republican dilemma ever since 1936. So many Americans were now working in federal programs that he risked offending about ten million voters if he argued for cutting programs to balance the budget. But if he agreed to continue the programs, then the balanced budget crowd would be unhappy and the people on the programs, although no longer angry, would still have no real incentive to ditch the man who created so many of their federal jobs. As one reporter quipped: "Don't switch Santa Clauses in mid-stream." Roosevelt accurately attacked Landon in Syracuse as follows: "You cannot promise to repeal taxes before one audience and promise to spend more of the taxpayers' money before another audience. . . . You simply cannot make good on both promises at the same time."[46]

On election day, Roosevelt seemingly crushed Landon by the largest margin in any two-party race in American history—523 to 8 in the electoral college, and an eleven million vote margin (better than 3–2) in the popular vote. Such a lopsided margin, many argued, made FDR perhaps the most popular president in U.S. history.[47]

After the election, author and editor David Lawrence made a detailed study of the vote. He recognized that the 1936 election was something new in American politics, a situation where the president had unprecedented "means of extending billions of dollars in money benefits to the voters." That fascinated Lawrence, and compelled him to ask this fundamental question: "To what extent was the campaign a reflection of a new trend in American politics, a trend in which the federal government's paternalistic interest in the citizen brought an amazing reward to the party in power?"[48]

To answer this question, Lawrence first broke down the popular vote by county. He started with the solid South and noted that Roosevelt's 82.4 percent vote—while very strong—was actually less than the 82.9 percent that he received in 1932, when he ran against Hoover.[49]

Second, Lawrence then wrote to city and county clerks, federal government officials, and other "authoritative sources" all over America to correlate federal benefits—especially AAA and WPA money—by county for every nonsouthern city and county in America. His results were revealing and fascinating: cities and rural areas that were bountifully blessed with federal tax dollars gave Roosevelt a much larger vote than those that weren't.[50]

Lawrence started by correlating the Roosevelt vote in every nonsouthern county with the amount of AAA money that county received in 1934 and 1935. He found that 708 counties received $500,000 or more in AAA money; 601 counties received between $100,000 and $500,000 in AAA funds; 675 counties secured some funds, but they were less than $100,000; and finally 68 counties received no AAA money. Lawrence correlated these four levels of funding with voting, and his results were as follows:

County Funding Level	Roosevelt Vote	Landon Vote
Highest-funded AAA counties	60%	40%
Medium-funded AAA counties	57	43
Low-funded AAA counties	54	46
Counties with no AAA funds	47	53

Roosevelt did best in counties that secured a large amount of AAA money, and weakest in those few counties that imported no AAA dollars. In fact, as Lawrence's data reveal, Landon actually carried the 3 percent of the counties that received no AAA support—an interesting point when one considers that before 1929 no county in America received any direct federal subsidy for agriculture.[51]

Then Lawrence compiled the same data for the cities. Since all 297 nonsouthern cities over 25,000 in population received at least some federal aid, Landon broke the cities into three groups and did a correlation of the vote with the WPA dollars received:

Ranking of Counties in Relief Money	Roosevelt Vote	Landon Vote
Lower than average $ for relief	62.0%	38.0%
Higher than average $ for relief	67.8	32.1
Extra high $ for relief	70.7	29.3

Again, as the aid for relief went up in American cities, so did Roosevelt's vote. When the federal funds were not so overwhelming, Landon did better. The thirty-eight cities with extra-high relief, Lawrence discovered, accounted for close to half of Roosevelt's victory margin over Landon.[52]

Lawrence next did a special study of the key state of Pennsylvania. Hoover had carried Pennsylvania in 1932. Roosevelt, Farley, and Hurja all believed that if Pennsylvania could be shifted into the Democratic column, Roosevelt would win reelection. For 1936, WPA appropriations increased 3,000 percent in Pennsylvania—greater than in any other state in the union. Lawrence found that Roosevelt's investment in Pennsylvania paid big dividends. For example, the Democrats registered so many new voters that turnout increased by a whopping 50 percent from 1932 to 1936. These new voters, and many of the old ones, too, cast a large vote for Roosevelt, who won the state easily.[53] If we break down the vote in Pennsylvania by the amounts of relief the 67 counties received, we find the following results:

Pennsylvania Counties	Roosevelt Vote	Landon Vote
19 highest-relief counties	62%	38%
23 medium-relief counties	52	48
25 lowest-relief counties	45	55

Those counties that received the highest amounts of relief went overwhelmingly for Roosevelt, and those with low relief Landon actually carried by a large margin. What this suggests is that if all of Pennsylvania had received only limited amounts of federal aid, Landon might have easily carried the state.

In Vermont, one of the two states that Landon actually carried, the story was similar. High-relief counties went for Roosevelt and those that received less relief went for Landon.[54]

Vermont Counties	Roosevelt Vote	Landon Vote
3 highest-relief counties	51%	49%
7 medium-relief counties	40	60
4 low-relief counties	34	66

In other words, when federal aid seeped into the traditionally Republican state of Vermont, even strong Republicans sometimes switched to Roosevelt. Perhaps if the Democrats had targeted the lower-relief counties in Vermont harder, the president could have carried Vermont. If he had done the same in Maine, perhaps Roosevelt would have won all forty-eight states.

Roosevelt was able to do especially well in the cities because federal programs could be concentrated and targeted by loyal political bosses. Roosevelt needed big-city politicians for his votes, and the bosses needed Roosevelt for their federal aid. As political scientist Sean Savage noted, "Through the WPA, PWA, and later the U.S. Housing Authority, Chicago, Jersey City, Kansas City, and other machine-controlled cities built new public schools, public hospitals, water and sewer systems, bridges, expressways, subway extensions, parks, and housing projects."[55]

An example from New Jersey may illustrate the point. New Jersey was historically a swing state. For instance, if we look at the vote along the eastern edge of New Jersey, Roosevelt narrowly carried Bergen, Essex, and Union counties; Landon eked out victories in Monmouth and Ocean counties. But in Hudson County, the home of Mayor Frank Hague, Roosevelt's loyal boss, the balance swung to the president. Roosevelt carried Hudson County by an astonishing 233,390 to 65,110 margin over Landon. Hague controlled New Jersey patronage for Roosevelt, and in turn Hague had about 90,000 WPA jobs a year given to New Jersey. From 1935 to 1939, the WPA alone plowed $47 million into Hudson County; even more came from the PWA, CCC, and other federal programs. For example, the PWA helped Hague expand the Jersey City Medical Center, which became so well endowed it actively provided free medical aid to many Jersey City residents. On October 2, 1936, one month before the presidential election, Hague declared a public holiday to celebrate the arrival of President Roosevelt, who dedicated the new hospital and praised Mayor Hague for having "done a great service not only to you good people who are alive today in Jersey City and Hudson County, but a service that is going to last for many, many generations to come."[56]

The 1936 election, then, is very revealing about the role of patronage in reelecting Roosevelt. First, he did especially well in large cities, where federal aid could be concentrated and targeted to gain votes. Bosses like Ed Kelly in Chicago, Tom Pendergast in Kansas City, Ed Flynn in the Bronx, and Frank Hague in Jersey City delivered their areas to Roosevelt by record amounts in 1936. Most of Roosevelt's margin over Landon was in America's larger cities, where blacks were also concentrating. Second, southerners remained solidly Democrat, but they gave their votes to Roosevelt by a slightly lower margin in 1936 than 1932. Third, Roosevelt scored well in rural counties that received AAA benefits, especially those that received massive benefits. Fourth, Roosevelt lost those counties without AAA benefits, and he ran about even with Landon in those more urban counties receiving only small amounts of federal aid. Yes, Roosevelt was popular, but so was Santa Claus, and both might have been ignored during November and December had it not been for their bags of presents.

The following equation seems to be true: FDR + $ in patronage = reelection. What if he had had much less federal patronage to distribute? Another Democrat, Grover Cleveland, was in that position as president forty years earlier when America had what was then a record-high 18 percent unemployment—less than FDR's 22 percent unemployment in 1934. Unlike Roosevelt, Cleveland lost 113 House seats in his midterm election, and his party was ousted from office in the next presidential election. Granted, Cleveland had to face the 1894 midterm election with an economy that was getting worse; Roosevelt, in contrast, seemed in 1934 and 1936 to be presiding over an improving economy. Nonetheless, if we study those areas in Pennsylvania and Vermont where Roosevelt distributed little or no patronage, we find Roosevelt sometimes did as poorly as Cleveland did forty years earlier. Perhaps FDR minus money in patronage would have equaled FDR a one-term president.

FDR STUMBLES:
COURT PACKING, THE PURGE, AND THE ISSUE OF RACE

February 5, 1937, started as a normal day in American political life. President Roosevelt, fresh from his landslide victory, had invited six key Democrat leaders to the White House, perhaps, they thought, to help him plan his second term. Seated in the Oval Office, they experienced a shock—the president did not invite them to consult them, but to tell them of his plan to pack the Supreme Court. All of the men listened with dismay, some in horror, as Roosevelt unveiled his surprise plan to appoint up to six new justices, one for each current member over age seventy who chose not to retire. Through patronage and political success, Roosevelt already was exerting unprecedented leverage over Congress. He presented his reform as a plea for judicial efficiency, but what he wanted was to neutralize the pesky justices who had struck down some of his cherished New Deal programs.[1]

As the six startled men, instructions in hand, left the White House, Representative Hatton Sumners of Texas said, "Well, boys, here is where I cash in my chips." Others in the House and Senate would agree. During the five months of wrangling over the Court packing, or "Court emasculating" issue, most other New Deal programs were on hold as Roosevelt cajoled and manipulated Congress to support his plan. So many congressmen were beholden to Roosevelt for patronage and political favors that for a while he seemed certain to win. The small band of Republicans in the House and Senate shrewdly decided to be quiet; they let Burton Wheeler (D-Mont.), a strong New Dealer, lead the public opposition to Court packing. To win, Wheeler knew he would somehow have to counter Roosevelt's promises of patronage for supporters. As Senator Wheeler told Senator Harry Byrd of Virginia, "Most members of the Senate are lawyers. Deep down, they agree with you and me, but they're like a lot of mercenaries. They want patronage. A small army that believes in principle can lick a bunch of mercenaries, and we'll lick them."[2]

Wheeler's views would be tested quickly when the debate began. Many senators, including many prominent Democrats, began expressing reservations about the bill. Jim Farley, who was helping with Senate patronage, was annoyed that so many needy Democrats were denigrating the plan. When a reporter asked Farley how the Court fight stood, Farley said he had an off-the-record question: How could Senators Patrick McCarran of Nevada and Joseph O'Mahoney of Wyoming "afford not to vote for the bill if they ever wanted anything from the administration?" To Farley's surprise, the reporter published his comment on the record. McCarran was furious. He had been bedridden but, against doctor's orders, he rose up, went to the Senate floor, and said he didn't care if what he said meant political death. "I think this cause is worthy of any man's life," McCarran urged. "When Farley said that if I asked for something for my humble state there would be a different viewpoint, he wrote my death warrant and he knew it, and I may today be delivering my valedictory by reason of a mandate of Mr. Farley." Nonetheless, McCarran was more than ever determined to fight the Court-packing plan, even if he lost all of his federal patronage.[3]

Roosevelt had some success charming more malleable politicians such as young Florida senator Claude Pepper. Roosevelt invited the wavering Pepper into the Oval Office and turned on the charm. It helped even more when he turned on the spigot. "The president," Pepper recalled, "was not above a little logrolling, promising to help me win re-election in 1938 and, in my presence, notifying the army that he wanted to see some favorable action on a Florida canal project that I had been pushing." Pepper ended up backing Roosevelt.[4]

In the midst of the Court fight, Roosevelt's Senate engineer, Majority Leader Joseph Robinson, died of a heart attack—many believe the strain of lining up votes for Roosevelt contributed to his poor health. Thus, the Senate Democrats would have to choose a replacement, and Roosevelt's political skills would again be tested. Two candidates to replace Robinson quickly emerged—the assistant majority leader, Alben Barkley of Kentucky, and Pat Harrison of Mississippi, chairman of the Finance Committee. Both men had faithfully supported Roosevelt, but Barkley more so, especially on Court packing. Still, Roosevelt had previously endorsed both men in their political careers; he was comfortable working with both men and funneled patronage through both men in their respective states. Roosevelt, therefore, gave "absolute assurance" to both candidates, and to others, that he would stay out of the contest for majority leader. It was the Senate's business. Farley, as head of the DNC, consulted with Roosevelt, who reassured him he would be neutral, that either man was capable of promoting Roosevelt's programs.[5]

Roosevelt then changed his mind. He was still seething over the Court fight and decided that Barkley, who had shown gusto for battle, would fight harder than Harrison for the plan. Roosevelt chose an odd way to suggest his new leanings for Barkley. The president wrote a "Dear Alben" letter in which he deplored the political canvassing already going on among the senators for the position of majority leader so soon after Robinson's death—and wished Barkley the best now that he was acting majority leader. Senator Charles McNary of Oregon, the Republican minority leader, observed, "If there's been any political activity, it's been at the White House." Many observers correctly read the president's maneuver as a subtle sign of support for Barkley, and Barkley, of course, tried to leverage Roosevelt's "endorsement" with undecided senators, who did not want to cross the president. In other words, Roosevelt was subtly campaigning for Barkley by writing a letter to Barkley condemning the campaign to select a new majority leader. After Roosevelt's artful endorsement, Senator Morris Sheppard of Texas told Harrison, "I am sorry, Pat, but the President's wishes come first with me." Other Democrats, especially Harrison supporters, resented Roosevelt's interference. Senator Frederick Van Nuys of Indiana said, "We'll elect our own leader and dispose of the Court bill in our own way without any dictation by any source whatsoever."[6]

Meanwhile, supporters of Harrison and Barkley solicited their colleagues' votes in private offices, in the Senate cloakroom, and on the train to Joe Robinson's funeral in Little Rock. The day before the July 21 election, Roosevelt insisted to reporters that he was not intervening, that he was neutral and that it was "very obvious" he had been so "from the very beginning." In a feigned show of impartiality, Roosevelt even invited Barkley and Harrison to the White House for a conference on future legislation.[7]

Behind the scenes, however, Roosevelt was maneuvering with his big-city bosses to swing votes for Barkley. First, the White House called Tom Pendergast of Kansas City to sway Missouri senator Harry Truman toward Barkley. "I can't do it Tom," Truman responded. "I've given my word to Pat Harrison." Truman, like other Democrat senators, resented executive interference and he called Steve Early, the president's press secretary, and said, "Tell him [FDR] to stop treating me like an office boy."[8]

Next, Roosevelt called Farley: "Jim," he said, "I want you to call

[Mayor] Ed Kelly of Chicago right now. It's necessary to get him to put the pressure on Senator [William] Dieterich [of Illinois] to get him to vote for Barkley.""I can't do it," Farley said. "I said I wouldn't turn a hand either way, for Barkley or Harrison.""Dieterich's weakening," Roosevelt insisted; "all we need is a phone call.""I can't help it, I can't call Kelly," Farley pleaded. "You mean you won't," Roosevelt retorted. "Boss, I just can't," Farley said. "I gave my word—my word to Harrison, Barkley, [South Carolina senator James F.] Byrnes, and Guffey on the train. You yourself said it was right for me to take no sides." "Very well," Roosevelt said abruptly. "I'll get Harry Hopkins to do it," and he hung up immediately. Perhaps even Hopkins found the deceitful task too distasteful. In a private diary entry, Harold Ickes claimed Tom Corcoran was the one who made the calls to Kelly and Dieterich.[9]

The White House caller made clear to Kelly and Dieterich that WPA funds were at stake. Without WPA funds, Kelly could not control Chicago, and without Kelly, Dieterich could not hope to be reelected. In fact, Howard Hunter, a key WPA official, applied further pressure on Dieterich. Thus Dieterich, who had pledged to support Harrison, changed his vote to Barkley. The next day, when the Senate vote was taken, Barkley eked out a 38–37 win over Harrison. The Dieterich switch had been vital, as Roosevelt suspected. Harrison, as White House strategist Charles Michelson recognized, "was probably the most popular member of the body," and many senators deplored the president's "meddling."[10]

The success of Roosevelt's manipulations was short-lived. Barkley had become, in the minds of many senators, an "errand boy" for the president. In his first two efforts as majority leader, he failed the president twice. First, Roosevelt had vetoed a bill to renew special interest rates on farm loans; the Senate overrode Roosevelt's veto, and Barkley couldn't stop it. Second, the Senate, perhaps with resentment, voted to recommit his Court-packing bill by a lopsided 70-20 vote.[11]

Harrison quietly voted against Roosevelt on both of these bills, and he was not done yet. Next, he spoke out publicly against Roosevelt's minimum wage bill, which the Senate had been debating. The day before his speech he said, "I'm going to give Franklin Roosevelt a licking tomorrow. . . . I just can't take any more." On the Senate floor, he spoke effectively against the president's bill, arguing that it would harm business and encourage more unemployment. Roosevelt's minimum wage bill never even came up for a vote in the Senate.[12]

Shortly thereafter, the Senate considered a sugar act to protect American growers from imports. Roosevelt was against it, and Harrison decided he was for it with minor alterations. According to Harold Ickes, who was reflecting the president's view, the sugar quotas in Harrison's plan were "unconscionable and unfair and rotten." Roosevelt, therefore, opposed Harrison's bill, but the wily Harrison deftly maneuvered the sugar bill through the Finance Committee by a 16 to 1 vote, and the Senate then passed it almost by acclamation. Roosevelt, not wanting to have the Senate override another veto, signed it reluctantly at the last minute. Finally, as chairman of the Finance Committee, Harrison persuaded the Senate to repeal Roosevelt's much-desired tax on the undistributed profits of corporations (the House restored a weakened version of the tax). This series of political defeats for Roosevelt made the 1937 Congress bitterly disappointing for him. As Roosevelt said in the midst of Harrison's onslaught, "Pat Harrison has gone off the deep end."[13]

From Harrison's standpoint, it was Roosevelt who went off the deep end. As the head of one branch of government, he tried to snatch power from each of the other two. The Senate finally rebelled and defeated most of his legislative program that year. Roosevelt began 1937 on the wave of a great landslide victory; he had almost four-to-one margins in the House and Senate. Yet his Court-packing scheme failed and then bill after bill with his support failed to pass Congress.

At the beginning of 1938, Roosevelt increasingly contemplated a "purge" of those Senate Democrats who had opposed his 1937 program, especially the Court-packing bill. He was reluctant to get too involved and risk further embarrassment, but he encouraged others to do so. He wanted to support his faithful subordinates with endorsements and patronage, and undermine those who had opposed him. Roosevelt confidant Donald Richberg, according to reporter Raymond Clapper, said the president "feels bitter about [the] court fight and that those who did not go down the line won't get any consideration. . . . This is a test issue with R[oose]v[el]t and he won't give court opponents any break." [14]

One of the first races of 1938 was Claude Pepper's campaign for reelection. Roosevelt had promised to endorse Pepper if he voted for Court packing, which he did. Pepper earnestly sought presidential support, and even publicly backed his minimum wage bill, which Harrison and others had defeated in the last year. James Roosevelt, the president's son, came to Florida and endorsed Pepper. So did others close to the president. Tom Corcoran then helped raise private money for Pepper; then he helped put the "full strength of the federal machine behind Pepper." That included IRS officials, federal attorneys, and the WPA. Farley personally came down to Florida to dedicate new post offices and to praise Pepper. When Pepper won his primary (which was tantamount to election in the one-party South), Roosevelt called him in and said, "Claude, if you were a woman, I'd kiss you." [15]

That victory alerted many congressmen, and made them sensitive to the continuing power of the president and also to his minimum wage bill. Eight days after Pepper's victory, May 11, the House passed a minimum wage bill. The next month the Senate did, too, and Roosevelt signed it into law. [16]

Pepper's victory pleased the president and led him to believe his whole program—from Court packing to minimum wage—was as popular as ever. Therefore, Roosevelt did not move toward reconciliation with the Senate; instead he began to believe that those senators who had obstructed some of his bills, especially Court packing, should be denied his patronage and his support. Cautiously at first, and then with increasingly direct pressure and patronage, he tried to oust the obstructionists and elect 100 percent New Dealers. Roosevelt's Brains Trusters encouraged him to do this, and even began doing it themselves. Harry Hopkins, an Iowa native, intervened in the Iowa primary to support the opponent of Senator Guy Gillette, who had been favorable to most New Deal measures, but had opposed Court packing. Gillette won handily anyway despite Hopkins's maneuver. Then Harold Ickes spoke out in the Oregon primary to oppose Governor Charles Martin, who had annoyed Ickes by refusing to support a government-owned power plant from being constructed at the Bonneville Dam. Ickes helped organize federal workers behind Martin's opponent, Henry Hess, who narrowly won the primary but lost to the Republican in November.[17]

By late June, Roosevelt was still seething over his rebuke on Court packing. He therefore decided to directly enter many midterm races, to travel the country, and to endorse some candidates and oppose others. In trying to sell his purge to the public, Roosevelt decided to underplay his unpopular Court-packing plan and tell voters he was campaigning for political liberalism, an increased role for government in the economy. In a fireside chat on June 24, he told the country he would campaign for liberal Democrats only in order to make the Democrats a more liberal party. However, some of the Democrats he would oppose tended to be liberals who had supported most of the New Deal, but had opposed changing the Supreme Court. In fact, the common thread among those Democrats Roosevelt would try to "purge" would not be political philosophy, but personal loyalty to the president, especially on the issue of Court packing.[18]

Another thing that may have prompted Roosevelt to campaign directly was the dangerous political race faced by Alben Barkley, the majority leader. Roosevelt had invested much political capital in backing Barkley over Harrison for majority leader. Yet Governor

A. B. "Happy" Chandler, a popular and charismatic politician, had challenged Barkley for his Senate seat. Roosevelt wanted to prevent the personal embarrassment of having his right-hand man in the Senate ousted.[19]

Roosevelt's strong support for Barkley immediately brought the WPA into the election. The state WPA director was a Barkley enthusiast, and by late May, Chandler's campaign manager complained that "every agency of the Federal government dispensing relief is resorting to methods and policies that are crudely reprehensible to force the citizens of the great commonwealth to support Senator Barkley." The WPA director denied the charges and Harry Hopkins insisted he didn't permit such things, but a Senate committee investigated and concluded that not only the WPA, but also Federal Housing Administration and even state IRS officials were campaigning for votes and money for Barkley's campaign.[20]

Interestingly, Chandler, who understood well how the new political game was being played, had his own state machine generating votes and contributions from state employees, especially in the highway department. Chandler also had state employees hand deliver government checks—and solicit support for the governor while doing so. When the president visited Kentucky to campaign for Barkley, the wily Chandler quickly barged into the presidential motorcade and plopped himself in between the president and Barkley.[21]

With the issue of federal programs paramount in the campaign, Roosevelt reminded Kentuckians that since he had become president, $300 million of federal money had gone to Kentucky in relief and jobs alone. Barkley was even more specific, and in his speeches around the state he handed out flyers that listed the job totals and the federal tax dollars received by each county in the state. "Those are the policies I helped to write," Barkley bragged, "and those are the policies for which I will continue to stand for the next six years."[22]

The furor over the WPA and vote buying became so loud that

Senator Carl Hatch of New Mexico introduced a bill barring WPA workers, and certain other appointees, from political activity. Barkley denied he was personally manipulating the WPA, but he initially opposed the Hatch Act. So did Roosevelt. From Barkley's standpoint, if he were barred from using the WPA to promote his campaign, he would be at a disadvantage to Chandler, who would still have his state patronage to use.[23]

Meanwhile, the Scripps-Howard newspaper chain sent reporter Thomas Stokes to Kentucky to interview federal and state employees alike, and learn the truth. Stokes found massive evidence that the WPA was strongly behind Barkley, and that state employees were working for Chandler. Stokes called it "a grand political racket in which the taxpayer is the victim." Many WPA offices, Stokes discovered, were "open and flagrant" in soliciting votes for Barkley. Stokes personally supported Barkley, Roosevelt, and the New Deal. Thus, after he inspected various WPA projects, "it was a keen disappointment to find that the WPA was being exploited for politics and to ponder the ultimate effects to our [d]emocracy if such a large group, dependent upon the administration in power, should be hereafter utilized and organized politically." Since Harry Hopkins had said publicly that he didn't want WPA projects to be used for political purposes, Stokes was saddened that an embarrassed Hopkins denounced him, and "when friends within the New Deal turned on me. . . . They sought refuge in the seductive philosophy that the end justifies the means and, under this philosophy, they condoned the political organization of relief workers."[24]

In the election, Barkley ultimately defeated Chandler by a 56 to 44 percent vote. Chandler claimed that without WPA involvement he would have won. Chandler may or may not have been right, but one thoughtful estimate was that WPA efforts gave Barkley 200,000 votes—over half of his total vote. Many cried out for reform. In fact, 70 percent of Americans polled in early 1939 said they "favor a law prohibiting any relief official from contributing money to political campaigns." As a result, that year Congress finally passed the Hatch Act, and Thomas Stokes won the Pulitzer Prize for journalism for his coverage of the corrupt Kentucky campaign. The WPA, one New Deal agency at least, would, starting in 1939, have to sit on the political sidelines.[25]

During 1938, however, Roosevelt was everywhere but on the sidelines. As part of his purge campaign, he rode a train across the country to endorse some candidates, ignore others, and receive adulation from curious Americans, most of whom had never seen a president. Roosevelt studiously avoided those senators who had opposed Court packing—in Nebraska, Wyoming, and Montana, for example, the president avoided Democrat senators Edward Burke, Joseph O'Mahoney, and Burton Wheeler.[26]

During the summer, Roosevelt mapped his strategy to challenge about a dozen incumbent Democrats in both the Senate and the House—men who, Roosevelt contended, had not been faithful recently to the New Deal. Three special targets were Senators Millard Tydings of Maryland, Walter George of Georgia, and Ellison DuRant "Cotton Ed" Smith in South Carolina. Roosevelt not only went into these states and campaigned against these men, he helped persuade loyal New Dealers to run against them. Of the three, Tydings, indeed, was an anti–New Deal Democrat: He voted against the NRA, TVA, and AAA. One can understand the president's desire to oust him. But Senators George and Smith tended to be New Deal supporters. The Court-packing and minimum wage bills were the exceptions. Smith and George, therefore, were both outraged at Roosevelt's meddling. "I have supported 80 percent of New Deal measures," Smith confessed; George also boasted of having backed "most of the major reform issues of the last six years." He compared Roosevelt's arrival to Sherman's march to the sea.[27]

Roosevelt, meanwhile, tried to repeat his strategy that worked so well in Barkley's victory. The president personally campaigned in Maryland, Georgia, and South Carolina; he attacked the loyalty of the incumbents, praised the liberalism of the challengers, and used the power of the federal government to elect them. As Farley observed, "On every hand I heard complaints that the vast power of the administration in the manipulation of patronage and funds was being mobilized to purge the party of all but one hundred percent New Dealers."[28]

The Tydings campaign seemed to be most important to Roosevelt, and he actively used the power of the federal purse. First, he sent a message to all federal employees in Maryland by firing the director of the state's Federal Housing Administration office, who was a Tydings appointee. The president replaced him with the campaign manager for Congressman David Lewis, who was Tydings's opponent in the election. Lewis then had support from federal appointees (postmasters and IRS workers) to help him campaign against Tydings. Second, Roosevelt dangled the promise of two major bridges in the Chesapeake area as a possible reward for loyal Marylanders. In offering subsidies for votes, the president was following a campaign report prepared for him by Theodore Huntley, a reporter for the *Washington Times-Herald.* The "practical thing to do," his report advised, "is to take the organization away from Tydings through judicious use of federal patronage, thus bringing influential leaders into line."[29]

In Georgia and South Carolina, the president again tested the effectiveness of political patronage. Harry Hopkins appeared on the scene right before the primary with promises of 200,000 WPA jobs to help southern farmers. "Mr. Hopkins," the *Charleston News and Courier* noted, "will continue to relieve the distressed, especially—on the eve of important primaries." PWA funds also came into Georgia in the election month of September. Roosevelt wanted a united front of federal workers behind his chosen candidate. When two officials with the RFC and National Emergency Council (NEC) openly supported George for Senate they were fired and replaced with men loyal to the president.[30]

The incumbents had strong local support and struck back vigorously. Tydings, for example, went on the attack. He demanded a Senate investigation into how the president's supporters were pressuring federal officials to campaign against him. He, George, and Smith also mobilized state officials indebted to them and used state and local patronage to offset the large federal presence. Commentators watched the federal spending spree with interest. Frank Kent, a columnist for the *Baltimore Sun*, described Roosevelt's "unprecedented interference in the politics of the states and an unparalleled use of federal machinery in the effort to have his way."[31]

The WPA and other federal agencies were not as effective for Roosevelt's purge candidates as they were for Barkley because the incumbent senators had strong support among many federal officials long before Roosevelt began his purge. And unlike the Barkley model, Roosevelt's handpicked candidates were not nearly as strong as Barkley.

On election day, Tydings, George, and Smith soundly thrashed all three of Roosevelt's purge candidates. One of the president's challengers couldn't even come in second place. Such a drubbing captured much attention. The *Philadelphia Inquirer* observed, "The Administration's attempt to dictate the selection of popular representatives, even to the extent of using PWA grants as lures, looks to be a monumental political blunder."[32] Raymond Clapper, the syndicated columnist, was impressed that Tydings, Smith, and George were able to overcome the onslaught of federal aid. "They have shown that federal officeholders, reliefers, promises of bridges, and the magic of that radio voice do not add up to inevitable victories."[33] On Tydings's election in particular, Clapper noted that "Roosevelt's promise of a bridge on the eastern shore didn't make a dent, except as it affronted many voters. In politics the pay-off is not unwelcome, but it must not be offered too crudely."[34]

And so it went in state after state. Roosevelt snubbed Senator Alva Adams in Colorado, but Adams won reelection anyway. Roosevelt endorsed Senator William McAdoo in California, but he was upset by a relative unknown named Sheridan Downey. Roosevelt ignored Senator Patrick McCarran of Nevada, but he won renomination easily. Roosevelt anointed Senator James Pope in Idaho for reelection, but D. Worth Clark beat him in the primary. Only in a House race, that of John J. O'Connor (D-N.Y.), did Roosevelt's man James Fay win—and that only happened because Bronx boss Ed Flynn enlisted WPA workers to raise money and solicit voters for Fay. In other words, Roosevelt's purge campaign was a flop, and Democratic senators were in disarray.[35]

Jim Farley, who had pleaded with FDR to avoid the purge campaign, described how Vice President John Nance Garner cornered him: "The boss has stirred up a hornet's nest by getting into these primary fights," Garner fumed. "There are now twenty men—Democrats—in the Senate who will vote against anything he wants because they are mad clean through." Some voters were feeling the same way. Roosevelt had told Farley that even divided he thought the Democrats in 1938 would hold their losses to about one Senate seat and sixteen House seats. However, on election day, the Democrats lost eight Senate seats and eighty-one House seats. The president, however, blamed neither himself nor his purge campaign. At his cabinet meeting, he announced, "Well, I've been giving a lot of time to the study of the election returns and I find they demonstrate the result around the country was due in every case to local conditions."[36]

If we study the political abilities of Franklin Roosevelt in the first half of his second term, we see a poor performance. He began with a landslide mandate for the New Deal and almost four-to-one margins in both houses of Congress. He was popular within his party, incumbents cultivated his favor, and he had almost destroyed his opposition. True, the Supreme Court had struck down some of his programs, but the margins were often five to four, and Roosevelt was clearly going to get his way soon to replace some of the elderly justices. No president in over one hundred years had such an opportunity to achieve his political program.

Instead of pursuing ideas, however, or a plan of recovery, he pursued power—he gambled the second term of his presidency on his ability to push through an unpopular plan to pack the Supreme

Court. He used much political capital seeking votes, and then he interfered in the contest to pick a Senate majority leader. The president became resented more than adored, and soon Congress was altering his legislation and overriding his vetoes. He did push through his wages-and-hours bill, but lost on almost everything else.

Granted, Roosevelt could be a shrewd and smooth politician, but his anger and vindictiveness overrode his political judgment, and he mounted a campaign to snub or purge most of the senators and some House members who opposed his Court-packing plan. Even though he was already appointing a new Supreme Court justice in 1937, he still bore a grudge.

Roosevelt tried to mask his motives by claiming the purge campaign was an effort to make the Democrats a more liberal party, not just an effort to punish those who defected on Court packing. That is partly true. Roosevelt had become increasingly liberal, but hostility to Court packing was not just a conservative issue. It united many liberals and conservatives who argued that preserving the separation of constitutional powers was more important than promoting a political philosophy.[37]

But there is a more important point. If Roosevelt wanted to pursue liberal ideas, why was he so unhelpful to black Americans on racial issues? Granted, some New Deal programs involved blacks, and did so against prevailing traditions of segregation. But FDR, liberal rhetoric notwithstanding, did little to advance civil rights. Why, for example, did he refuse to endorse the antilynching bills that were filibustered by southern Democrats in the Senate in 1937 and 1939? That would have been politically possible and politically desirable for someone determined to promote liberal ideas.[38]

Lynchings of black Americans without due process of law were contrary to the whole notion of individual rights that Americans had enshrined in their legal codes and in their Constitution. In the Hoover years, lynchings had actually dropped, but they still happened to blacks at a rate of almost one per month. In Roosevelt's first term, lynchings of black Americans shot back up over 40 percent to almost 1.4 per month. Black Americans implored Congress to make lynching a federal crime, and thereby create the federal machinery to enforce justice in areas that refused to punish lynch mobs. That would expand government, which appealed to liberals, and would improve civil liberties for a persecuted American minority, which also appealed to liberals. Furthermore, from a political angle, blacks had just begun voting for Democrats in the 1930s. Alf Landon in his presidential campaign, and other Republicans later, were clamoring for an antilynching bill. Roosevelt had a good opportunity to steal their thunder, solidify blacks in the New Deal coalition, and pursue a noble, liberal idea.[39]

When Senator Robert Wagner of New York introduced an antilynching bill in 1937, and when the Democrat filibuster stopped it, Roosevelt could have used his political capital to step in, support the bill, and cajole the Senate to pass it. Gallup polls conducted in early 1937 showed 72 percent of northerners and a surprising 57 percent of southerners favored an antilynching law. Eleanor Roosevelt urged her husband to lend his support, and she publicly endorsed the bill herself. By refusing to join her, he was clearly sacrificing what was possibly the most noble liberal idea of the twentieth century.[40]

Many indicators suggest that if Roosevelt had used his political strength in 1937 to endorse the antilynching bill, instead of pursuing his futile Court-packing scheme, he could have easily twisted the arms to push the bill through Congress—without even having to entice recalcitrant southerners with more WPA money.

Granted, some southern senators were resisting the bill, and race baiting was still a vote getter in their states. But less so. Black literacy had risen from 20 to 84 percent from 1870 to 1930, and Booker T. Washington and others had been promoting self-help and black upward mobility for decades. The excuses for abusing blacks and discriminating against them were slowly diminishing.[41]

By the 1930s, the time was probably right for a federal anti-lynching bill to become law. Alben Barkley became the first southern senator to actually support the bill. Interestingly, Happy Chandler, when he ran against Barkley in 1938, refused to use that issue against Barkley even though it would have won him some votes at the time. That was one visible sign of improved race relations.[42]

Here was another one. In the midst of the antilynching debate in 1937, two blacks accused of killing a white merchant in Mississippi were heinously killed by a blowtorch. That kind of thing had happened before, but this time several white groups in Mississippi—including the Methodist Women's Society—petitioned the governor for federal action to prosecute lynchers. In September 1937, Senator Harrison told his fellow Mississippians publicly that Congress would pass an antilynching bill in the next session. "There is no way to stop it," he lamented. But with a six-week filibuster in early 1938, Harrison and his southern colleagues did stop the antilynching bill from reaching the Senate floor. Roosevelt again refused to endorse the bill, or use any political capital to make it pass. He would antagonize southern senators to promote his wages-and-hours bill—which did nothing to reduce unemployment—but he ignored antilynching.[43]

In January 1940, even Vice President Garner, a Texan, had decided that a federal antilynching bill ought to be passed. He said so in a private conference with Roosevelt that month, and Roosevelt's reaction was very revealing. At a dinner party, Roosevelt announced to Farley:

> Jim, I have the grandest joke for you. I had Garner, Barkley, and Rayburn in this morning for a conference on the anti-lynching bill. And you'll never guess what Jack [Garner] said. Very seriously he said that he had given considerable thought to the legislation and that he felt that the colored vote in the border states and in the northern cities was such that he thought the legislation had to be passed.

Then, Farley observed, "Roosevelt threw back his head and laughed till tears came to his eyes."[44]

Farley may have been startled at such a reaction because Roosevelt then said, "Don't you love it? Jack has done a complete about face on it now that he's out looking for votes." Garner would indeed be a candidate for president in 1940, and Roosevelt, who would run for a third term, was ridiculing his future opponent's switch on antilynching because "he's out looking for votes." What's interesting about this exchange is that (1) Garner thought it politically expedient to support a federal antilynching law—more votes were there to gain than to lose; and (2) that Roosevelt did not disagree with that conclusion, but instead was amused by Garner's straddling. That means that Roosevelt must have thought it at least *possible*, and maybe probable, that joining the antilynching crusade really was, in fact, as the Gallup polls suggested, politically expedient. Yet he still refused to do so himself.

Roosevelt also refused to publicly support a constitutional amendment to abolish the poll tax, a device that had been used for decades to keep blacks from voting. That was another chance for Roosevelt to show that liberal political ideas, not just patronage and personal loyalty, were guiding his presidency. In a similar vein, Roosevelt refused to pressure the racist American Federation of Labor "to let the Negro enter skilled trades," even when urged to do so.[45] Perhaps, then, his Court-packing scheme and his purge had more to do with personal pique and the centralizing of power than with Roosevelt's public pronouncements that he was acting in order to transform the Democrats into a liberal party.

Roosevelt's hesitancy to court black voters is puzzling. As shrewd as the president was in mobilizing different groups into his New Deal coalition, he tended to keep blacks at a distance. He did win the black vote anyway, so his election-winning skills came through. When we consider that his support from southern whites was always strong, however, it is odd that he would risk sending black voters back to the Republicans by ignoring civil rights issues.

Even though he occasionally met with a so-called "black cabinet" he tended to ignore them and other black spokesmen as well. The two most prominent blacks in the 1930s were track star Jesse Owens and heavyweight boxing champion Joe Louis. Owens won four gold medals in Berlin at the 1936 Olympics, defying Adolf Hitler and the overtly racist Germans. Yet Roosevelt refused to invite Owens to the White House, or even to send him a congratulatory telegram. Owens that year opposed Roosevelt and endorsed Landon for president. Vote-hungry Republicans paid Owens to speak around the country for Landon and to try to dislodge black voters from Roosevelt's grasp.[46]

The story is similar with Joe Louis. Roosevelt gave Louis little attention until he revealed astonishing popularity with whites as well as blacks. Only then did the president invite the champ to the White House. Louis, like Owens, supported the Republican Party. "Win by a knockout," Louis telegrammed Wendell Willkie in 1940. "It will mean freedom from the WPA and for American Negro rights." Interestingly, after Owens and Louis began supporting the Republican Party, they both underwent IRS investigations. Of course, that could just be coincidence—both had large taxable incomes, and both managed money poorly. Also, the IRS investigations did turn up financial irregularities, and that in itself would justify the audits. But other free-spending athletes, such as Babe Ruth (who was apolitical, but tended to support Democrats), had little problem with the IRS.[47]

Owens's IRS payment was only a few thousand dollars, but Louis, by the 1940s, owed about a half million dollars. He claimed to have made large donations to both the Army and Navy during World War II, and was not properly credited with deductions. In any case, his debt was so large he had to continue boxing just to pay the interest. Louis was in debt to the IRS for the rest of his life. Roosevelt could have won much praise from the black community by pardoning Louis, or at least calling off the IRS as he did for Lyndon Johnson.[48]

Along these lines, Roosevelt could also have earned praise by responding to petitions from black reporters to integrate his press conferences during the 1930s. But Roosevelt chose not to ask the White House Correspondents' Association to admit even one black reporter. Opera singer Marian Anderson did get to sing at the Lincoln Memorial in 1939, but Eleanor, not Franklin, created that symbolic gesture. Roosevelt did give race some recognition by meeting from time to time with college president Mary McLeod Bethune and Democrat Arthur Mitchell, the only black congressman, but both said the president dominated the conversations with chatty stories and rarely gave them a chance to speak. For whatever reasons, Roosevelt was wary of forming close political ties with black Americans and he used no political capital to support civil rights during the New Deal years.[49]

During Roosevelt's second term, his ambition seems to have trumped his good judgment. The president's political instincts, which were so acute in his first term, deserted him after his landslide reelection. He passed up the chance to support civil rights and instead used his political capital to promote Court packing and to make Alben Barkley the Senate majority leader. Such tampering with the other two branches of government triggered a large opposition, both overt and subtle, from many sources. The New Deal was essentially over. The president's honeymoon with both the press and Congress had ended.

HOW FDR'S DECEPTION TARNISHED
THE PRESIDENCY FOREVER

On August 18, 1920 in Deer Lodge, Montana, Franklin D. Roosevelt, the Democrat candidate for vice president of the United States, claimed he wrote Haiti's Constitution himself adding, "if I do say so, I think it a pretty good Constitution." Roosevelt made the same statement in the nearby towns of Helena and Butte. Such a false claim, the Republicans cried, revealed Roosevelt's poor character. Meanwhile, Roosevelt decided to deny he ever made the claim, and the Associated Press sent an extra reporter to follow Roosevelt in case he had another burst of creativity.[1]

Did Roosevelt's character improve during the next twelve years? Personalities shape presidencies, and Roosevelt's did so more than most. His dogged optimism ("We have nothing to fear but fear itself") and his charm (via his fireside chats) were very real assets and invigorated his presidency. In shaping his leadership style, was his character an asset or a liability?

In the 1932 campaign, Roosevelt's emphatic promise to balance the budget became a major test of his character. At the same time, with unemployment high, Roosevelt tended to promise audiences that he would use the federal government to create jobs. For example, in September Roosevelt declared that Americans had a "right to a comfortable living." President Hoover, of course, was on the defensive and, to shift attention from his weak performance, he attacked Roosevelt's schemes of "political log-rolling." He accused Roosevelt of "yielding to sectional and group raids on the public treasury." [2]

Under these kinds of attacks, two weeks before the election, Roosevelt decided to take a clear and unwavering stand for balancing the budget. In Pittsburgh, on October 19, he addressed "Republican leaders" and "American voters" about the federal budget. He began with an attack on the Hoover administration. In four recent years, Roosevelt observed, federal expenses had increased by $1 billion "and that I may add, is the most reckless and extravagant past that I have been able to discover in the statistical record of any peacetime Government anywhere, any time." What's more, this figure was increasing. Hoover had, Roosevelt concluded, burdened the country with "a deficit so great that it makes us catch our breath."

What was causing these astonishing deficits, Roosevelt asked? "It arises from one cause only," he admonished, "and that is the unbalanced budget and the continued failure of this Administration to take effective steps to balance it." Hoover was "committed to the idea that we ought to center control of everything in Washington as rapidly as possible—Federal control. That was the idea that increased the cost of Government by a billion dollars in four years." [3]

Roosevelt's solution: cut expenses and balance the budget. "I shall approach the problem of carrying out the plain precept of our Party, which is to reduce the cost of current Federal Government operations by 25 percent." To help achieve this, Roosevelt vowed that any person entering his cabinet must pledge "absolute loyalty to the Democratic platform," which promised a balanced budget and a 25 percent reduction of expenses. "I regard reduction in Federal spending as one of the most important issues of this campaign. In my opinion it is the most direct and effective contribution that Government can make to business." Roosevelt did say that in an emergency of "starvation and dire need" he might have to ask for new funds for relief. But clearly he did not anticipate this—and indeed unemployment had roughly peaked in late 1932. It was "necessary," Roosevelt said, "to eliminate from Federal budget-making during this emergency all new items except such as relate to direct relief of unemployment." That way, Roosevelt concluded, the budget would be balanced, federal expenses reduced, and "I hope that it will not be necessary to increase the present scale of taxes." [4]

When Roosevelt took office in March 1933 he did not fill his cabinet with persons pledged to balancing the budget, but he did appoint Lewis Douglas, a four-term congressman from Arizona, as director of the budget. Douglas was committed to fulfilling the president's pledge to balance the budget and cut federal spending. When Roosevelt and his advisors put together the massive federal spending and administrative expansion of his first hundred days in office, Douglas provided a counterpoint, arguing and pointing FDR back to his promises made in Pittsburgh. Indeed, Douglas did win a few cuts in salaries and administrative expenses, but usually he watched in horror as the president expanded the federal government and ran up deficits much greater than those of Hoover. Roosevelt was bemused by Douglas's efforts to make the Democrats keep their promises. Somewhere between Douglas's "efforts to spend nothing," Roosevelt quipped, "and the point of view of the people who want to spend ten billions additional on public works, we will get somewhere." [5]

Sometimes after talking with Roosevelt, Douglas would come away convinced that spending cuts were finally coming. But then Tugwell, Hopkins, and others would come to the president wanting more money to spend, and Douglas would be thwarted. In the spring of 1934, after more than one full year on the job, Douglas finally coaxed an official White House memorandum "ordering an across-the-board cutback in federal spending." That translated to hundreds of millions of dollars in spending cuts. At last, Douglas contended, the budget might get balanced. An elated Douglas called in Turner Catledge, a *New York Times* reporter, to give him the "exclusive story on this major decision." Catledge wrote the story on the spending cuts, and was reading it the next morning, when he received a call to see the president. The story is best told in Catledge's words: "When I entered the President's office, he threw out his hand in a welcoming gesture. 'Hello, Turner,' he called out happily, 'where have you been so long? I said to Steve [Early] just this morning, "What's happened to old Turner Catledge? Why doesn't he come around any more? Get him over here."'" Young Catledge was "immediately skeptical" because he barely knew the president and had never had a private meeting with him. Roosevelt

pointed to the clipping, patting it with his fingertips, and said he was curious how such fantastic stories got around. He said, most affably, that I needn't have swallowed such a cock-and-bull story, for all I had to do was call him and check the facts, as I was always free to do. This was news to me.

He went on to say that the final budget plans couldn't be fixed until an estimate had been made of the needs of the relief program. My story about an agreed-on cutback, he said, was made up out of whole cloth. I told him the story might be wrong but it wasn't made up out of whole cloth—I'd gotten it from what I considered a responsible source. "Exactly," he said. "But you should be more careful where you get your stories, shouldn't you?"

He then suggested that I do another story, to the effect that the budgeting process was under way but no final decision had been made. I was not to attribute this to him, but he assured me this was the "real McCoy." I later confirmed that Roosevelt had led Douglas to believe he'd accepted his budget cuts while also leading the spenders to think he was on their side.[6]

Catledge was astonished at his first meeting with the president. Not just the remarkable "What's happened to old Turner Catledge?" part. Roosevelt had denied the official memo he had sent to Douglas, then said no final decision on the budget had been made, and then urged Catledge to print a retraction, but not to attribute it to Roosevelt himself.

Catledge was in for more surprises. Henry Morgenthau, the secretary of the treasury, called Catledge later that day and asked for a lunch date the next day. Catledge accepted and here is his account of the meeting:

> We had hardly placed our napkins on our laps when Morgenthau brought up my budget story—the one I'd gotten from Douglas. Morgenthau said he wanted to thank me for absolving him and his department of any part in that "leak." He said the President had called him to assure him that Catledge had given him and the Treasury a clean bill of health. He said he was most relieved at this, because the President didn't take kindly to leaks.
>
> I listened for a few minutes, then I told him, "Mr. Secretary, this is very interesting, but it's not true. I didn't mention you to Roosevelt and he didn't mention you to me. He didn't treat the story as a leak—he said it was made up out of whole cloth."
>
> Morgenthau's face lapsed into a sickly grin. Morgenthau worshipped FDR and I suppose he never knew why the President would invent a fictitious conversation with me when there was no need to. But it was Roosevelt's way—perhaps that small fiction was quicker or easier than simply telling Morgenthau the truth.
>
> Apparently Morgenthau came to understand Roosevelt better in time, for he later told of an exchange in which Roosevelt said, "Never let your left hand know what your right hand is doing." "Which hand am I, Mr. President?" Morgenthau said. "My right hand," Roosevelt replied, "but I keep my left hand under the table." Morgenthau added: "This is the most frank expression of the real FDR that I ever listened to."[7]

After a year and a half working as budget director, Douglas finally resigned in frustration in August 1934. Douglas and Morgenthau were not the only ones who felt manipulated by the president. Many reporters, like Turner Catledge, discovered Roosevelt liked to use them to launch his "trial balloons." William Chenery, editor of *Collier's*, observed the president's craftiness firsthand.

> He played with public opinion as a cat with a mouse. I have heard him tell a secretary to let the White House reporters get an intimation that this or that might be done. The secretary was specifically instructed, in my presence and doubtless for my enlightenment, not to permit any official name to be used as an authority for this statement. Then the popular reaction could be watched. Within a couple of days the rumor could be confirmed or denied as the public response indicated.

After Douglas had resigned, Morgenthau, as treasury secretary, was often involved in Roosevelt's maneuvers. Sometimes, like Douglas, he was frustrated over the deficits; always he was frustrated when the facts stood on one side, and the president's statements stood on the other.[8]

For example, in January 1935, Rexford Tugwell, who took charge of the Resettlement Administration that year, persuaded Roosevelt to send him $67 million. When Morgenthau found out, he called the president and persuaded him that "Hopkins and Ickes are going to be sore" and that "you are going to need this money badly for relief before July 1." Roosevelt agreed and then devised a plan whereby Tugwell "cannot obligate a single cent of this money unless it is passed on by the [Bureau of the] Budget." Of course, Roosevelt then made sure Morgenthau would persuade the Bureau of the Budget not to approve the funding Roosevelt had promised to Tugwell.

Morgenthau was glad to stop the $67 million to Tugwell, but was distressed at Roosevelt's hypocrisy. "This is so typical of the President," Morgenthau lamented.

He assured me and Harry Hopkins that he would not allot any more money until we had another meeting. I understand a couple of weeks ago he allotted Hopkins $125,000,000 secretly. Next Tugwell appeals to him directly and he gives him what he wants. The result is that everybody is angry and frothing at the mouth. Then when I draw his attention to it, instead of doing the straightforward thing and canceling Tugwell's authorization which could not have yet reached him, he double crosses Tugwell by telling me to tell [assistant budget director Daniel] Bell that Tugwell cannot have one cent until the budget passes on it. This ma[k]es a complete circle and everybody will be sore and nobody will be satisfied.[9]

From time to time Roosevelt admitted that he lied. But he always said he did so for higher purposes—that necessity was the mother of his inventions. During World War II, for example, Roosevelt said, "I am perfectly willing to mislead and tell lies if it will help win the war." That argument is at least understandable; but often Roosevelt was "willing to mislead and tell lies" merely to secure a short-term advantage. For example, at a press conference in early 1935, with the NRA under fire, Roosevelt said he would not support state NRA laws. However, when Democratic governor Paul McNutt of Indiana protested vigorously, Roosevelt sent him a telegram repudiating his position. The president alleged an "extraordinary misinterpretation put upon my reply at press conference."[10]

A few months later, according to Senator Pat Harrison, chairman of the Senate Finance Committee, the president called him in to push for immediate passage of a "soak-the-rich" tax bill. Harrison, who tended to be cautious on tax issues, was perplexed because the president had earlier promised he would submit no new tax bill in 1935. Roosevelt obviously took delight in Harrison's discomfort—in having to support Roosevelt's plan for steep taxation—because he told a treasury official, "Pat Harrison's going to be so surprised he'll have kittens on the spot." Harrison, however, as a loyal Senate leader, reluctantly accepted the president's change of mind and began preparing his fellow senators for the surprise tax bill. As news of the tax hike became public, however, suddenly a deluge of public criticism came forth, some from New Dealers themselves, and Roosevelt quickly rushed to shelter; he denied ever having suggested tax reform. Neither he nor anyone else at the White House, he alleged, had "ever intimated in any shape, manner or form" that they wanted a new tax bill. Ever the dramatist in his denial, the president said, "Heavens above, I am not Congress. I am just an innocent, peaceful little fellow down here that makes recommendation." Harrison, who was left alone holding the tax bill, "has once more taken the rap," wrote Arthur Krock at the *New York Times*. Harrison, however, as the loyal lieutenant, refused to criticize the president. He simply dropped the tax bill and said, "Let us close this chapter, and let us not talk about the matter any more."[11]

Harold Ickes, the secretary of the interior, like Harrison was a strong supporter of Roosevelt and, like Harrison, Ickes was always troubled to discover the president's willingness to go back on his word. Ickes expressed this sadness in his diary:

> It is distressing to hear from so many quarters expressions that the President's word cannot be relied upon. The number of people in the country who believe this seems to be growing. Unfortunately, based on my own experience, I regret to say there are occasions when he does seem to regard his word lightly. I regret to say this about my Chief, the President of the United States, but unfortunately it is true.[12]

Roosevelt's deceitfulness on issues large and small created a climate of uncertainty among New Dealers as to what was really going to happen from week to week or even from day to day. As Roosevelt once admitted, "We seldom know, six weeks in advance, what we are going to do." Therefore, he never considered himself bound by any statement or commitment he had made. To complicate matters further, Roosevelt, as Arthur Krock observed, "was often devious when it was not necessary." Turner Catledge, who attended many of the president's press conferences, believed Roosevelt's first instinct when under pressure was to lie. Certainly Catledge's lunch with Henry Morgenthau revealed the president's unnecessary lie to Morgenthau. Charles Edison, the secretary of the Navy, saw this tendency as well. When Edison was appointed, Roosevelt told him needlessly that he had offered the job first to Joseph Martin, the Republican House leader. But when Edison later checked this point, Martin was stunned and said he knew nothing about it.[13]

Sometimes Roosevelt invented not just a fact or two, but whole stories, complete with detailed dialogue. James Farley, the postmaster general, related an event where Roosevelt fabricated a story for the $100 a plate Washington Democratic Victory Dinner to announce he would not seek a third term.

Roosevelt could have simply told the audience he discussed the third-term issue with advisors and that he decided not to run for a third term. Instead, he built the story around an invented character named "John." Roosevelt, Farley explained, sometimes created the imaginary "John" when he needed a straight man for his stories. At the dinner, according to Farley, Roosevelt began his ruse this way:

> "A few days ago a distinguished member of Congress came to see me. . . . I said to him, 'John, I want to tell you something that is very personal to me—something that you have a right to hear from my own lips. I have a great ambition in life. . . . John, my ambition relates to January 20, 1941!'"

He paused dramatically. There was not a sound in the room. Everyone leaned forward to listen. He was speaking in studied earnestness; but he later acknowledged to me he knew he had his audience in the palm of his hand and was enjoying himself immensely.

> "I could just feel what horrid thoughts my friend was thinking.

> So in order to relieve his anxiety, I went on to say, 'My great ambi-
> tion on January 20, 1941, is to turn over this desk to my successor,
> whoever he may be. . . .'"[14]

In defense of Roosevelt, one can argue that his fabrication in this
case was harmless, the action of a raconteur, and that his eventual
"change of mind" on running for a third term was perhaps understandable because conditions changed during his second term. A
larger point is that during his presidency he never felt bound by the
truth in pursuing his ends, and that his subterfuge took a variety of
forms, some perhaps harmless and others more serious.

Given the deception that permeated his presidency, we need to
ask how Roosevelt was able to escape without paying a steep political price. The first reason is that Roosevelt was very quick-witted
and often talked his way out of contradictions. In 1936, for example, when he ran for reelection he had to explain away his skyrocketing deficits in light of his promise to cut spending and balance
the budget. When the president asked Samuel Rosenman, a Brains
Truster, to help him explain his Pittsburgh speech, Rosenman responded, "Mr. President, the only thing you can say about the 1932
speech is to deny categorically that you ever made it." But Roosevelt
showed boldness and remarkable ingenuity in returning to Pittsburgh on October 1, 1936, and explaining himself this way: "The
only way to keep the Government out of the red is to keep
the people out of the red. And so we had to balance the budget of
the American people before we could balance the budget of the
national Government."[15]

Shortly after this sleight of hand came an emotional appeal:

> In those dark days between us and a balanced budget stood mil-
> lions of needy Americans, denied the promise of a decent American
> life. To balance our budget in 1933 or 1934 or 1935 would have
> been a crime against the American people. To do so we should ei-
> ther have had to make a capital levy that would have been confisca-

tory, or we should have had to set our face against human suffering with callous indifference. When Americans suffered, we refused to pass by on the other side. Humanity came first.[16]

Thus Roosevelt wriggled out of his earlier promise by saying that when choosing between people and his promise of a balanced budget he chose people and that to have done otherwise "would have been a crime against the American people." Roosevelt had asked the listeners to look at the funding of many federal programs to create jobs and not at the high excise and income taxes extracted from scores of millions of Americans, some of them very poor, to fund these programs. His tactic worked, and when Roosevelt was overwhelmingly reelected he had fewer constraints than ever on his obligation to keep his word.

A second reason Roosevelt was able to survive his deceptions was that he controlled a great deal of power and patronage; his allies in his cabinet and in Congress had strong incentives to gloss over the president's lies, or even to cover for him. As we have seen, Pat Harrison, the high-ranking senator from Mississippi, willingly took the heat for Roosevelt's reversal on his proposed tax hike. Harrison (until he tried to become majority leader) was glad to be working with a Democrat president and appreciated the patronage Roosevelt flowed through Harrison into Mississippi.[17]

Along similar lines, the president's cabinet reluctantly but willingly bore the brunt of many of the president's fabrications. It was to Garner, initially, whom Roosevelt confided his story that fifty men had put $5 million in a pot to destroy his administration. To Morgenthau, the president earlier pegged his list of conspirators at two thousand. To prove his point that rich people were not paying 79 percent of their marginal income in taxes, Roosevelt seems to have invented another man, not named "John" this time. To Morgenthau, the president alleged that he had a casual conversation with this unnamed man, who revealed to the president that he earned $900,000 the previous year, but was not paying his share of about $700,000 in taxes. Roosevelt, in his account to Morgenthau, discerned the man was keeping back more, accused him of doing so, and then asked how he did it. The man, caught in the act, confessed that he had sheltered some of his income in tax-exempt bonds. That, Roosevelt told Morgenthau, meant that the 79 percent marginal tax rate was not really onerous because tax-exempt bonds were a loophole. Morgenthau listened patiently to this self-serving story; as a loyalist, he never made Roosevelt's invented stories public until after his death.[18]

A third reason Roosevelt's duplicity was rarely exposed related to what we call today his charisma, especially with reporters. Roosevelt had remarkable charm and his strong, likable personality often overwhelmed reporters and others who encountered the president's penchant for deception. Person after person who met Roosevelt described his warmth, optimism, energy, and likability. Even adversaries were captivated by Roosevelt. An excellent example was Arthur Krock, the Washington bureau chief for the *New York Times*. Krock won an unprecedented four Pulitzer Prizes (two in the 1930s); he was strong-willed, cynical, and almost impossible to manipulate. Roosevelt, who often tried to manage the news, was often frustrated with Krock and twice tried to get him fired. Nonetheless, Krock admired the president's persuasive skills and had to work to avoid being swirled into his orbit. One time, Roosevelt asked Krock why he no longer attended the president's press conferences. "Because," Krock replied, "I can't keep my objectivity when I'm close to you and watching you in action. You charm me so much that when I go back to write a comment on the proceedings, I can't keep it in balance."[19]

Roosevelt had trouble snaring Krock, but at twice-a-week press conferences the president was amiable, attentive, and effective with the scores of reporters who attended. Even though most newspaper publishers opposed Roosevelt, most reporters (some have estimated over 90 percent) supported the president, and they often wrote their stories while under his enchanting spell.[20]

FDR used his charm on the mostly friendly reporters to circumvent hostile publishers and thereby secure pro–New Deal stories in print. To help do this, the president artfully hired scores of reporters to join his administration and filter the news to their reporter friends who covered the White House. Stephen Early, for example, was a longtime UP and AP reporter before Roosevelt hired him and made him the first-ever White House press secretary. Early had an affable touch with his friends in the news business. Roosevelt also hired many reporters to become press agents for cabinet members and for the heads of New Deal agencies. Since salaries in government were much higher than most publishers offered, the New Deal became a great job source for reporters. The president was able to hire talented newsmen to present his ideas in attractive form. Many in the press, confident in the judgment of Roosevelt's newly hired press agents, willingly accepted and printed almost verbatim in their news stories the press releases issued daily from the various cabinet and department officials.[21]

The gregarious Roosevelt loved using the personal touch with reporters, both friendly and hostile. He warmly greeted them by name, and often asked about their families and jobs. The president regularly invited influential reporters for private lunches and Sunday dinners, sometimes at Hyde Park, where he would give them a personal tour of the grounds. Eleanor used this tactic as well with women reporters. Both Franklin and Eleanor sent flowers and personal letters to reporters on special occasions. In 1934, Roosevelt introduced an annual dance for reporters and chatted with them informally throughout the evening. Henry Morgenthau began sponsoring an annual clambake on his farm in New York for reporters, and Roosevelt sometimes took charge of the event to ensure the atmosphere there was convivial and entertaining.[22]

Some reporters literally joined the Roosevelt family. John Boettiger of the *Chicago Tribune* divorced his wife to marry Anna Roosevelt, the president's daughter. Boettiger left the *Tribune* and, with the president's financial and personal support, became publisher of the *Seattle Post-Intelligencer*. Also, Lorena Hickok, reputed to be the highest paid female reporter, left the Associated Press to live part-time at the White House and cover the FERA for Harry Hopkins. Part of her goal was to promote Roosevelt politically among journalists. Biographer Doris Faber discovered that Hickok "along her travels had enlisted a small corps of strategically located journalists to alert Washington directly when something struck them as potentially an embarrassment—if possible, before the story got printed." Arthur Krock, who observed these kinds of situations firsthand, concluded as early as 1935 that the Roosevelt administration was guilty of "more ruthlessness, intelligence, and subtlety in trying to suppress legitimate unfavorable comment than any other I have known."[23]

Krock, however, made only a general observation. What were some of the specific ways the press helped FDR? First, the press cooperated with him in his effort to portray himself as a healthy and whole man. They rarely mentioned his crippling disease of polio and they never printed pictures of him in a wheelchair. In 1931 and 1932, when questions were raised about Roosevelt's fitness, Fulton Oursler, editor of the popular *Liberty* magazine, published two articles that stressed Roosevelt's vigor and good health. Remarkably, Oursler let Roosevelt edit the first article before publication. In that article, Oursler's author initially wrote that Roosevelt "never entirely recovered from infantile paralysis." Roosevelt went into deception mode. According to Oursler, FDR "banged his great fist on the desk and shouted: 'Never recovered what?' Now he leaned forward and pointed a finger at me as he added in a mild and mincing tone, 'I have never recovered the complete use of my knees. Will you fix that?' " The obliging Oursler later was rewarded with special invitations to private White House dinners and with insider comments and articles from Roosevelt for *Liberty* magazine. The press followed Oursler's lead: the subject of Roosevelt's polio almost did not exist in news stories.[24]

Second, the press sometimes actively promoted Roosevelt's political success. Cissy Patterson, publisher of the *Washington Times-Herald*, systematically retouched photos of Eleanor to make her appear more attractive to readers. Joseph Patterson, Cissy's brother, was publisher of the *New York Daily News*, and his coverage of the president was so favorable that Roosevelt asked him to join his cabinet. One of Cissy's reporters, Theodore Huntley, wrote the president a "secret strategy report" to help unseat Senator Millard Tydings of Maryland, whom, as we saw earlier, Roosevelt actively tried to defeat in 1938.[25]

In addition, sometimes helpful reporters actually determined New Deal policy. For example, in January 1936, when the Supreme Court struck down the AAA, New Dealers were frantic to think up a way to continue paying farmers not to produce. Felix Belair of the *New York Times* and J. Russell Wiggins of the *St. Paul Pioneer Press* discovered a passage in the obscure Soil Conservation Act that allowed Roosevelt to continue his crop reduction program in a more constitutional manner. They took their discovery to the Department of Agriculture; the startled officials then passed it along to the president; and in Roosevelt's next press conference he was presenting the new farm program of crop reduction for soil conservation.[26]

Just as many journalists tried to help the New Deal subsidies to succeed, some New Dealers tried to use subsidies to help journalists succeed. Jesse Jones, the head of the RFC, often tried to lend money and even a business or two to Walter Trohan of the *Chicago Tribune*. "I didn't think I would be honest in accepting," Trohan concluded. No such ethical issues bothered J. David Stern, publisher of the *Philadelphia Record*. Stern strongly supported the New Deal and he was eager to take federal help. Roosevelt obliged and pressured Jesse Jones to make a $1 million RFC loan to Stern.[27]

A third way the press helped Roosevelt was by refusing to cover the awkward family relationship between Franklin and Eleanor. The president and his wife had a "marriage of convenience." Franklin would sometimes work with Eleanor, and she did bring him useful reports from her travels, but Franklin often avoided her, sometimes for days and weeks at a time. He also would ridicule her publicly. Their tensions were exempt from coverage, however, and Franklin often exploited this exemption. For example, when Walter Lippmann, the highly respected columnist with the *New York Herald Tribune*, criticized Roosevelt's reversal on tax policy, the president invited Lippmann to Hyde Park for a private lunch and personal tour. At one point, when Eleanor joined them and expressed an opinion, Roosevelt interrupted, "Oh, Eleanor, shut up. You never understand these things anyway."[28] The president correctly concluded that Lippmann would not quote his rebuke in print.

Even more important, Roosevelt had cooperation from the press not to report his liaisons with other women, particularly Lucy Mercer. After his affair with Mercer, he continued to see her despite his promise to Eleanor that he wouldn't. The press knew all about the romance. Eleanor's first cousin, Alice Roosevelt Longworth, told it to, among others, Cissy Patterson, publisher of the *Washington Times-Herald*. Walter Trohan of the *Chicago Tribune* said that he first heard about it in 1934 from fellow *Tribune* reporter John Boettiger, who, as we have seen, married the president's daughter. In fact, the day Boettiger revealed the story to Trohan they both were covering Hyde Park, and Boettiger pointed to the second floor of Roosevelt's house and said Eleanor was gone and that the president was with Lucy Mercer as they spoke. Since Lucy Mercer was also married, there was risk for her as well as the president, but the press and the Secret Service kept the story, and their meetings, quiet during Roosevelt's lifetime. Trohan, with a tip from the Secret Service, saw Lucy visit the president once at night and began collecting evidence on the affair. But even Robert McCormick, publisher of the *Chicago Tribune*, perhaps the newspaper most hostile to the president, refused to print the story.[29]

By 1941, the president had become even bolder with women. After the fall of Norway to the Nazis, Roosevelt invited Crown

Princess Martha of Norway and her young children to Washington. Shortly thereafter, Trohan had a tip that Roosevelt was having an affair with her. According to Trohan, "week after week, I would watch FDR make his way slowly down the ramp of his private car . . . to his auto. Then the train door would open and Martha would dart out, invariably in high-heeled slippers and black silk hose. . . . She would race to the car, leap in and off it would go." Trohan decided to write stories merely mentioning that the crown princess was visiting the president, not necessarily insinuating a romantic relationship. Soon, however, Stephen Early, the White House press secretary, was urging Trohan to stop mentioning the crown princess; when that didn't work, Early and other White House staffers tried, without success, to deflect Trohan so that he would not see the crown princess's train arrive. As a last resort, according to Trohan, Early pleaded with him, "My God, after Eleanor, isn't he entitled to a bit of femininity?"

Trohan could have persisted on grounds of national security. According to columnist Joseph Alsop, Roosevelt discussed diplomatic and military secrets with Lucy Mercer. If he did the same with the princess of Norway, he indeed put his country at risk.[30]

With so much help from most reporters in so many areas, Roosevelt sometimes became careless in telling the truth. Merriman Smith, White House correspondent for the United Press, gives us a fascinating example of Roosevelt caught in the act of deception in a press conference. According to Smith,

> During the early stages of the war when inflationary trends were first showing themselves in force, he [Roosevelt] told a press conference a story. He swore it was true.
>
> It seems a garage mechanic friend of his "dropped in" for a chat. Now, how in the world a mechanic ever dropped in on Mr. Roosevelt was beyond explanation. He claimed a lot of friends in comparatively low stations of life. I regarded them as his imaginary play-

mates because I doubted seriously one of them ever existed. He told often of a Chinese laundryman he knew, a baseball player, a small dirt farmer, a garage man.

This mechanic, he said, had come to him complaining about the high price of strawberries in February. His "missus," the mechanic was alleged to have told the President, was having to pay a God-awful price for strawberries.

The President said he lectured his mechanic friend sharply. Since when could mechanics afford strawberries out of season? Why didn't they eat something else? Why throw away their defense plant wages in such a foolish fashion?

The President used this to prove that the price line actually was being held, but that too many people were spending their money on unnecessary luxuries.

About six months later, the inflation question came up again in a press conference. Someone wanted to know whether the President really thought the price line was being held, and how much longer it would last.

The President declined to comment directly. He thought for a moment and added that there were too many people like a master mechanic he knew.

This man, he said, had dropped in "to chat" and complain about the high price of asparagus. His "missus," the President said of the mechanic, was complaining bitterly about having to pay such a dear price for asparagus.

And since when, the President said he told the mechanic, did he find it necessary to have asparagus, out of season, on his menu? Why didn't they eat something else? Why contribute to inflation by wasting their defense plant wages on unnecessary luxury items?

I could not resist it. I knew it was presumptuous and bordered on the disrespectful, but I had to ask the question.

"Mr. President," I said, "is that the same mechanic who came in a few months back complaining about the price of strawberries?"

The press conference exploded into roars of laughter. Mr. Roosevelt turned a little pink and shouted over the guffaws:

"My God, Merriman. It's true. It *is* true. It was the same man."[31]

Smith, who admits elsewhere that he was completely charmed by Roosevelt, interestingly seems to chide himself rather than the president for this episode. He said, "I knew it was presumptuous and bordered on the disrespectful, but I had to ask [Roosevelt] the question." If the president was entitled to invent information, was the reporter who challenged it "presumptuous" and bordering "on the disrespectful"? Such a view of life, which Roosevelt obviously fought hard to encourage, gave the president a strong advantage.

Roosevelt used a carrot-and-stick approach with the press. He preferred using the carrot, turning on his charm, and gently encouraging reporters to write friendly stories of his New Deal. Sometimes he would tell them in a press conference, "Now if I were writing this story, here is the way I would do it" and then proceed to advance his point of view. As we have seen he also had other persuasive tools: White House dinners, private meetings, jobs in his administration, and even government loans. If these did not work, the president used the stick. The press conferences, for example, sometimes produced awkward questions for Roosevelt. In some cases, if he didn't like the direction of the discussion, he would tell a reporter, "put on the dunce cap and sit in the corner." He also banned a reporter from a future press conference.[32]

Social pressure was a useful weapon as well. In 1938, when Thomas Stokes of the Scripps-Howard newspapers exposed the WPA for paying workers to campaign for Democrats, he won a Pulitzer Prize for his detailed and thorough reporting. To Stokes, the buying of votes "imperil[ed] the right of the people to a free and unpolluted ballot," but he was disappointed when Harry Hopkins and others in the Roosevelt administration "turned upon me. I was an outlaw, a pariah." Delbert Clark of the *New York Times* pointed out that even though Stokes had previously been sympathetic toward the New Deal, after his WPA stories he "was ostracized by his former friends in the administration."[33]

In special cases, the IRS made calls on Roosevelt's press adversaries. For example, William Randolph Hearst had a thorough investigation into every "crevice and corner" of his huge newspaper empire. Hearst's books however, were in order and he escaped penalties. Publisher Moses Annenberg of the *Philadelphia Inquirer* wrote pungent editorials against Roosevelt, and did much damage to the Democrat Party in Pennsylvania. Annenberg, however, had been careless in his finances, as we have seen in chapter 11. When Roosevelt and Morgenthau put the IRS on his case, Annenberg went to jail and the president did much better in Pennsylvania in the next election. Even Fulton Oursler, who helped the president hide his true polio condition from the public, may have been targeted by the IRS. Eleanor had written some articles for his *Liberty* magazine, and he refused to give her what she thought they were worth. Then Oursler had an unpleasant visit from an aggressive IRS agent. Afterward, Oursler stormed into the White House; when he confronted Louis Howe, Howe told Oursler that he had "miserably treated" Eleanor and said, "I resent it for her." Oursler couldn't prove it, but he always suspected that Howe triggered the IRS challenge because of the alleged underpayment to Eleanor.[34]

After Roosevelt's first term, his prevarications began to catch up with him. In part that is because they were more public and more obvious in his second term. For example, when Roosevelt announced his Court-packing plan, he did not argue for it in a forthright manner. He could have used his reelection landslide to argue that the Supreme Court was hopelessly reactionary in striking down some of his New Deal programs. Given that the Supreme Court had been altered in size before, why not add a few more justices now to make it more progressive and more in line with the overwhelming mandate the president had just received?[35]

Instead, Roosevelt at first relied solely on an efficiency argument, that the justices were overloaded with case work and that if he could add more justices they would help ease the strain on the current nine justices. Sociologist Robert Nisbet watched Roosevelt in action and summarized a widely held view in these words: "Presidents before FDR were charged with everything from sexual immorality to blind political stupidity, but not with calculated deception of the public. When Roosevelt declared to the people that his reason for wishing to see the Supreme Court enlarged was a desire for greater judicial efficiency, he lied and everyone knew it." [36]

The Court-packing lie, then, was qualitatively different from other Roosevelt claims. Most of his false statements were made to an individual or a small group for the purpose of securing a short-term advantage. Among Roosevelt's riskier public deceptions, such as his pledge to balance the budget and his later promise not to raise taxes, he could always say that circumstances changed from the time he made the promise to the time he broke it. After all, voters sometimes change their minds and they understand that circumstances can cause changes in presidential plans as well. With Court packing, however, Roosevelt's purpose was clearly to appoint new justices to change the Court's philosophy, not to increase its efficiency. In the past two years he had attacked the Supreme Court regularly for striking down some of his programs; he had yet to make an appointment to the Court and all political observers knew he wanted to put many of his followers on the Court.

Thus, as Nisbet and scores of others have noted, Roosevelt told a deliberate and premeditated lie on a major subject and everyone knew it. Those who jumped to the president's defense knew they were defending a falsehood, that judicial efficiency was merely a means to an end. Those who became critics of the plan could attack it directly as a willfully deceptive effort by Roosevelt to increase his political power and control not only the executive branch, but the legislative branch (through patronage and power) and the judicial branch. [37]

Most of the first shots fired against Court packing came from the press. Syndicated columnist Walter Lippmann, one of the most respected political writers in the country, concluded "that the intoxication of personal power has gone to Mr. Roosevelt's head." Lippmann added, "I do not say that Mr. Roosevelt is a dictator or that he wishes to be one. But I do say that he is proposing to create the necessary precedent, and to establish the political framework for, and to destroy the safeguards against, a dictator." Frank Kent of the *Baltimore Sun* agreed: "The simple truth is that if Mr. Roosevelt secures passage of both of these bills [Court packing and its companion, executive reorganization] he will have all the power there is." David Lawrence of *U.S. News* concluded, "if the Supreme Court goes, all other American institutions begin to crumble one by one."[38]

One by one, reporters and newspaper editors began to accuse Roosevelt of trying to become a dictator. Those charges lingered and were repeated during the next year and beyond. Even when Roosevelt revealed his real motives and began attacking the Supreme Court for its decisions, not just its inefficiency, the charges of "dictator" continued. Gallup polls began to ask Americans if they thought their country was in danger of dictatorship (significantly, as we have seen, 45 percent said "yes" at one point). At 1:00 A.M. one night in March 1938, Roosevelt felt compelled to call reporters to announce he had "no inclination to be a dictator" and "none of the qualifications."[39]

Some congressmen joined in the criticism of Court packing, but most, as we saw in chapter 13, hesitated because they did not want to lose federal patronage and did not want Roosevelt campaigning against them when they ran for re-election. When Burton Wheeler agreed to lead the Senate charge against Court packing, he correctly surmised that his control of federal patronage in Montana was threatened and that Roosevelt would also try to defeat him in his next election.[40] Reporters were more insulated from these threats, and they were able to lead the attack against Court packing more safely.

Interestingly, those in the radio business were poorly positioned to oppose Court packing, or any other New Deal program. Newspaper reporters had relative freedom; radio operators did not. Roosevelt persuaded Congress to pass the Communications Act of 1934, and that act set up the Federal Communications Commission (FCC) and sharply restricted the political freedom of radio stations. The man the Roosevelt administration appointed as secretary of the FCC was Herbert L. Pettey, who had been director of publicity for the Democratic National Committee during the 1932 election. Pettey and his cohorts at the FCC had, in the words of the *New York Herald Tribune*, "the power of life and death over every broadcasting station in the land." They could grant or revoke licenses. Right away, the FCC reduced the renewal period of broadcasting licenses from three years to six months.[41] Richard Steele, who did a study of Roosevelt and radio licenses, concluded that friends of the New Deal were granted licenses and renewals quickly, but those critical of the New Deal faced problems and some had their licenses and renewals denied. Radio became, in Steele's words, "the informational propaganda medium *par excellence*." NRA officials, for example, estimated that they received over $2 million worth of radio time free. As historian Betty Winfield concluded, Roosevelt "could control exactly what was said on the air." Radio operators needed to protect their licenses, which explains why so little opposition to Court packing was heard on radio.[42]

Even after Roosevelt's Court-packing fiasco, he chose to use deception again in his next crisis—the appointment of a new Senate majority leader. As we saw in chapter 13, Senate Majority Leader Joseph Robinson died while leading the fight for Court packing. The two candidates to replace him, Senators Alben Barkley and Pat Harrison, were both loyal New Dealers and Roosevelt publicly promised he would be neutral and not interfere with the Democratic senators as they chose a replacement. Secretly, however, Roosevelt wanted Barkley to win and when the president pressured Senator William Dieterich of Illinois to switch sides, Barkley won the vote, 38-37. The problem was, as we saw in the last chapter, that Pat Harrison then proceeded, with lots of help from disgruntled senators, to undermine the president's legislative program and Roosevelt accomplished little of significance during 1937 and 1938. The strategy of deception failed again. The New Deal was virtually over.[43]

Tom Corcoran, who helped lead the president's efforts to influence senators on the Court-packing and majority-leader fights, must have been puzzled by the outcomes. He had assumed that the president, with all of his power and patronage, would easily prevail. Two months before the Court-packing fight, Corcoran told Raymond Moley: "I've learned a lot about politics from being down there. When a politician makes a promise, he knows that he is not binding himself, and the man to whom he makes the promise knows it too. That is one of the things you've got to learn. There aren't any binding promises in politics. There isn't any binding law. You just know that the strongest side wins."[44] Roosevelt, who was clearly the "strongest side" after the 1936 election, may have come to believe that statement so thoroughly that he couldn't imagine losing the Court fight or the majority-leader fight, even though he built both on open duplicity.

As a result of so many falsehoods, Roosevelt was increasingly disbelieved when he made policy statements. During the Court fight and the majority-leader dispute, the president kept promising again and again he would balance the budget in 1938. "I have said fifty times that the budget will be balanced for the fiscal year 1938," Roosevelt promised his vice president. "If you want me to say it again, I will say it either once or fifty times more." The budget, however, was again unbalanced in 1938. But Roosevelt again had his argument ready that special circumstances intervened and made balancing the budget less desirable than more federal spending.[45]

In Roosevelt's first term, his style of leading by deception did not cost him many votes. He had charm; he had power; and he artfully used both. In his second term, however, when he tried to increase his power, his duplicity almost shattered his presidency.[46]

In the 1790s, George Washington had argued that morality, especially among leaders, was indispensable to the survival of the American republic. Even before Roosevelt, of course, some presidents had fallen short of Washington's high standard. But during the 1930s, the increased role of government made Washington's pledge of morality seem antiquated. Roosevelt, by centralizing power in the executive, by providing subsidies for votes, and by his charismatic radio addresses, took attention away from his *character* and focused it on his *intentions* in his dramatic New Deal. After Roosevelt, fewer presidents would be bound by public promises, by constitutional restraints, or by providing exemplary conduct in their personal lives.

WHAT FDR SHOULD HAVE DONE:
CUT SPENDING, TAX RATES, AND THE TARIFF

If the evidence suggests that the New Deal failed, that raises a legitimate question: What should Roosevelt have done about the Great Depression? Put another way, what better path might Roosevelt have taken to achieve economic recovery?

Such a question is, of course, speculative and counterfactual. No one can be sure what alternatives would have produced a stronger economy and less unemployment. The Great Depression was a complicated, worldwide crisis and difficult to handle. It's easy many decades later to see errors in policy. Also, Roosevelt and other leaders were constrained politically and economically. They did not have the hindsight we have today. For example, few politicians of the 1920s and 1930s saw the damage done by the Federal Reserve, and not just in the higher interest rates, but in its demand that banks change their reserve ratios. Few saw at the time how the declining money supply, a by-product of Fed actions, damaged the economy and hindered recovery. In any case, however, because the

Fed is independent, no one can really fault Hoover or Roosevelt for problems created by the new federal banking system.

Given the constraints on Roosevelt, then, and the confusion created by this unique depression, what could Roosevelt have done to achieve better recovery for the economy and more employment? Some comparisons might help. In the Panic of 1893, U.S. unemployment briefly hit what was then the all-time high of 18.4 percent, but the panic was over in a little more than five years. In the mini-recession of 1921, unemployment reached 11.7 percent, but hard times lasted less than two years. In both of these economic downturns, Presidents Cleveland and Harding cut federal expenses and, in the case of Harding, cut the income tax rate as well. Soon investments in business became attractive again, capital slowly flowed back into the American economy, and it bounced back. In recessions before 1893 and 1921, presidents followed roughly the same plan and the crises were short-lived.[1]

In 1929, however, after the stock market crash, President Hoover did the opposite of Cleveland and Harding. Hoover increased federal spending—through the Federal Farm Board, the Reconstruction Finance Corporation, and public works. Then in 1932 he agreed to sharply increase both income and excise taxes to help pay for his costly programs. With the top income tax rate hiked to 63 percent, and with almost all Americans paying some excise taxes for the first time in U.S. history, private investment did not bounce back and unemployment reached 25 percent. Thus Roosevelt had an especially difficult task when he entered the White House. Some of his emergency measures—the banking holiday and taking the United States off the gold standard (to stop the outflow of gold)—may have been in order. His New Deal, however, is another story because there he applied ideas from underconsumption theory.

What if, instead of expanding Hoover's programs and starting many new ones of his own, Roosevelt had kept his campaign promises to cut spending, reduce taxes, and lower the Smoot-Hawley tariff immediately? In the Democrat Party platform, and in speech after speech during the campaign, Roosevelt promised these three things.

On taxes, for example, Roosevelt seemed to understand that lower taxes would attract business investments. On the campaign trail, he said, "Taxes are paid in the sweat of every man who labors because they are a burden on production and are paid through production. If those taxes are excessive, they are reflected in idle factories, in tax-sold farms, and in hordes of hungry people, tramping the streets and seeking jobs in vain." In Sioux City, Iowa, Roosevelt announced that if elected president, "I propose to use this position of high responsibility to discuss up and down the country, in all seasons and at all times, the duty of reducing taxes, of increasing the efficiency of Government, of cutting out the underbrush around our governmental structure, of getting the most public service for every dollar paid in taxation. That I pledge you, and nothing I have said in the campaign transcends in importance this covenant with the taxpayers of the United States."[2]

In describing his "covenant" with the taxpayers, Roosevelt often became specific. He pledged to "reduce the cost of current Federal Government operations by 25 percent." The Democrat Party platform also promised Americans "a saving of not less than 25 percent in the cost of the federal government," and Roosevelt viewed that platform as a binding document. In Pittsburgh, Roosevelt announced, "Before any man enters my Cabinet he must give me a two-fold pledge:

1. Absolute loyalty to the Democratic platform and especially to its economy plank.
2. Complete cooperation with me, looking to economy and reorganization in his Department."

He further said he would "eliminate from Federal budget-making during this emergency all new items except such as relate to direct relief of unemployment."[3]

These pledges, this "covenant with the taxpayers," freed Roosevelt to attack the "reckless and extravagant" spending of the Hoover administration. "It is committed to the idea that we ought to center control of everything in Washington as rapidly as possible—Federal control." If, as president, Roosevelt had used his influence to cut spending and then cut the tax rate on top incomes from 63 percent back to about 25 percent, that would probably have encouraged investors to seek returns on new capital ventures. When Harding and Coolidge introduced such tax cuts during the 1920s, that helped the American economy go from 11.7 percent unemployment in 1921 to an average of 3.3 percent unemployment from 1923 to 1929.[4] If Roosevelt had slashed tax rates, many Americans could also have given more to private charities; states and cities would have had more room to ask wealthy citizens for contributions to assist the hungry people in their cities. Governor Joseph Ely of Massachusetts, as we have seen, fully embraced that line of reasoning. In fact, Roosevelt himself seemed to be making these connections during the campaign.

The tariff needs discussion as well. In Seattle, Sioux City, and elsewhere, Roosevelt blasted the "outrageous rates" of the Smoot-Hawley tariff. He showed a keen understanding of the dynamics and unintended consequences of Hoover's signing the highest tariff in U.S. history. "Now, the ink on the Hawley-Smoot-Grundy tariff bill was hardly dry before foreign nations commenced their program of retaliation," Roosevelt observed. And the Hoover administration "had reason to know that would happen. It was warned. While the bill was before Congress, our State Department received 160 protests from 33 other nations, many of whom after the passage of the bill erected their own tariff walls to the detriment or destruction of much of our export trade." What's more,

Roosevelt observed that American manufacturers responded to foreign retaliation against American-made products by relocating their American businesses—and jobs—to friendlier foreign countries. Americans had established "258 separate factories" in other parts of the world from 1930 to 1932 to escape retaliation. Lost American factories and diminished American business was not the only harm.[5]

Farmers were most hurt by the Smoot-Hawley tariff because so much of American agriculture was exported. Forty nations, Roosevelt noted, had set up high tariffs against U.S. imports. "For example," Roosevelt said in Seattle, "our next-door neighbor, Canada, imposed retaliatory tariffs on your peaches . . . [and] on asparagus, and on other vegetables and other fruits, so high that practically none of your agricultural product can be sold to your logical customers, your neighbors across the border." Roosevelt added, "Embargoes by France, embargoes by other European nations on apples and other products of the Pacific Coast, make it impossible to ship your surplus apples abroad. . . ." Earlier we saw how Senator Harry Byrd, because of the Smoot-Hawley tariff, lost much of his market for Virginia apples and had to reduce wages and lay off workers. Roosevelt proposed reducing tariff duties "through [a] negotiated tariff, with benefit to each nation." He pledged "immediate action," on this point, and he observed that public sentiment was such that tariff reform "policy will be initiated on March 4, 1933."[6]

Roosevelt does deserve some credit for pursuing reciprocal tariff reduction. But he waited until 1934 to promote a law to authorize the secretary of state to negotiate reciprocal trade agreements. By 1940, the United States had negotiated tariff reductions with twenty-one nations that affected almost 60 percent of American exports. But such changes came slowly and unevenly. High tariff rates still dominated in 1940. Economist Douglas Irwin, perhaps the foremost expert on the Smoot-Hawley tariff, concluded, "there is no evidence that trade was a particularly strong component of the economic recovery." With the Smoot-Hawley tariff the law of the land for so long, Europeans also refused to pay their debts to the United States from World War I. How could they earn the money to pay the $10 billion they owed us if the Americans refused to trade with them? Much of that, of course, was Hoover's fault. But when Roosevelt was elected, instead of rapidly pursuing tariff reduction, as promised, he promoted the AAA and paying farmers not to produce.[7]

If, during 1933, Roosevelt had pursued the cutting of spending, taxes, and tariffs, as he had promised in the campaign, we have, of course, no guarantee that he would have ended the Great Depression that year, or even the next. The issue is a complex one. But if Roosevelt had tried to fulfill his "covenant with the taxpayers," he might have set in motion forces to stimulate employment, encourage foreign trade, and make more money available for investment. In past economic downturns, that strategy clearly helped, and it is reasonable to assume that low tax rates, balanced budgets, and a much lower tariff would have eased America's path to recovery during the Great Depression as well.

Let's compare Roosevelt's performance in international terms. The United States under Roosevelt fared worse than did almost any other European country in recovering from the Depression during the 1930s. The League of Nations kept data on unemployment and the table below reveals that in 1929 the United States had the lowest unemployment rate among the sixteen countries studied. In 1932, the U.S. had dropped to eighth place. By 1937, after Roosevelt's first term, the U.S. had sunk to tenth place; the next year it fell further to thirteenth place. In more specific terms, the world index in unemployment for 1938 was 11.4 percent, but the United States had a sharply higher rate of 19.8 percent (and would rise higher in the months ahead).

TABLE 1.

Percentage of Workers Unemployed

Country	1929	1932	1937	1938
World index	5.4	21.1	10.1	11.4
Australia	11.1	29.0	9.3	8.7
Austria	12.3	26.1	20.4	15.3
Belgium	1.9	23.5	13.1	17.6
Canada	4.2	26.0	12.5	15.1
Czechoslovakia	2.2	13.5	8.8	8.5
Denmark	15.5	31.7	21.9	21.4
France	—	—	—	8.0
Germany	9.3	30.1	4.6	2.1
Japan	4.0	6.8	3.7	3.0
Netherlands	5.9	25.3	26.9	25.0
Norway	15.4	30.8	20.0	22.0
Poland	4.9	11.8	14.6	12.7
Sweden	10.7	22.8	11.6	11.8
Switzerland	3.5	21.3	12.5	13.1
United Kingdom	10.4	22.1	10.5	12.6
United States	1.0	24.9	13.2	19.8

Source: League of Nations, *World Economic Survey: Eighth Year, 1938/39* (Geneva, 1939), 128.

These statistics, of course, must be used with caution. Different countries used different methods of measuring unemployment, and the gradual approach of World War II began to influence unemployment rates in some countries. But the trend is clear—the U.S. economy under Roosevelt did poorly not only in an absolute sense, but in a relative sense as well.

Let's put the issue this way: In 1938, five years after Roosevelt took office, the League of Nations, as we have seen, reported an average of 11.4 percent unemployment for the 16 nations it surveyed. U.S. unemployment, at 19.8 percent, was almost twice the rate for the rest of the world. Was the better U.S. strategy for recovery a 79 percent top income tax rate, a doubled national debt, unbalanced budgets, the only undistributed profits tax in the world, and only slow tariff reform—all of which Roosevelt delivered—or tax cuts, balanced budgets, and immediate tariff reduction, all of which Roosevelt promised?

WHAT FINALLY DID END THE GREAT DEPRESSION?

If Roosevelt's New Deal programs did not break the Great Depression, then what did? Most historians have argued that America's entry into World War II was the key event that ended it. Federal spending drastically increased as twelve million U.S. soldiers went to war, and millions more mobilized in the factories to make war materiel. As a result, unemployment plummeted and, so the argument goes, the Great Depression receded.

William Leuchtenburg, who has written the standard book on the New Deal, claims, "The real impetus to recovery was to come from rapid, large-scale spending." Roosevelt, according to Leuchtenburg, was reluctant to take this step. When, at last, Pearl Harbor was bombed, "The war proved that massive spending under the right conditions produced full employment."[1]

Recently, David M. Kennedy, in his Pulitzer Prize–winning book on Roosevelt, echoed Leuchtenburg's argument. "Roosevelt," Kennedy insisted, "remained reluctant to the end of the 1930s to engage in the scale of compensatory spending adequate to restore the economy to pre-Depression levels, let alone expand it." At the end of his book, Kennedy concluded, "It was a war that had brought [Americans] as far as imagination could reach, and beyond, from the ordeal of the Great Depression. . . ." More specifically, "The huge expenditures for weaponry clinched the Keynesian doctrine that government spending could underwrite prosperity. . . ."[2]

Economists, Keynes notwithstanding, have always been less willing to believe this theory than historians. F. A. Hayek, who won the Nobel Prize in economics, argued against this view in 1944 in *The Road to Serfdom*. Economist Henry Hazlitt, who wrote for the *New York Times* during the Roosevelt years, observed, "No man burns down his own house on the theory that the need to rebuild it will stimulate his energies." And yet, as historians and others viewed World War II, "they see almost endless benefits in enormous acts of destruction. They tell us how much better off economically we all are in war than in peace. They see 'miracles of production' which it requires a war to achieve." Thus, in Hazlitt's argument, the United States merely shifted capital from private markets, where it could have made consumer goods, to armament factories, where it made tanks, bombs, and planes for temporary use during war.[3]

Along these lines, economist Robert Higgs has observed, "Unemployment virtually disappeared as conscription, directly and indirectly, pulled more than 12 million potential workers into the armed forces and millions of others into draft-exempt employment, but under the prevailing conditions, the disappearance of unemployment can hardly be interpreted as a valid index of economic prosperity." A supporting point for this idea is that real private investment and real personal consumption sharply declined during the war. Stock market prices, for example, in 1944 were still below those of 1939 in real dollars.[4]

If not World War II, what did end the Great Depression? This question is still open to research and original thinking. Higgs argues, "It is time for economists and historians to take seriously the hypothesis that the New Deal prolonged the Great Depression by creating an extraordinarily high degree of regime uncertainty in the minds of investors."[5] Roosevelt, as we have seen, regularly attacked business and steadily raised income tax rates, corporate tax rates, and excise taxes during the 1930s. He added the undistributed profits tax and conducted highly publicized tax cases that sent many investors to prison. During World War II, Roosevelt softened his rhetoric against businessmen, whom he needed to wage the war, but he did issue an executive order for a 100 percent tax on all personal income over $25,000. When Roosevelt died, and Truman became president, the hostile rhetoric toward businessmen further declined and no new tax hikes were added. During the war, in fact, Roosevelt had switched from attacking rich people to letting big corporations monopolize war contracts. Under Truman, businessmen were even more optimistic. They expanded production, and the U.S. economy was thus able to absorb the returning soldiers and those who had previously worked to make war equipment.

That, in a nutshell, is Higgs's thesis, and he has two persuasive pieces of evidence on his side. First, many leading industrialists of the 1930s openly explained how the president's efforts to tax and regulate were stifling the nation's economic expansion. For example, Lammot Du Pont, who revolutionized the textile industry in the 1940s with the invention of nylon, was one of many businessmen who complained about Roosevelt's policies. "Uncertainty rules the tax situation, the labor situation, the monetary situation, and practically every legal condition under which industry must operate," Du Pont protested in 1937. "Are new restrictions to be placed on capital, new limits on profits? . . . It is impossible to even guess at the answers."[6]

Second, Higgs cites poll data that show a sharp increase in optimism about business after Roosevelt died and Truman became president. For example, the American Institute of Public Opinion (AIPO) did solid polling of attitudes on business and its findings are impressive. In March 1939, for example, AIPO asked a national sample, "Do you think the attitude of the Roosevelt administration toward business is delaying business recovery?" More than twice as many respondents said "yes" as said "no." In May 1945, however, one month after Roosevelt's death, the AIPO pollsters asked, "Do you think Truman will be more favorable or less favorable toward business than Roosevelt was?" On this poll, Truman had eight times more yeses than nos. *Forbes* and *Fortune* also did polls of businessmen and found similar results. What that meant was that after the war, American businessmen expanded production and thereby absorbed into the workforce the returning soldiers. The Great Depression was over at last.[7]

Other nations recovered from the Great Depression more quickly than did the United States. During the late 1930s, the League of Nations collected statistics from the United States and from many other nations on industrial recovery. Much of that data supports the idea that Roosevelt's New Deal created economic uncertainty and was in fact uniquely unsuccessful as a recovery program. In the table below, we can see some of the aftermath of the depression within a depression in 1937, when the stock market lost one-third of its value. During late 1938, the United States had some recovery, but in early 1939 recovery again lagged. By May 1939, unemployment again reached 20 percent, industrial production had fallen about 10 percent from the first of the year, and Henry Morgenthau confessed, "We are spending more than we have ever spent before and it does not work."

This table helps clarify the one in chapter 15. The U.S. economy was in a tailspin six years after FDR became president and the country suffered more unemployment than most of the other ones studied by the League of Nations.

Industrial Production in the United States
Date (1929 = 100)

June 1938	65
December 1938	87
January 1939	85
February 1939	82
March 1939	82
April 1939	77
May 1939	77
June 1939	81

Source: League of Nations, *World Economic Survey, 1938/39* (Geneva, 1939), 110–11.

Some historians, trying to defend Roosevelt, point out that unemployment in the United States slightly dropped each year from 1933 to 1937, which suggests some progress in fighting the Depression. Unemployment was 25.2 percent in 1933, 22 percent in 1934, 20.3 percent in 1935, 17 percent in 1936, and 14.3 percent in 1937. That 14.3 percent, however, is alarmingly high and—outside of the 1930s—was only exceeded for a brief period in all of American history during the Panic of 1893. What's worse, the business uncertainty during Roosevelt's second term stifled that modest recovery of his first term.

To be fair, if we describe the downward move of unemployment during Roosevelt's first term, we must present the steady upward move of unemployment during most of his second term. Unemployment was 15.0 percent in September 1936, 15.1 percent in January 1937, 17.4 percent in January 1938, 18.7 percent in January 1939, and 20.7 percent in April 1939. Thus, more than six years after Roosevelt took office, and almost ten years after the stock market crash of 1929, unemployment topped the 20 percent mark. The League of Nations study, which tried to explain the poor performance of the U.S. economy, cited the "uneasy relations be-

tween business and the [Roosevelt] Administration." As Yale economist Irving Fisher bluntly wrote Roosevelt, "You have also delayed
recovery."

Why was the performance of the U.S. economy—especially
relative to other nations—so miserable? What were some of the
ingredients in America's unique "regime uncertainty"? The first
place to start is tax policy. One reason that the United States lagged
behind other countries in recovery from the Great Depression is
that Roosevelt strongly emphasized raising revenue by excise taxes.
According to another League of Nations study, the U.S. increased
its revenue from excise taxes more rapidly than did any of the other
nine nations surveyed. Britain and France, for example, decreased
their dependency on excise taxes from 1929 to 1938. Japan, Germany, Italy, and Hungary did increase their excise revenues, but
only slightly. The United States, however, had a whopping 328 percent increase in excise revenue from 1929 to 1938. "The very large
increases of yield [in tax revenue] which are shown in the case of
Belgium [310 percent] and the United States [328 percent] are due
to substantial increases in the rate of duty," the study concluded.
Since these taxes fell heavier on lower incomes, that may have contributed to the poorer rate of recovery from the Great Depression
by the United States.[8]

Other tax problems contributed to "regime uncertainty." Corporate taxes went up, the estate tax was increased to a top rate of
70 percent, and the United States alone among nations passed an
undistributed profits tax. Businessmen watched the top rate of the
federal income tax increase from 24 to 63 percent in 1932 under
Hoover and then to 79 percent in 1935 under Roosevelt. The president regularly castigated businessmen and threatened to raise rates
further. On April 27, 1942, Roosevelt issued an executive order
that would tax all personal income over $25,000 at 100 percent.
All "excess income," the president argued, "should go to win the war."
Furthermore, Roosevelt's use of the IRS to prosecute wealthy

Americans, especially Republicans, created incentives for business-men to shift their investments into areas of lesser taxation. All of this created "regime uncertainty," and the Great Depression per-sisted throughout the 1930s.[9] As we have seen in the League of Nations study, in 1929 the United States had the lowest level of unemployment of any of the sixteen nations surveyed. The U.S. dropped to eighth place by 1932, eleventh place in 1937, and then to thirteenth place in 1938.[10]

In retrospect, we can see that Roosevelt's special-interest spend-ing created insatiable demands by almost all groups of voters for special subsidies. That, in itself, created regime uncertainty. Under the RFC, for example, the federal government made special loans to banks and railroads; then the AAA had price supports for farm-ers; soon the operators of silver mines were demanding special high prices for their product. At one level, as we have seen, Roosevelt used these subsidies as political tools to reward friends and punish enemies. But beyond that, where would the line be drawn? Who would get special taxpayer subsidies and who would not? As Wal-ter Waters, who led the veterans' march on Washington in 1932, observed, "I noticed, too, that the highly organized lobbies in Washington for special industries were producing results: loans were being granted to their special interests and these lobbies seemed to justify their existence. Personal lobbying paid, regardless of the justice or injustice of their demand."[11]

Roosevelt became trapped in a debt spiral of special-interest spending. He often did not try to escape because of the political benefits received when he supported subsidy bills to targeted inter-est groups. In 1935, when the veterans came clamoring again for a special subsidy, Roosevelt cast only a tepid veto—how could he justify the cash to all the other groups, but deny the veterans? Therefore, an obliging Congress voted the veterans a special bonus of $2 billion—a sum exceeding 6 percent of the entire national debt. As the St. Louis Post-Dispatch observed, "Here is a superb example of how a powerful minority, in this case the veterans' organizations, has been able . . . to win Congress over to a proposition in defiance of logic, good sense and justice." Such an unwarranted subsidy was, the editor feared, a "grave defect in our system."[12] We can better understand Henry Morgenthau's frustration in May 1939. He could just as easily have said, "We have tried spending and it creates frantic lobbying and a never-ending cycle of more spending."

WHY HISTORIANS HAVE MISSED THE MARK

If we study carefully Roosevelt's character and his failed New Deal programs, we have to wonder why historians almost uniformly rate him as the best or one of the best presidents in U.S. history. As early as 1948, just three years after Roosevelt's death, historian Charles Beard, who was especially irritated by Roosevelt's foreign policy, had already noticed the almost cultlike attachment of historians to FDR. "It is clear," Beard wrote to Ray Moley, "that anybody who deviates a hair's breadth from the Roosevelt line is in trouble, not only from the professional smear Bund but also from 'scholars.' I have been through the mill myself."[1] The situation may be worse today because so many historians have written books and articles favorable to Roosevelt—or ranked him highly in presidential polls—that to have Roosevelt discredited is to undermine their work and their careers.

We need to be clear here. Not all writers on the New Deal are friendly to Roosevelt. Some of his contemporaries, such as John Flynn, wrote critical accounts of him and his programs. Even today, authors such as Jim Powell and Amity Shlaes have written books critical of the New Deal.[2] Beard, however, is referring to trained historians and political scientists with Ph.D.s. These scholars tend strongly to support the legend of the New Deal, that it was a very constructive political and economic program for the United States. Those criticisms that historians have made are not that Roosevelt did too little, but that he should probably have done more to redistribute wealth and restructure society.

For historians to carry the discussion in that direction is to ignore many facts readily available. Unemployment lines, for example, were long and steadily lengthening during Roosevelt's *second* term. From November 1937 to August 1939, monthly unemployment numbers always ranged from 17 to 21 percent—the highest in U.S. history except for Roosevelt's first term, one year in Hoover's presidency, and one year in the 1890s. The tax rates on entrepreneurs were also higher than at any previous time in U.S. history. With the rise in income tax rates, revenue to the federal government had steadily declined. Excise tax rates on middle- and lower-income earners were also higher than ever before in U.S. history. With restrictive income and excise taxes, how could historians expect anything other than skyrocketing unemployment rates?

Why would so many historians heap so much praise on Roosevelt? Most historians are, along with Roosevelt, influenced by the "progressive view of history" that began to dominate American life during the presidency of Woodrow Wilson. Before the early 1900s, the constitutional views of the Founders dominated American political thought. In writing the Declaration of Independence and Constitution, the Founders emphasized natural rights—the process of ensuring God-given rights to life, liberty, and property to every American. "If men were angels, no government would be necessary," Madison wrote. But men were not angels, so to protect natural rights, the Constitution was written with power widely dispersed to prevent a strong president or legislature from increasing its authority and gradually turning the United States into a tyranny.[3]

In crafting the Constitution, the Founders emphasized process, not results. If we follow the Constitution, we won't have a perfect society, which is unattainable by imperfect humans. But we will provide opportunity for people to use their natural rights to pursue the acquisition of property and their personal happiness. The results may yield sharp inequalities of income, but the process will guarantee chances for almost everyone. During the 1800s, Americans increasingly acknowledged the natural rights of black Americans and guaranteed more rights for women. Both were logical outflows of the Declaration of Independence and the limited government enshrined in the Constitution. The Founders emphasized the lessons of experience, not the opportunity to create a utopia; they stressed fidelity and the rules of the game more than good intentions (sincerity). The process, not results, were what most American leaders from the Founders to Grover Cleveland wanted to protect.[4]

Woodrow Wilson—both as a Ph.D. in history and as a two-term president—represented a break with the Constitution and its constrained view of history. Government, in Wilson's progressive view, did not exist merely to protect rights. "We are not," Wilson insisted, "bound to adhere to the doctrines held by the signers of the Declaration of Independence." The limited government enshrined in both the Declaration and the Constitution may have been an advance for the Founders, Wilson conceded, but society had evolved since then. Separation of powers was inefficient and hindered modern government from promoting progress. "The only fruit of dividing power," Wilson asserted, "was to make it irresponsible." A strong executive was needed, Wilson believed, to translate the interests of the people into public policy. The president was the opinion leader, the "spokesman for the real sentiment and purpose of the country." And what the country needed was "a man who will be and who will seem to the country in some sort of an embodiment of the character and purpose it wishes its government to have—a man who understood his own day and the needs of his country."[5]

In the White House, Wilson intended to be a strong president working with a "living Constitution." Contrary to the written Constitution, he promoted the expanding of "beneficent" government into new areas—regulating overseas shipping rates, subsidizing loans to farmers, and fixing an eight-hour day for railroad workers. In Wilson's progressive view, government was not to be used to limit executive or legislative activity, but to improve the lives of its people. Results, not process, mattered to Wilson. The Federal Reserve was created to regulate banking "for the general good"; the first income tax was also passed under Wilson. He promoted it as a progressive tax, and had it raised repeatedly until the wealthiest Americans were paying a 77 percent marginal tax on their annual incomes during World War I.

Roosevelt served in the Wilson administration and believed deeply in Wilson's progressive view of the Constitution. When Chief Justice Charles Evans Hughes was swearing in Roosevelt for his second term, he apparently read with great emphasis the words "promise to support the Constitution of the United States." Roosevelt met Hughes's challenge and repeated these words with force. Later the president said he wanted to shout, "Yes, but it's the Constitution as *I* understand it. . . ."[6] In a fireside chat on Court packing, Roosevelt dropped his argument for judicial efficiency and called the Constitution "a system of living law." He added, "We must have Judges who will bring to the courts a present-day sense of the Constitution."[7]

In other words, Roosevelt understood the Constitution the way Wilson did, and applied progressive ideas to expand the role of government in American society. When, during the 1936 campaign, Roosevelt was asked by a Canadian editor to state his objectives, Roosevelt responded that they were

> to do what any honest Government of any country would do; try to
> increase the security and the happiness of a larger number of people
> in all occupations of life and in all parts of the country; to give them

more of the good things of life, to give them a greater distribution not only of wealth in the narrow terms, but of wealth in the wider terms; to give them places to go in the summer time—recreation; to give them assurance that they are not going to starve in their old age; to give honest business a chance to go ahead and make a reasonable profit, and to give everyone a chance to earn a living.[8]

Roosevelt, more than Wilson, gave lip service to the Founders. He conceded that the United States "grew to its present strength under the protection of certain inalienable political rights" but then argued that "these political rights proved inadequate to assure us equality in the pursuit of happiness." Thus, in the 1932 campaign Roosevelt described a new "right to a comfortable living." In 1944 he elaborated an Economic Bill of Rights that included "the right to a useful and remunerative job . . . The right of every family to a decent home . . . The right to a good education."[9]

Roosevelt's new progressive rights, unlike those of the Founders, imposed obligations on society to provide jobs, buy homes, and pay for educations. Government, by necessity, had to increase in size to tax some citizens to provide newly discovered "rights" for others. Where the Founders wanted government limited mainly to protect rights, Roosevelt and the progressives wanted expanded government to provide jobs, recreation, education, and houses. Where the Founders were skeptical of human nature, the progressives were optimistic that a president, or a small group of administrators, could use government to create the good life for Americans and preserve liberty as well. Results, in Roosevelt's view, were more important than process; intentions more important than protecting natural rights; plans and new ideas more important than experience. When Roosevelt moved to centralize power by changing the rules for appointment to the Supreme Court, he was reflecting the progressive view that dispersed power was inefficient and centralized power was needed to accomplish good works for the citizens.

Most modern historians, following Woodrow Wilson's lead, have embraced the progressive view of history; therefore they have praised Roosevelt's efforts at government intervention, and wish he had done more of it. William Leuchtenburg and Arthur Schlesinger, Jr., as we have seen—the two most prominent and conspicuous New Deal historians—have promoted the progressive view of history. Most historians, Leuchtenburg has admitted, "are liberal Democrats." Schlesinger and Leuchtenburg both became active in the 1940s in the liberal Americans for Democratic Action, Schlesinger as a founding member and Leuchtenburg as a full-time official. Earlier, in 1939, Leuchtenburg, as a freshman at Cornell University, secured a federal job with the National Youth Administration "cleaning out test tubes in a laboratory." His loyalty to Roosevelt was firm "despite the 'inadequacies' of the New Deal."[10]

Leuchtenburg uses the term "inadequacies" because, he believes, "the real impetus to recovery was to come from rapid, large-scale spending." By 1938, Leuchtenburg argues, "Roosevelt was moving more or less in a Keynesian direction, but while he may have grasped the idea that *spending* could be a good thing, he probably never grasped the concept that *deficits* were a good thing."[11] Thus Leuchtenburg, like many progressives, embraced the Keynesian view that massive deficit spending benefited the economy. Most economists today, even beyond the Austrians and the monetarists, dispute the value of deficit spending. The Founders, even more so, saw deficits and a large national debt as a dreadful thing. Washington, in his farewell address, warned against "the accumulation of debt" and the next six presidents so limited government that by the 1830s the United States briefly became debt-free, and actually ran surpluses. Roosevelt and the progressives represented a sharp break with the earlier American tradition, and most historians endorse that break.

In the progressive view, intentions and sincerity are among the noblest virtues a president can possess. According to Schlesinger, "In the welter of confusion and ignorance [during the Great Depression], experiment corrected by compassion was the best answer." Experiment is valued by Schlesinger more than experience, and compassion, not results, is described as "the best answer." Leuchtenburg follows a similar line and notes, "many workingmen, poor farmers, and others who felt themselves to have been neglected in the past regarded Roosevelt as their friend. They sensed that his was a humane administration, that the President cared what happened to them." Historians seem to focus on "caring" and "compassion" more than on the unprecedented lack of recovery for the eleven years from 1929 to 1940.[12]

Irving Bernstein, who has written a three-volume history of the 1920s and 1930s, uses the title *A Caring Society* for his book on Roosevelt and the New Deal. "Roosevelt," Bernstein wrote, "consciously undertook the creation of his caring society in order to preserve both American democracy and American capitalism." Bernstein concluded, "Ordinary people with no power and lots of trouble believed that someone in Washington with power cared." The emphasis here is not on the 18 percent or more of the people who were unemployed during much of Roosevelt's second term; the emphasis is on the caring intentions of his programs. Many of the caring programs, however, from the Resettlement Administration to the NRA to the AAA, had unintended consequences that increased unemployment. George McJimsey, who has recently written a book on Roosevelt's presidency, also wrote a biography of WPA chief Harry Hopkins, which he subtitled *Ally of the Poor and Defender of Democracy*. McJimsey's main focus, then, is on the good intentions, not the politicized results of the WPA.[13]

When results are lacking, intentions may be a good place to focus. David Kennedy, in his Pulitzer Prize–winning book on Roosevelt, recognizes that the New Deal did not produce recovery from the Great Depression, but he seems pleased with Roosevelt anyway. "Security was the leitmotif of virtually everything the New Deal attempted," Kennedy argues. "The New Deal was a welcoming mansion of many rooms, a place where millions of his fellow citizens could find at last a measure of . . . security. . . ." Was this "security" present for small businessmen harassed by the NRA; larger entrepreneurs trying to invest in the midst of an undistributed profits tax and a 79 percent marginal income tax; or the ten million Americans, like Kennedy's father, who were steadily unemployed during the 1930s?[14]

The constitutional view of the Founders gives little weight to intentions. Good intentions assume that the leader, or leaders, know what is best for society. All they need is the authority to implement their ideas and reconstruct society. People with good intentions, however, can be busybodies who use the power of government to do more harm than good. In the case of Harry Hopkins, McJimsey calls him "ally of the poor" in his book title, but his WPA cost taxpayers over $4.8 billion in the 1935 appropriation alone (almost 15 percent of the entire national debt)—and Hopkins often produced little to show for the money. Constitutionalists believe taxpayers are better stewards of their money than government. Since people, even very wise people, are limited in what they can know about complex societies, voluntary giving is the proper way for an individual to become an "ally of the poor."

Constitutionalists stress fidelity to process, obeying the rules, and the importance of duty and integrity. Consistent application of rules means people know what to expect and how to plan their businesses and their lives. Honest rulers help establish the integrity of the system and serve as examples to emulate for personal behavior. If they declare a "covenant with the taxpayers," they try to keep it. George Washington saw himself as playing a role when he was president. Duty, for Washington, and fidelity to the new constitutional system were necessary to make it work. Grover Cleveland's last words were "I've tried hard to do what is right."[15] Cleveland's fidelity to the Constitution was so scrupulous that he vetoed 414 bills in his first term alone to stop what was, in his view, the unconstitutional spending of Congress. The good intentions of congressmen in providing relief to their constituents counted for nothing with Cleveland.

Roosevelt, by contrast, gave much weight to intentions and little weight to experience, rules, and the constitutional process. He proclaimed, "We cannot reach a millennium or utopia in any four years, or eight years; but at least I have felt that people in responsible positions ought to start the ball rolling. . . ."[16] Constitutionalists would wonder how Roosevelt could know what a millenium or utopia ought to be; and if he did, would he know for sure how to get there? His, or anyone else's, efforts to get there might create unintended negative consequences. For the constitutionalists, the better way for a president is to avoid utopias, work within the system, follow the path of duty, and be a good role model. Let millions of Americans make their economic choices and follow the path of supply and demand rather than empower small groups of policy makers to set prices or move production in ways they conceive to be in the public interest.

During the New Deal era, Republicans had a dilemma. Many argued that New Deal programs failed to promote recovery and needed to be scrapped, not expanded. Landon, in his presidential campaign, briefly argued that way in 1936 about the AAA. But Landon quickly discovered that the AAA, illogical and costly though it was, had many vocal farmers who benefited from being paid not to grow crops. Thus Landon and the Republicans backed off—and lost anyway.

Since the New Deal years, Republicans have continued to argue publicly that most federal programs, from the 1930s on, have failed. But they have dreaded the idea of antagonizing Roosevelt's New Deal coalition; thus Republicans have usually refused, when elected, to eliminate the very programs they gingerly attacked during the election campaign. Republicans have had the most electoral success when they have challenged federal programs, as Ronald Reagan did in 1980 and as congressional Republicans did in 1994. "A government bureau," Reagan quipped, "is the nearest thing to eternal life we'll ever see on this earth."

More typical of Republican presidents has been to try to break the New Deal coalition by outspending—or spending more shrewdly—than the Democrats. President Dwight Eisenhower initiated the interstate highway program; President George H. W. Bush expanded the Department of Education; President George W. Bush initiated a prescription drug discount for senior citizens. President Richard Nixon tried to beat the post–New Deal Democrats by outmaneuvering them. In 1972, an election year, Nixon raised social security benefits by 20 percent, with the new payments starting the month before the November election, but with the tax increase not payable until after the election was over. Such a ploy was reminiscent of Roosevelt and the WPA in 1936. On the IRS, Nixon emulated Roosevelt's audit of Moses Annenberg. "John [Ehrlichman]," Nixon said, "we have the power. Are we using it now to investigate contributors to Hubert Humphrey, contributors to [Edmund] Muskie—the Jews, you know, that are stealing in every direction? Are we going after their tax returns? . . . I can only hope that we are, frankly, doing a little persecuting."[17] What all of this suggests is that the forces set in motion by Franklin Roosevelt and the New Deal have changed U.S. political and economic life forever. The progressive historians were always well intentioned, but once power is centralized, the unintended consequences are many.

THE NEW DEAL AND REPERCUSSIONS
FOR TODAY'S ECONOMY

The New Deal has been the greatest political force in America during the last one hundred years, and Franklin Roosevelt has probably been the most influential president during this time. We can see how FDR and the New Deal defined the Great Depression and the 1930s. But even though FDR died in 1945, the New Deal lived on. Many New Deal programs, even though they did much economic damage during the Great Depression, became part of the American political fabric in the generations that followed. Some, like farm subsidies, cost billions of dollars with no real benefit to the nation. Others, like Aid to Families with Dependent Children (AFDC), not only cost billions but do actual harm to the recipients. Still others, such as labor union monopolies and minimum wage laws, tended to help targeted groups and then hindered others who paid higher costs or taxes and were often explicitly excluded, as blacks were for example, from benefits.

Few New Deal programs were ever repealed (the WPA and

RFC were exceptions). Most were continued, expanded, and energized with new federal support. They took on an aura of indispensability. They had been the creations of Franklin Roosevelt himself. The myth that these programs were once valuable, that they helped end the Great Depression, and that they restored prosperity to the United States has been enough to keep them going. In the 1960s, President Lyndon Johnson built on the New Deal to create the Great Society, which began food stamps and other programs designed to wage a "war on poverty." Of course, once a federal program is in place, even a bad one, bureaucrats within the program flock to defend it; those receiving benefits from the program strive to retain it. Thus the legacy of the New Deal was an expanded federal government.

Minimum wage. The minimum wage law, as we have seen, contributed to unemployment during the Great Depression. The minimum wage has risen steadily since 1938 and its rise has continued to promote unemployment. The effect has been especially pernicious on black teenagers and others with low skills trying to enter the labor force. In 1950, for example, Congress almost doubled the minimum wage from 40 to 75 cents per hour. Unemployment for nonwhite teenagers also doubled from 7 to 14 percent. Six years later, when minimum wage was next raised, unemployment for nonwhite teenagers spiked again to over 24 percent. That high rate has never sustained a decline, and today black teenage unemployment is almost 30 percent.

As economist Thomas Sowell noted, employers are willing to take a chance on hiring *and training* unskilled youths if doing so is not costly. If hiring them is costly, employers will either mechanize their operations or hire fewer and more skilled workers. Minimum wage laws prevent many unskilled workers from getting a start in the workforce. A poll of more than three hundred economists at the American Economic Association in 2000 revealed that almost 75 percent of them fully or at least partly agree that "a minimum wage increases unemployment among young and unskilled workers." The support, however, for this New Deal program is still so strong that the minimum wage was increased from $5.15 in 2007 to $7.25 in 2009.

Social security. Social security began as a low-cost insurance program: employees paid 1 percent on their first $3,000 of earnings, a maximum of $30 per year (and employers matched this). The payments—from both employee and employer—have steadily increased (with a Medicare tax now included) to more than 7.5 percent on an employee's first $102,000. The program has also proven to be financially unsound—no longer do accrued funds pay for future retirement as was intended in the 1930s. Furthermore, the return on social security is small relative to that of other retirement plans. Black Americans, whose life expectancy is lower than whites, often pay in much more—an estimated $12,000 more—than they ever receive. Chile, which has privatized its social security system, has a much higher rate of return than its counterpart in the United States. In 1981, Galveston and two other Texas counties opted out of social security and entered into another retirement plan; benefits for these Texas counties have clearly exceeded those under the regular social security system. President Bush in 2005, perhaps noting the results of the Galveston experiment, recommended that the United States partly privatize social security. Bush pointed out that more money is paid out than is collected—the system, at this rate, will be bankrupt at some point in the 2020s.

Labor unions. The labor union monopoly created by the Wagner Act during the New Deal endured thereafter (somewhat restricted by the Taft-Hartley Act in 1947). Ever since the Wagner Act, labor unions have been exempt from taxation or antitrust laws. Unions, once voted in for a corporation, can mandate membership and dues payments from all members—even those who voted against the union. Labor unions have often driven the wages for their members higher than the value produced. Thus, by the 1970s, the U.S. steel and auto industries, for example, became increasingly uncompetitive in selling their products in foreign markets. The UAW, for example, has lost about one million members in the last twenty years as carmakers in Japan, with a lower minimum wage, have been steadily making better cars for lower costs. Foreign competition, then, has sharply driven down membership in private-sector unions.

Public-sector unions, because they can enforce and protect monopoly profits, have actually grown since the New Deal years. Members of the National Education Association (NEA), for example, have done better protecting their monopoly in education because they have limited their competition. Private schools must raise their own money while public schools receive lavish local, state, and federal payments. The quality of public education, however, has steadily declined since the 1960s, and private schools and homeschooling have greatly expanded despite the obstacles for parents in pursuing those options. The NEA endorsed Jimmy Carter for president in 1976—its first presidential endorsement in its 119-year history—and President Carter in return established the Department of Education, which has sharply increased the flow of funds to public education.

Industries with labor unions have tended to be less productive than those industries without unions. The twenty-two states with right-to-work laws have, on the whole, much more economic growth as a group than those twenty-eight states with closed shops.

Farm subsidies. The legacy of the AAA has persisted from the 1930s to today. Farm subsidies have proliferated and some people buy farmland to make money on it by receiving federal payments for taking part of it out of use. Even though almost no one can defend farm subsidies in the abstract, many farmers continue to be paid not to produce. In fact, these farm subsidies, which were created during the worst depression in U.S. history, have grown and expanded even during prosperous decades. By 1989, the Department of Agriculture gave the top 29,000 farmers an average of more than $46,000 each. Farmers have also secured subsidies for producing extra amounts of some crops. In recent years, for example, corn farmers have argued that ethanol made from corn provides an alternative to oil, which often must be imported. Thus the federal government has begun providing subsidies to grow corn, which earlier administrations paid farmers not to produce. Today, with the creation of the huge ethanol subsidies, corn farmers alone have received over $7 billion in farm subsidies—which comes to $1.45 added to each gallon of ethanol in subsidy alone.

AFDC. Aid to Families with Dependent Children became the welfare policy that ultimately emerged from the New Deal. Unwed mothers received direct federal aid for each child under age eighteen. These payments increased over time, and this provided incentives for births out of wedlock. The big change came in the 1960s. Through the Supreme Court and Congress, the law changed so that unwed mothers could live with boyfriends without reducing their federal benefits, and these women could also earn some income and not have it counted against their welfare payments. Food stamps, Medicaid, rent subsidies, and increased payments per child were also added to the package during the 1960s. As a result, out-of-wedlock births skyrocketed from one in twenty in 1960 to one in three by 1995. Serious welfare reform in 1996 (TANF— Temporary Assistance for Needy Families) shifted authority for welfare from federal to state administration. TANF removed some women from the welfare rolls and limited the payments and the time women would be allowed to receive federal payments. Welfare rolls in some states declined by about one-third by 2007.

Tariffs. The Smoot-Hawley tariff, the highest tariff in U.S. history, made the Great Depression much more severe than it had to be. Foreign countries retaliated by refusing to buy U.S. exports, and the Great Depression worsened. FDR supported the Reciprocal Tariff Act in 1934, and through mutual tariff reduction, the United States improved its trading steadily with other countries. After World War II, both Republicans and Democrats tended to support lower tariffs, and in 1994, under President Bill Clinton, the North American Free Trade Agreement (NAFTA) went into effect—the U.S., Canada, and Mexico have agreed to slash tariffs on agriculture (which has tended to help American exports) and some manufacturing and industry, which has sometimes given incentives to U.S. corporations to locate parts of their businesses in Mexico, with its lower labor costs. That exchange has increased worldwide free trade.

In 2008, both major Democrat candidates for president attacked NAFTA and urged higher tariffs for at least some American industry. Thus, we have a return to the arguments that led to the passage of the Smoot-Hawley Tariff Act in 1930.

Federal Reserve. The Fed created problems during the Great Depression. When the Fed raised interest rates in the late 1920s and early 1930s, it hampered investment and caused the closing of thousands of banks, which led to the shrinkage of the money supply by about one-third. The Bank of the United States collapsed in late 1930 and the Fed refused to bail it out; this contributed to runs on banks throughout the country and 1,400 banks closed in 1931. Fed policy became more interventionist after the Great Depression. In 1984, for example, when the Continental Illinois National Bank, the seventh largest bank in the country, went broke, the Fed bailed it out and the economy had no negative repercussions from that, and no other banks went under. In 2008, Bear Stearns failed, and the Fed guaranteed its holdings. Also, in the midst of stock market declines and the subprime mortgage crisis, the Fed began lowering interest rates—exactly the opposite of its strategy during the Great Depression.

FDIC. Federal deposit insurance started at $2,500 under the New Deal, but politicians increased the coverage over time without increasing the commensurate costs to the banks. By 1980, the FDIC and the Federal Savings and Loan Insurance Corporation were promising savers coverage of $100,000. That gave bankers incentives to reduce their reserves and lend out more money in a risky manner. If the investments failed, the government would pick up the tab. During the 1980s, more than one thousand savings and loans went broke, and picking up the tab cost the taxpayers an estimated $800 billion. If the federal government had merely required banks to have adequate private insurance, the results, according to economists George Benston and George Kaufman, would likely have been much better.

SEC. The Securities and Exchange Commission may have helped provide security for investors by having new companies jump through many hoops to secure approval. The downside is that jumping through hoops—especially if the hoops are narrow—may make it harder for good new companies to come into existence. Nobel laureate George Stigler argued that once the SEC was in place, fewer companies were able to raise capital through the stock market. What's more, the rate of return for companies in the 1920s was almost the same as those created after 1933 that had to jump through the SEC hoops. Also, the SEC protected brokerages in charging high commissions and this fixing of commissions continued until 1975.

Taxes. FDR's desire to increase the progressive income tax persisted throughout his presidency. As we saw earlier, in 1942, he signed an executive order taxing all personal income over $25,000 at 100 percent. Congress balked at that rate and later lowered it to 90 percent at the top level. In 1943, the president and Congress also approved of withholding taxes and they introduced a new 20 percent rate on all annual income starting at $500. After that dramatic move, most American families were paying federal income tax. Presidents Kennedy and Reagan cut taxes on all income groups. The Kennedy tax cuts lowered the top rate to 70 percent and Reagan lowered it to 28 percent. After both of these tax cuts, the revenue to the government shot up. Investment also increased and the 1980s, with fax machines, computers, VCRs, CDs, Walkmans, and cell phones became one of the most innovative decades in U.S. history. The top tax rate was hiked to 31 percent under President George H. W. Bush and to 39.6 percent under President Clinton.

Revenue to the government leveled off, although the late 1990s was a prosperous time. George W. Bush cut the top tax rate back to 35 percent and, under both Clinton and Bush, the capital gains tax was cut as well. Revenue from income taxes and from the sales of stocks increased sharply after these cuts.

Character. A big change in the New Deal was the lowered emphasis on strong character to be president. Before the Great Depression, the personal integrity of the president was a key ingredient in his ability to be nominated by a major party and elected by the voters. This did not mean that presidents were necessarily paragons of virtue. In the rumble and tumble of political life, compromises and changes of policy created problems for many presidents among voters in the area of character and consistency. But Americans nonetheless expected presidents to be men of virtue, and Washington and others said that without that the American system would fail. The massive increase of the federal government into American life in the 1930s created new incentives for presidents. As FDR discovered, he could promise one thing in an election and deliver something quite different and get away with it as long as many political constituencies received their subsidies. Constituents, who previously had little or no direct economic interest in a presidential candidate (except for occasional tariffs and infrequent subsidies), now had many reasons to look at what presidential candidates were promising to do with the increased tax revenue flowing into the federal treasury. Would different voting groups receive more than they paid out? That question led many voters to look more closely at money promised than at the integrity of the presidential contenders.

NOTES

Chapter 1: The Making of the Myth

1. John M. Blum, *From the Morgenthau Diaries: Years of Crisis, 1928–1938* (Boston: Houghton Mifflin, 1959), 30–34. The two men, according to Eleanor Roosevelt, were Morgenthau and Louis Howe.

2. Morgenthau Diary, May 9, 1939, Franklin Roosevelt Presidential Library, hereinafter RPL. For the unemployment data, see Richard K. Vedder and Lowell E. Gallaway, *Out of Work: Unemployment and Government in Twentieth-Century America* (New York: Holmes & Meier, 1993), 77.

3. U.S. Bureau of the Census, *Historical Statistics of the United States: Colonial Times to 1970* (Washington, D.C.: U.S. Government Printing Office, 1975), I, 126.

4. Studs Terkel, *Hard Times* (New York: Avon, 1970), 488; Robert S. McElvaine, ed., *Down and Out in the Great Depression* (Chapel Hill: University of North Carolina Press, 1983), 117, 159, 161, 170–71. Unemployment, of course, hit some parts of the economy harder than others. See Richard J. Jensen, "The Causes and Cures of Unemployment in the Great Depression," *Journal of Interdisciplinary History* 19 (Spring 1989), 553–83.

5. *Historical Statistics*, II, 651, 716, 912, 958–59, 1007.

6. *Historical Statistics*, II, 1105, 1117.

7. *Historical Statistics*, II, 884.

8. *Historical Statistics*, I, 10, 15.

9. *Historical Statistics*, I, 58; McElvaine, ed., *Down and Out in the Great Depression*, 103–4.

10. *Historical Statistics*, I, 55.

11. *Historical Statistics*, I, 55.

12. *World Economic Survey: Eighth Year, 1938/39* (Geneva: League of Nations, 1939), 128.

13. *Historical Statistics*, I, 64, 77, 414, 415.

14. David A. Shannon, ed., *The Great Depression* (Englewood Cliffs, N.J.: Prentice-Hall, 1960), 58–61.

15. Henry Steele Commager and Richard B. Morris, "Editors' Introduction," in William E. Leuchtenburg, *Franklin Roosevelt and the New Deal, 1932–1940* (New York: Harper & Row, 1963), ix–x. For a useful biography of Commager, see Neil Jumonville, *Henry Steele Commager: Midcentury Liberalism and the History of the Present* (Chapel Hill: University of North Carolina Press, 1999).

16. Here is just one example of Leuchtenburg's wide influence. In his book *The FDR Years: On Roosevelt & His Legacy* (New York: Columbia University Press, 1995), Leuchtenburg dedicates the work "to my students who have written about the New Deal era and who have taught me so much." This impressive list of students alone includes eighty-nine names of scholars who have written books or articles on the New Deal. See also Jumonville, *Henry Steele Commager*, 31–36, 132–33.

17. Arthur M. Schlesinger, Jr., *The Crisis of the Old Order, 1919–1933* (Boston: Houghton Mifflin, 1957), 159–60, 67; John A. Garraty, *Interpreting American History: Conversations with Historians* (London: Macmillan, 1970), 171.

18. Leuchtenburg, *Franklin Roosevelt and the New Deal*, 347; Samuel Eliot Morison, *The Oxford History of the American People* (New York: Oxford University Press, 1965), 953; Joseph R. Conlin, *The American Past*, 6th ed. (Belmont, Calif.: Wadsworth, 2001), 833. Morison co-authored a major U. S. history text, *A Concise History of the American Republic*, 7th ed. (New York: Oxford University Press, 1977), with both Commager and Leuchtenburg.

19. Arthur M. Schlesinger, Jr., *The Coming of the New Deal* (Boston: Houghton Mifflin, 1958), 572; Conlin, *The American Past*, 818; Leuchtenburg, *Franklin Roosevelt and the New Deal*, 90.

20. Morison, *The Oxford History of the American People*, 986; Leuchtenburg, *Franklin Roosevelt and the New Deal*, 327–28, 346; Frank Freidel, *Franklin D. Roosevelt: A Rendezvous with Destiny* (Boston: Little, Brown, 1990), 94.

21. Conlin, *The American Past*, 818; Leuchtenburg, *The FDR Years*, 34. Most New Left historians, although they are critical that FDR did not accomplish more, still basically accept the four points in the New Deal legend. See Barton J. Bernstein, "The New Deal: The Conservative Achievements of Liberal Reform," in Barton J. Bernstein, ed., *Towards a New Past: Dissenting Essays in American History* (New York: Vintage, 1968), 263–88.

22. Leuchtenburg, *Franklin Roosevelt and the New Deal*, 347; Thomas A. Bailey, David M. Kennedy, and Lizabeth Cohen, *The American Pageant*, 11th ed. (Boston: Houghton Mifflin, 1998), 823.

23. David M. Kennedy, *Freedom from Fear: The American People in Depression and War, 1929–1945* (New York: Oxford University Press, 1999), xi, 378;

George McJimsey, *The Presidency of Franklin Delano Roosevelt* (Lawrence: University Press of Kansas, 2000), 287–88, 295.

24. Arthur M. Schlesinger, Jr., *The Politics of Upheaval* (Boston: Houghton Mifflin, 1988 [1960]), x.

25. Arthur M. Schlesinger, Jr., "Rating the Presidents: Washington to Clinton," *Political Science Quarterly* 112 (1997), 182; David E. Hamilton, ed., *The New Deal* (Boston: Houghton Mifflin, 1999), 231. The Schlesinger poll, the oldest presidential poll, was begun in 1948 by Arthur Schlesinger, Sr., continued in 1962 by Schlesinger, and conducted again in 1996 by his son. The poll asks leading historians to rank presidents as great, near great, average, below average, or failure.

26. Anthony J. Badger, *The New Deal: The Depression Years, 1933–1940* (New York: Hill & Wang, 1989), 314.

27. Ray A. Billington, *American History after 1865* (Totowa, N.J.: Littlefield, Adams, 1968), 193.

Chapter 2: FDR's Rise to Power

1. Some of the useful biographies of Roosevelt include Frank Freidel, *Franklin D. Roosevelt: A Rendezvous with Destiny* (Boston: Little, Brown, 1990); James MacGregor Burns, *Roosevelt: The Lion and the Fox* (New York: Harcourt, Brace, & World, 1956); Arthur Schlesinger, Jr., *Crisis of the Old Order, 1919–1933* (Boston: Houghton Mifflin, 1957), 273–485; Ted Morgan, *FDR: A Biography* (New York: Simon & Schuster, 1985); and Conrad Black, *Franklin Delano Roosevelt: Champion of Freedom* (New York: Public Affairs, 2003). See also Paul Conkin, *The New Deal* (Wheeling, Ill.: Harlan Davidson, 1992 [1967]), 1–21.

2. Geoffrey C. Ward, *Before the Trumpet: Young Franklin Roosevelt, 1882–1905* (New York: Harper & Row, 1985), 125–26.

3. Ward, *Before the Trumpet*, 71.

4. Ward, *Before the Trumpet*, 211; Kenneth S. Davis, *FDR: The Beckoning of Destiny, 1882–1928* (New York: Random House, 1972), 28–29.

5. Geoffrey C. Ward, *A First-Class Temperament: The Emergence of Franklin Roosevelt* (New York: Harper & Row, 1989), 139.

6. Ward, *Before the Trumpet*, 180–81, 185, 208.

7. Ward, *Before the Trumpet*, 215, 236; Davis, *FDR*, 129–67.

8. Ward, *Before the Trumpet*, 204.

9. Ward, *First-Class Temperament*, 62.

10. Ward, *First-Class Temperament*, 77; Davis, *FDR*, 209–13.

11. Nathan Miller, *F.D.R.: An Intimate History* (Garden City, N.Y.: Doubleday & Co., 1983), 61–62.

12. Ward, *First-Class Temperament*, xv.

13. Ward, *First-Class Temperament*, 112–23. Hyde Park was, of course, a small town in a large district.

14. Hugh G. Gallagher, *FDR's Splendid Deception* (New York: Dodd, Mead, 1985).

15. Alfred B. Rollins, Jr., *Roosevelt and Howe* (New York: Knopf, 1962); and Freidel, *Franklin D. Roosevelt*, 22.

16. Davis, *FDR*, 749–58, 819–23.

17. Ward, *First-Class Temperament*, 677.

18. Ward, *First-Class Temperament*, 776–77; Davis, *FDR*, 485–95; Gallagher, *Splendid Deception*, 142.

19. Ward, *First-Class Temperament*, 676–77.

20. Ward, *First-Class Temperament*, 658, 756, 768–69, 793; Elliott Roosevelt and James Brough, *An Untold Story: The Roosevelts of Hyde Park* (New York: Dell, 1974), 252–57.

21. Ward, *First-Class Temperament*, 215–16, 659n.

22. Ward, *First-Class Temperament*, 552n, 656.

23. Roosevelt and Brough, *An Untold Story*, 219–20.

24. Roosevelt and Brough, *Untold Story*, 220–23; Ward, *First-Class Temperament*.

25. Ward, *First-Class Temperament*, 497, 529, 534.

26. Ward, *First-Class Temperament*, 535.

27. Ward, *First-Class Temperament*, 535–36.

28. Oscar Handlin, *Al Smith and His America* (Boston: Little, Brown, 1958).

29. Ward, *First-Class Temperament*, 126.

30. Handlin, *Al Smith and His America*, 127–43.

Chapter 3: What Caused the Great Depression?

1. H. G. Moulton and Leo Pasvolsky, *War Debts and World Prosperity* (New York: Century Co., 1932). For a brief overview of the Allied debt issue, see Thomas A. Bailey, *A Diplomatic History of the American People* (New York: Appleton-Century Crofts, 1964), 656–71.

2. Alan Reynolds, "What Do We Know About the Great Crash?" *National Review*, November 9, 1979, 1416–21; and Joseph M. Jones, Jr., *Tariff Retaliation: Repercussions of the Hawley-Smoot Bill* (Philadelphia: University of Pennsylvania Press, 1934).

3. Reynolds, "What Do We Know About the Great Crash?"; Jones, *Tariff Retaliation*; and Allan Nevins and Frank Ernest Hill, *Ford: Decline and Rebirth, 1933–1962* (New York: Charles Scribner's Sons, 1963), 4. The car sales figures include trucks.

4. Jude Wanniski, *The Way the World Works* (New York: Simon & Schuster, 1978); Douglas A. Irwin, "The Smoot-Hawley Tariff: A Quantitative Assessment," *Review of Economics and Statistics* (May 1988), 326–34; and Larry Schweikart, "A Tale of Two Tariffs," *The Freeman* 52 (June 2002), 46–48.

5. Milton Friedman and Anna J. Schwartz, *Monetary History of the United States* (Princeton: Princeton University Press, 1963). A more recent essay is Christina D. Romer, "What Ended the Great Depression?" *Journal of Economic History* 52 (December 1992), 757–84.

6. Lawrence W. Reed, "Great Myths of the Great Depression," Mackinac Center for Public Policy, 2005; Gary Dean Best, *Peddling Panaceas: Popular Economists in the New Deal Era* (New Brunswick, N.J.: Transaction, 2005); Rexford Tugwell, *The Battle for Democracy* (New York: Columbia University Press, 1935), 78–96, 265, 285; Stuart Chase, *A New Deal* (New York: Macmillan, 1932).

7. Thomas B. Silver, *Coolidge and the Historians* (Durham, N.C.: Carolina Academic Press, 1982), 124–36.

8. Peter Temin, *Did Monetary Forces Cause the Great Depression?* (New York: Norton, 1976), 4, 32; Peter Temin, *Lessons from the Great Depression* (Cambridge, Mass.: MIT Press, 1989). See also Gene Smiley, *Rethinking the Great Depression* (Chicago: Ivan Dee, 2002).

9. For Tugwell's underconsumptionist ideas, see Rexford Tugwell Diary, "Introduction," 6–10, in Rexford Tugwell Papers, RPL. For a critique of underconsumptionist ideas, see Stanley Lebergott, *Men Without Work: The Economics of Unemployment* (Englewood Cliffs, N.J.: Prentice Hall, 1964), and Lebergott, *The Americans: An Economic Record* (New York: Norton, 1984). On the origins of the brains trust, see Samuel Rosenman to Rexford Tugwell, January 16, 1969, in Samuel Rosenman Papers, RPL.

10. Benjamin M. Anderson, *Economics and the Public Welfare: A Financial and Economic History of the United States, 1914–1946* (Indianapolis: Liberty Press, 1979 [1949]); Henry Hazlitt, *Economics in One Lesson* (San Francisco: Laissez Faire, 1996 [1946]); Isaac Lippincott, *The Development of Modern World Trade* (New York: D. Appleton-Century, 1936); and Irving Fisher to Franklin Roosevelt, June 16, 1936, April 30, 1933, and December 19, 1937, in Irving Fisher Papers, RPL. Of these four economists, Hazlitt was not formally trained in economics. See also David Laidler, *Fabricating the Keynesian Revolution: Studies of the Inter-war Literature on Money, the Cycle, and Unemployment* (Cambridge, England: Cambridge University Press, 1999). Laidler points out that John Maynard Keynes's ideas evolved during the 1920s, and that others were involved in working out what became the Keynesian revolution.

11. Samuel I. Rosenman, ed., *The Public Papers and Addresses of Franklin D. Roosevelt* (New York: Random House, 1938), I, 626, 645–46.
12. Rosenman, *Public Papers*, I, 650.
13. Rosenman, *Public Papers*, I, 651–59.
14. Rosenman, *Public Papers*, I, 648; Kirk H. Porter and Donald B. Johnson, *National Party Platforms, 1840–1968* (Urbana: University of Illinois Press, 1970), 331.
15. Geoffrey C. Ward, *Before the Trumpet: Young Franklin Roosevelt, 1882–1905* (New York: Harper & Row, 1985), 238n.
16. Herbert Hoover, *The Memoirs of Herbert Hoover: The Great Depression, 1929–1941* (New York: Macmillan, 1952), 341–43.
17. Murray R. Benedict, *Farm Policies of the United States, 1790–1950* (New York: Octagon, 1966 [1953]), 239–67.
18. James S. Olson, *Herbert Hoover and the Reconstruction Finance Corporation, 1931–1933* (Ames: Iowa State University Press, 1977); Harris Gaylord Warren, *Herbert Hoover and the Great Depression* (New York: Norton, 1967 [1959]); and Murray Rothbard, *America's Great Depression* (New York: Richardson & Snyder, 1972 [1963]). Olson and Warren tend to be favorable toward the RFC.
19. Rosenman, *Public Papers*, I, 751–52, 846. For a useful description of Roosevelt's economic thought in general, and his underconsumption views in particular, see Daniel Fusfeld, *The Economic Thought of Franklin D. Roosevelt and the Origins of the New Deal* (New York: Columbia University Press, 1954), esp. 245.
20. Rosenman, *Public Papers*, I, 751–52, 799, 809.
21. Geoffrey C. Ward, *A First-Class Temperament: The Emergence of Franklin Roosevelt* (New York: Harper & Row, 1989), 194.
22. Hoover, *Memoirs*, 336–43.

Chapter 4: The NRA

1. Samuel I. Rosenman, ed., *The Public Papers and Addresses of Franklin D. Roosevelt* (New York: Random House, 1938), II, 246.
2. Henry Steele Commager, ed., *Documents of American History* (New York: Appleton-Century-Crofts, 1968), II, 271–78; Bernard Bellush, *The Failure of the NRA* (New York: Norton, 1975).
3. Adam Smith, *An Inquiry into the Nature and Causes of the Wealth of Nations* (New York: Modern Library, 1937 [1776]), 137.
4. Butler Shaffer, *In Restraint of Trade: The Business Campaign Against Competition, 1918–1938* (Lewisburg, Penn.: Bucknell University Press, 1997),

108. See also Hugh Johnson, *The Blue Eagle from Egg to Earth* (Garden City, N.Y.: Doubleday, Doran, 1935), 190–219.

5. Rosenman, *Public Papers*, II, 251.

6. Bellush, *Failure of the NRA*, 10–12; Jim Powell, *FDR's Folly* (New York: Crown Forum, 2003), 120; Shaffer, *In Restraint of Trade*, 106. For a competent description of Johnson and the NRA, see John Kennedy Ohl, *Hugh S. Johnson and the New Deal* (DeKalb: Northern Illinois University Press, 1985). Germany was also experimenting with cartels, somewhat along the lines of the NRA. See Dan P. Silverman, *Hitler's Economy: Nazi Work Creation Programs, 1933–1936* (Cambridge, Mass.: Harvard University Press, 1998).

7. Powell, *FDR's Folly*, 118–19. For the story of Hugh Johnson and the failure of the Moline Plow Company in the 1920s, see Ohl, *Hugh Johnson*, 54–69.

8. Burton W. Folsom, Jr., *The Myth of the Robber Barons*, 5th ed. (Herndon, Va.: Young America's Foundation, 2007), 66–67; Harold Livesay, *Andrew Carnegie and the Rise of Big Business* (Boston: Little, Brown, 1975), 150, 165–66.

9. Shaffer, *In Restraint of Trade*, 125–27. U.S. Steel was also concerned about the possibility of antitrust prosecution. Perhaps that made Gary less aggressive in business.

10. Shaffer, *In Restraint of Trade*, 126.

11. Shaffer, *In Restraint of Trade*, 125; *New York Times*, April 14, 1915; Robert Hessen, *Steel Titan: The Life of Charles M. Schwab* (New York: Oxford University Press, 1975), 230, 265–66.

12. Burton W. Folsom, Jr., *Empire Builders: How Michigan Entrepreneurs Helped Make America Great* (Traverse City, Mich.: Rhodes & Easton, 1998), 144–48; George Gilder, *Recapturing the Spirit of Enterprise* (San Francisco: ICS Press, 1992), 189–98.

13. Henry Hazlitt, *Economics in One Lesson* (New Rochelle, N.Y.: Arlington House, 1979 [1946]), 58.

14. Marian C. McKenna, *Borah* (Ann Arbor: University of Michigan Press, 1961), 159–65, 307–9, 315. In the Borah Papers, at the Library of Congress in Washington, D.C., the estimated nine thousand letters to him on the NRA fill many boxes, and do not include the letters on the NRA written to other congressmen. See also Irving Fisher to Franklin Roosevelt, August 30, 1934, in Roosevelt Papers, RPL.

15. Allan Nevins and Frank Ernest Hill, *Ford: Decline and Rebirth, 1933–1962* (New York: Charles Scribner's Sons, 1963), 4; Folsom, *Empire Builders*, 157–61; Garet Garrett, *The Wild Wheel: The World of Henry Ford* (New York: Pantheon, 1952).

16. Carl Pharis to William Borah, September 12, 1934, in Borah Papers, Library of Congress, hereinafter LC.

17. Stuart S. Ball to William Borah, May 9, 1934, in Borah Papers, LC.

18. J. R. Isaacson to William Borah, July 14, 1934, in Borah Papers, LC.

19. F. H. Mills, Jr., to William Borah, August 17, 1934, in Borah Papers, LC.

20. Nevins and Hill, *Ford*, 19; Folsom, *Empire Builders*, 158–59.

21. *Complete Presidential Press Conferences of Franklin D. Roosevelt* (New York: Da Capo Press, 1972), II, 379; Nevins and Hill, *Ford*, 21, 38, 41; Garrett, *The Wild Wheel*, 153; Carol Gelderman, *Henry Ford: The Wayward Capitalist* (New York: Dial Press, 1980), 325.

22. At a dinner party, according to reporter Raymond Clapper, Hugh Johnson said the "American people would crack down on Ford, who refuses thus far to come in under the auto code." Raymond Clapper Diary, August 29, 1933, LC. See also Nevins and Hill, *Ford*, 20.

23. Fred Perkins to William Borah, May 5, 1934, and July 3, 1934; Senator David Reed to Fred Perkins, June 14, 1934; and *York Dispatch*, May 9, 1934, and June 10, 1934, in Borah Papers, LC. See also *Washington Post*, December 17, 1934.

24. Margaret Slamey to William Borah, April 28, 1934; and newspaper clipping, "Sentences 2 in NRA Price Cut: Judge Baer Orders Jail for Markowitzes in Dry Cleaning War," no date, Borah Papers, LC.

25. R. W. Johnson to N. J. Harkness, April 28, 1934, in Borah Papers, LC.

26. "Cruel and Unusual," *Washington Post*, April 22, 1934; "Tugwell Vs. Maged," *New York Herald Tribune*, April 23, 1934. See also newspaper clipping, "Jailing of Tailor Called Necessary," no date, Borah Papers, LC.

27. *Washington Post*, April 22, 1934; and *New York Herald Tribune*, April 23, 1934. Maged died of cancer in 1939 at the age of fifty-four. See *Time*, April 10, 1939.

28. Oneida Cedar & Lumber Company to Hugh S. Johnson, August 24, 1934; and A. Rollman to William Borah, August 28, 1934, in Borah Papers, LC.

29. C. J. Gilbert to William Borah, August, 10, 1934, in Borah Papers, LC.

30. Armand L. Friedlander to Borah, August 8, 1934, in Borah Papers, LC.

31. Irving Fisher to Roosevelt, August 30, 1934, in Irving Fisher Papers, RPL. Fisher added, "Except for such employers' and investors' fears, due to parts of the New Deal, we could, I think, have been practically out of the depression many months ago. . . ." See also Bellush, *The Failure of the NRA*, 66, 161, 142–46. For an excellent treatment of the Darrow commission, see Stephen J. Sniegoski, "The Darrow Board and the Downfall of the NRA," *Continuity* (Spring/Fall 1990), 63–83.

32. Bellush, *Failure of the NRA*, 136–41, 145, 148, 158–68; Ellis W. Hawley,

The New Deal and the Problem of Monopoly (Princeton, N.J.: Princeton University Press, 1966); Ohl, *Hugh Johnson.*

33. Hadley Arkes, *The Return of George Sutherland: Restoring a Jurisprudence of Natural Rights* (Princeton, N.J.: Princeton University Press, 1994), 84–86; Hawley, *The New Deal and the Problem of Monopoly*, 128–29.

34. Philip B. Kurland and Gerhard Casper, eds., *Landmark Briefs and Arguments of the Supreme Court of the United States* (Arlington, Va.: University Publications of America, 1975), vol. 28, 836–37. I thank Professor Hadley Arkes for calling my attention to this source.

35. Frank R. Kent, *Without Grease: Political Behavior, 1934–1936* (New York: William Morrow, 1936), 136, 140.

36. Kent, *Without Grease*, 173; Ohl, *Hugh Johnson*, 265–67.

37. James S. Olson, *Historical Dictionary of the New Deal* (Westport, Conn.: Greenwood, 1985), 223–25; Hazlitt, *Economics in One Lesson*, 99.

38. Paul Murphy, *The Constitution in Crisis Times, 1918–1969* (New York: Harper & Row, 1972), 137. A helpful book in trying to understand the points of view of both Roosevelt and his opponents is Thomas Sowell, *A Conflict of Visions: Ideological Origins of Political Struggles* (New York: William Morrow, 1987).

39. Morgenthau Diary, January 4, 1937, RPL.

Chapter 5: The AAA

1. Samuel I. Rosenman, ed., *The Public Papers and Addresses of Franklin D. Roosevelt* (New York: Random House, 1938), II, 74.

2. Henry Steele Commager, ed., *Documents of American History* (New York: Appleton-Century-Crofts, 1968), II, 242–55. See also John T. Schlebecker, *Whereby We Thrive: A History of American Farming, 1607–1972* (Ames: Iowa State University Press, 1975), 234–43; and Murray R. Benedict, *Farm Policies of the United States, 1790–1950* (New York: Octagon, 1966 [1953]), 207–401.

3. Schlebecker, *Whereby We Thrive*; Don Paarlberg, "Tarnished Gold: Fifty Years of New Deal Programs," in Robert Eden, ed., *The New Deal and Its Legacy* (Westport, Conn.: Greenwood, 1989), 39–47.

4. Anthony J. Badger, *The New Deal: The Depression Years, 1933–1940* (New York: Hill & Wang, 1989), 147; Joseph M. Jones, Jr., *Tariff Retaliation: Repercussions of the Hawley-Smoot Bill* (Philadelphia: University of Pennsylvania Press, 1934).

5. Harris Gaylord Warren, *Herbert Hoover and the Great Depression* (New York: Norton, 1967 [1959]), 172–77; Schlebecker, *Whereby We Thrive*, 236–37.

6. Henry A. Wallace, *New Frontiers* (New York: Reynal & Hitchcock, 1934), 172–73; Paul Findley, *The Federal Farm Fable* (New Rochelle, N.Y.: Arlington House, 1968), 17–46; Van L. Perkins, *Crisis in Agriculture: The Agricultural Adjustment Administration and the New Deal, 1933* (Berkeley: University of California Press, 1969); and William D. Rowley, *M. L. Wilson and the Campaign for Domestic Allotment* (Lincoln: University of Nebraska Press, 1970).

7. Wallace, *New Frontiers*, 163–64; John L. Shover, *First Majority—Last Minority: The Transforming of Rural Life in America* (DeKalb: Northern Illinois University Press, 1976); Schlebecker, *Whereby We Thrive*, 286–87. For the origin of the parity idea, see Rowley, *M. L. Wilson*; and Gilbert Fite, *George N. Peek and the Fight for Farm Parity* (Norman: University of Oklahoma Press, 1954).

8. Henry Hazlitt, *Economics in One Lesson* (New Rochelle, N.Y.: Arlington House, 1979 [1946]), 92.

9. Schlebecker, *Whereby We Thrive*, 245–46, 252, 297–98, 306, 312; Shover, *First Majority—Last Minority*, 152–58.

10. Badger, *New Deal*, 152; Schlebecker, *Whereby We Thrive*, 238.

11. *United States v. Butler*, 297 U.S. 1 (1936), 76.

12. Rosenman, *Public Papers*, IV, 432–33. A recent critique of Roosevelt's agricultural and industrial policy is in Kenneth Finegold and Theda Skocpol, *State and Party in America's New Deal* (Madison: University of Wisconsin Press, 1995).

13. Wallace, *New Frontiers*, 164.

14. Badger, *New Deal*, 153.

15. Badger, *New Deal*, 147–89; William E. Leuchtenburg, *Franklin D. Roosevelt and the New Deal, 1932–1940* (New York: Harper & Row, 1963), 74–75.

16. H. V. Kaltenborn, *Fifty Fabulous Years, 1900–1950* (New York: G. P. Putnam's Sons, 1950), 176–77.

17. Frank R. Kent, *Without Grease: Political Behavior, 1934–1936* (New York: William Morrow, 1936), 250. The importing of "wheat, corn, meat, and other foodstuffs" irritated Governor Alfred Landon of Kansas and may have helped prompt him to run for president in 1936. See "75th Anniversary of Kansas into the Union," undated, Box 14, Folder 5, in Alfred Landon Papers, Topeka, Kansas State Historical Society. Frank Knox, who was Landon's vice presidential nominee in 1936, was also appalled at the United States' having to import food in 1935. See Knox, "For an American Farm Policy," *Chicago Daily News*, September 30, 1935, and his speech to the Nebraska State Republican Rally, Kearney, Nebraska, November 22, 1935, in Frank Knox Papers, LC.

18. Schlebecker, *Whereby We Thrive*, 249–52, 263–64; Shover, *First Majority—*

Last Minority, 175–300; Badger, *New Deal*, 156–81; Theodore Saloutos and John D. Hicks, *Twentieth Century Populism* (Lincoln: University of Nebraska Press, 1951), 502–37. For a somewhat favorable view of the AAA, see Sally H. Clarke, *Regulation and Revolution in United States Farm Productivity* (Cambridge, England: Cambridge University Press, 1994). For a negative view of the impact of AAA on local retail sales, see Price V. Fishback, William C. Horrace, and Shawn Kantor, "Did New Deal Grant Programs Stimulate Local Economies? A Study of Federal Grants and Retail Sales During the Great Depression," *Journal of Economic History* 65 (March 2005), 36–71.

19. On July 18, 1935, the *Los Angeles Times* editorialized that if the AAA were struck down, "it will mean the end of taxation upon one class for the benefit of another." See also "An Unusual Report," *Omaha World-Herald*, January 5, 1936, 6; Badger, *New Deal*, 162; Schlebecker, *Whereby We Thrive*, 241–43; Shover, *First Majority—Last Minority*, 244–46; Findley, *Federal Farm Fable*, 27–46.

20. On the cotton land in Brazil, see Lewis W. Douglas, *The Liberal Tradition* (New York: D. Van Nostrand, 1935), 46–48. For the tenant problem, see David Eugene Conrad, *The Forgotten Farmers: The Story of Sharecroppers in the New Deal* (Urbana: University of Illinois Press, 1965); Perkins, *Crisis in Agriculture*.

21. Bernard Sternsher, *Rexford Tugwell and the New Deal* (New Brunswick, N.J.: Rutgers University Press, 1964), 263.

22. Diary of Rexford Tugwell, January 23, 1935, RPL.

23. Diary of Rexford Tugwell, September 10, 1935, RPL.

24. Sternsher, *Tugwell*, 273, 282, 285. A sympathetic view of Arthurdale is Nancy Hoffman, *Eleanor Roosevelt and the Arthurdale Experiment* (North Haven, Conn.: Linnet, 2001).

25. Kent, *Without Grease*, 296–97. Before 1935, the RA was preceded by the Federal Emergency Relief Administration.

26. Kent, *Without Grease*, 202–3; Sternsher, *Tugwell*, 262–306; Rexford Tugwell, *The Democratic Roosevelt* (Baltimore: Penguin, 1969 [1957]), 423–24, 435, 472–73.

27. Bernard Baruch to Samuel I. Rosenman, January 6, 1959, in Rosenman Papers, RPL.

28. Ronald L. Heinemann, *Harry Byrd of Virginia* (Charlottesville: University Press of Virginia, 1996), 7.

29. Heinemann, *Harry Byrd of Virginia*, 125–40.

30. Heinemann, *Harry Byrd of Virginia*, 133–36; Jones, *Tariff Retaliation*, 176–210, 226–34.

31. Harold L. Ickes, *The Secret Diary of Harold L. Ickes* (New York: Simon & Schuster, 1953), I, 475.

32. Rexford Guy Tugwell, "The Principle of Planning and the Institution of Laissez Faire," *American Economic Review* 22 (Supplement, March 1932), 75–92; Heinemann, *Harry Byrd of Virginia*, 166, 181–82.

33. Tugwell, *The Democratic Roosevelt*, 444n; Heinemann, *Harry Byrd of Virginia*, 137; James T. Patterson, *Congressional Conservatism and the New Deal* (Lexington: University Press of Kentucky, 1967), 29–30, 117, 200–2, 212, 216–17, 301–2, 319–20; 329, 348; A. Cash Koeniger, "The New Deal and the States: Roosevelt versus the Byrd Organization in Virginia," *Journal of American History* 68 (March 1982), 876–96.

34. Geoffrey Ward, *A First-Class Temperament: The Emergence of Franklin Roosevelt* (New York: Harper & Row, 1989), 264–67, 768–69; Mark Leff, *The Limits of Symbolic Reform* (Cambridge, England: Cambridge University Press, 1984); Walter Trohan, *Political Animals* (Garden City, N.Y.: Doubleday, 1975), 74; David Brinkley, *Washington Goes to War* (New York: Ballantine, 1988), 167–68.

Chapter 6: Relief and the WPA

1. Mark Noll, *A History of Christianity in the United States and Canada* (Grand Rapids, Mich.: Eerdmans, 1992); Josephine C. Brown, *Public Relief, 1929–1939* (New York: Octagon, 1971 [1940]), 3–38; and Robin Lampson, "Man at His Best," in Burton W. Folsom, Jr., ed., *The Spirit of Freedom: Essays in American History* (Irvington, N.Y.: Foundation for Economic Education, 1994), 103–8.

2. Federalist, No. 10, in Alexander Hamilton, James Madison, and John Jay, *The Federalist Papers*, with introduction by Clinton Rossiter (New York: New American Library, 1961), 79.

3. Marvin Olasky, *The American Leadership Tradition: Moral Vision from Washington to Clinton* (New York: Free Press, 1999), 160; and Alyn Brodsky, *Grover Cleveland: A Study in Character* (New York: St. Martin's, 2000).

4. Olasky, *The American Leadership Tradition*, 160.

5. Edward A. Williams, *Federal Aid for Relief* (New York: Columbia University Press, 1939), 33; Brown, *Public Relief*, 145–70.

6. Horace B. Powell, *The Original Has This Signature: W. K. Kellogg* (Englewood Cliffs, N.J.: Prentice-Hall, 1956); Joseph J. Fucini and Suzy Fucini, *Entrepreneurs: The Men and Women Behind Famous Brand Names and How They Made It* (Boston: G. K. Hall, 1985), 129.

7. Williams, *Federal Aid for Relief*, 48; Brown, *Public Relief*, 124–42; and

J. Joseph Huthmacher, *Senator Robert F. Wagner and the Rise of Urban Liberalism* (New York: Atheneum, 1968), 94–102.

8. Williams, *Federal Aid for Relief*, 51–53.

9. Charles H. Trout, *Boston, The Great Depression, and the New Deal* (New York: Oxford University Press, 1977), 85–87, 93. See also J. Joseph Huthmacher, *Massachusetts: People and Politics, 1919–1933* (Cambridge, Mass.: Harvard University Press, 1959), 221–24, 259.

10. Williams, *Federal Aid for Relief*, 51–52; Harold Gorvine, "The New Deal in Massachusetts," in John Braeman, Robert H. Bremner, and David Brody, eds., *The New Deal: The State and Local Levels* (Columbus: Ohio State University Press, 1975), 3–44.

11. Williams, *Federal Aid for Relief*, 58–86; and Brown, *Public Relief*, 145–298. A helpful study of the origins of welfare is Theda Skocpol, *Protecting Soldiers and Mothers: The Political Origins of Social Policy in the United States* (Cambridge, Mass.: Harvard University Press, 1992).

12. Joseph B. Ely, *The American Dream* (Boston: Bruce Humphries, 1944); and Williams, *Federal Aid for Relief*, 177, 217.

13. Williams, *Federal Aid for Relief*, 180–228; Frank R. Kent, *Without Grease: Political Behavior, 1934–1936* (New York: William Morrow, 1936).

14. Ely, *The American Dream*, 148; Jim Powell, *FDR's Folly: How Roosevelt and His New Deal Prolonged the Great Depression* (New York: Crown Forum, 2003), 95; and Jim F. Couch and William F. Shughart II, *The Political Economy of the New Deal* (Northampton, Mass.: Edward Elgar, 1998). I have benefited from discussions on New Deal relief with Professor Couch.

15. Ely, *The American Dream*, 180.

16. Samuel I. Rosenman, ed., *The Public Papers and Addresses of Franklin D. Roosevelt* (New York: Random House, 1938), IV, 19; James S. Olson, *Historical Dictionary of the New Deal* (Westport, Conn.: Greenwood, 1985), 147. Historian Bonnie Schwartz argued that the CWA did better than other New Deal relief agencies in matching the skills of the applicants with the needs of the jobs. One of her points is that the CWA was heavily run by engineers and industrial managers, not social workers. See Schwartz, *The Civil Works Administration, 1933–1934* (Princeton, N.J.: Princeton University Press, 1984).

17. Olson, *Historical Dictionary of the New Deal*, 549; Kent, *Without Grease*, 188–89; Nick Taylor, *American Made: The Enduring Legacy of the WPA* (New York: Bantam, 2008).

18. Kent, *Without Grease*, 189. John Faulkner, the brother of the Pulitzer Prize–winning William Faulkner, was a project engineer for the WPA in Missis-

sippi and observed the negative results firsthand. He later wrote a novel to portray the WPA. See John Faulkner, *Men Working* (Athens: University of Georgia Press, 1996 [1941]).

19. Henry Hazlitt, *Economics in One Lesson* (New Rochelle, N.Y.: Arlington House, 1979 [1946]), 32–33.

20. Hazlitt, *Economics in One Lesson*, 33.

21. Roy G. Blakey and Gladys C. Blakey, *The Federal Income Tax* (London: Longmans, Green & Co., 1940).

22. Olson, *Historical Dictionary of the New Deal*, 549; Kent, *Without Grease*, 133, 188–89. Many historians have recognized the corruption of the WPA. For a brief defense of Hopkins, see John Joseph Wallis, Price V. Fishback, and Shawn Kantor, "Politics, Relief, and Reform: Roosevelt's Efforts to Control Corruption and Political Manipulation during the New Deal," in Edward L. Glaesar and Claudia Goldin, eds., *Corruption and Reform: Lessons from America's Economic History* (Chicago: University of Chicago Press, 2006), 343–72.

23. Morgenthau Diary, April 12, 1938, RPL.

24. Seligman died in 1933, but Clyde Tingley, who was elected governor of New Mexico in 1934, explicitly pursued Seligman's strategy during the campaign and said that "only by returning a solid Democratic front can New Mexico get its full share of the money to be distributed by the federal government in the next two years" (*Washington Post*, October 10, 1935). See also James Patterson, *The New Deal and the States* (Princeton, N.J.: Princeton University Press, 1969), 82–83.

25. Gavin Wright, "The Political Economy of the New Deal Spending: An Econometric Analysis," *Review of Economics and Statistics* 59 (February 1974), 30–38. I would like to thank Jim Powell for calling my attention to this article.

26. Couch and Shughart, *The Political Economy of the New Deal*, 109; Lyle W. Dorsett, *Franklin D. Roosevelt and the City Bosses* (Port Washington, N.Y.: Kennikat Press, 1977), 102, 104.

27. *Newark Evening News*, October 19, 1938, in "WPA—Political Coercion, New Jersey," File 610, National Archives, College Park, Maryland.

28. Robert Hall to Harry Hopkins, October 29, 1938, in "WPA—Political Coercion, New Jersey," File 610, National Archives.

29. Clinton Hoffman to Aubrey Williams, October 31, 1938, and Aubrey Williams to Clinton Hoffman, November 8, 1938, in "WPA—Political Coercion, New Jersey," File 610, National Archives.

30. Mrs. William F. Reid to Franklin Roosevelt, February 11, 1939, and Elisa-

beth Reasoner to Mrs. William F. Reid, February 28, 1939, in "WPA—
Political Coercion, New Jersey," File 610, National Archives.

31. Aubrey Williams to Alicia Medilo, September 30, 1938, in "WPA—
Political Coercion, New Jersey," File 610, National Archives.

32. *Newark Evening News*, September 8, 1938, as quoted in telegram to Harry
Hopkins, in "WPA—Political Coercion, New Jersey," File 610, National Archives.

33. Sadie M. Kearney to Harry Hopkins, June 27, 1938, in "WPA—Political
Coercion, New Jersey," File 610, National Archives.

34. *Philadelphia Inquirer*, July 17, 1936. In campaigning for Alf Landon for president in 1936, Governor Ely said, "the Rooseveltian party has forsaken the
principles of the Democratic party." See also Patterson, *The New Deal and
the States*, 59.

35. Ely, *The American Dream*, 128; and Gorvine, "The New Deal in Massachusetts," 23, 27.

36. Wilbur L. Cross, *Connecticut Yankee* (New Haven, Conn.: Yale University
Press, 1943), 283–84.

37. Cross, *Connecticut Yankee*, 344.

38. Cross, *Connecticut Yankee*, 370. Other New Deal politicians encouraged, or
at least permitted, their names to be immortalized on public projects. The
presence of Norris Dam, Lake Barkley, the Joseph C. O'Mahoney Federal
Building, and McCarran International Airport, just to name a few, give testimony to that.

39. Cross, *Connecticut Yankee*, 281.

40. Monroe L. Billington, *Thomas P. Gore: The Blind Senator from Oklahoma*
(Lawrence: University of Kansas Press, 1967), 149.

41. Billington, *Thomas P. Gore*, 169–70.

42. Keith Bryant, Jr., "Oklahoma and the New Deal," in Braeman et al., eds., *The
New Deal*, 182–83.

43. Bryant, "Oklahoma and the New Deal," 166–97; Gavin Wright, "Political
Economy of New Deal Spending," 35; Powell, *FDR's Folly*, 101.

Chapter 7: More Public Programs That Fell Short

1. Felix Frankfurter to Arthur M. Schlesinger, Jr., June 18, 1963, in Felix Frank-
furter Papers, LC. See also Fulton Oursler, *Behold This Dreamer! An Autobi-
ography* (Boston: Little, Brown, 1964), 390; Samuel I. Rosenman, ed., *The
Public Papers and Addresses of Franklin D. Roosevelt* (New York: Random
House, 1938), I, 646. See also Leonard Mosley, *Lindbergh: A Biography*
(Garden City, N.Y.: Doubleday, 1976), 173–78; W. David Lewis and Wesley

Phillips Newton, *Delta: The History of an Airline* (Athens: University of Georgia Press, 1979), 24–29, 42–43.

2. Lewis and Newton, *Delta*, 25–29.

3. Franklin Roosevelt to Hugo Black, June 19, 1935, in Black Papers, LC; and Lewis and Newton, *Delta*, 42.

4. See *Scottish Rite News Bureau* (newsletters), January 22, 1934, and March 19, 1934, in Hugo Black Papers, LC; James A. Farley, *Jim Farley's Story* (New York: Whittlesey House, 1948), 46–48.

5. Edward V. Rickenbacker, *Rickenbacker: An Autobiography* (Englewood Cliffs, N.J.: Prentice-Hall, 1967), 184; Gary Dean Best, *Pride, Prejudice, and Politics: Roosevelt vs. Recovery, 1933–1938* (Westport, Conn: Praeger, 1991), 59.

6. Rickenbacker, *Rickenbacker*, 186–87; W. David Lewis, *Eddie Rickenbacker* (Baltimore: Johns Hopkins University Press, 2005), 312–13; A. Scott Berg, *Lindbergh* (New York: G. P. Putnam's Sons, 1998), 293.

7. Rickenbacker, *Rickenbacker*, 187.

8. Max Freedman, *Roosevelt & Frankfurter: Their Correspondence, 1928–1945* (Boston: Little, Brown, 1967), 210, 193. See also, Berg, *Lindbergh*, 294.

9. Rickenbacker, *Rickenbacker*, 190; Berg, *Lindbergh*, 295.

10. Donald J. Lisio, *The President and Protest: Hoover, Conspiracy, and the Bonus Riot* (Columbia: University of Missouri Press, 1974), 285.

11. Gary Dean Best, *FDR and the Bonus Marchers, 1933–1935* (Westport, Conn.: Praeger, 1992), xiv, 14. Best is my major source for the story of the Florida veterans. Also useful is Willie Drye, *Storm of the Century: The Labor Day Hurricane of 1935* (Washington, D.C.: National Geographic, 2002).

12. Best, *Bonus Marchers*, 73, 79, 78, 74, 102; Drye, *Storm of the Century*, 159–69.

13. Best, *Bonus Marchers*, 114, 128; Drye, *Storm of the Century*, 210.

14. Best, *Bonus Marchers*, 132.

15. Henry Ford, in collaboration with Samuel Crowther, *My Life and Work* (Garden City, N.Y.: Doubleday, 1926), 184; Allan Nevins and Frank Ernest Hill, *Ford: Expansion and Challenge, 1915–1933* (New York: Charles Scribner's Sons, 1957), 300–23.

16. William E. Leuchtenburg, *Franklin D. Roosevelt and the New Deal* (New York: Harper & Row, 1963), 165.

17. Henry Hazlitt, *Economics in One Lesson* (New Rochelle, N.Y.: Arlington House Publishers, 1979), 36.

18. William U. Chandler, *The Myth of TVA: Conservation and Development in the Tennessee Valley, 1933–1980* (Cambridge, Mass.: Ballinger, 1984), 50–53.

19. Chandler, *The Myth of TVA*, 57–59, 73–80.
20. Jim Powell, *FDR's Folly: How Roosevelt and His New Deal Prolonged the Great Depression* (New York: Crown Forum, 2003), 149–50.

Chapter 8: Financial Interference

1. John M. Blum, *From the Morgenthau Diaries: Years of Crisis, 1928–1938* (Boston: Houghton Mifflin, 1959), 68–74.
2. Jim Powell, *FDR's Folly: How Roosevelt and His New Deal Prolonged the Great Depression* (New York: Crown Forum, 2003), 65–74.
3. George Warren and Frank Pearson, *Prices* (New York: John Wiley & Sons, 1933).
4. Powell, *FDR's Folly*, 65–74; William E. Leuchtenburg, *Franklin D. Roosevelt and the New Deal* (New York: Harper & Row, 1963), 79–81.
5. Morgenthau Diary, January 14, 1935, RPL.
6. Morgenthau Diary, January 14, 1935, RPL; Leuchtenburg, *Roosevelt*, 80–81; Powell, *FDR's Folly*, 74.
7. *Washington Post*, January 13, 1935.
8. Morgenthau Diary, January 14, 1935, RPL.
9. *New York Herald Tribune*, February 19, 1935; Amanda Smith, ed., *Hostage to Fortune: The Letters of Joseph P. Kennedy* (New York: Viking, 2001), 149–51. Justice James McReynolds, who was in the minority on this vote, called the verdict "a repudiation of our national obligation." He further added, "It does not seem too much to say the Constitution is gone." For a summary of the Gold Cases, see James W. Ely, Jr., "Gold Clause Cases," in Kermit L. Hall, ed., *The Oxford Companion to the Supreme Court of the United States* (New York: Oxford University Press, 1992), 341.
10. Milton Friedman, *Money Mischief: Episodes in Monetary History* (New York: Harcourt Brace Jovanovich, 1992).
11. A good, brief account of the Silver Purchase Act is in Leuchtenburg, *Franklin D. Roosevelt and the New Deal*, 82–83. For fuller accounts, see John A. Brennan, *Silver and the First New Deal* (Reno: University of Nevada Press, 1969), 109, 119–36; Allan S. Everest, *Morgenthau, the New Deal, and Silver: A Story of Pressure Politics* (New York: King's Crown Press, 1950), 32–50; and Ray B. Westerfield, *Our Silver Debacle* (New York: Ronald Press, 1936), 35–105. See also Friedman, *Money Mischief*, 165.
12. Harold L. Ickes, *The Secret Diary of Harold L. Ickes* (New York: Simon & Schuster, 1954), II, 291–92; Leuchtenburg, *Franklin D. Roosevelt and the New Deal*, 82–83; Everest, *Morgenthau, the New Deal, and Silver*, 164–75.
13. League of Nations, *World Economic Survey, 1938/39* (Geneva, 1939),

192–93; James S. Olson, *Historical Dictionary of the New Deal* (Westport, Conn.: Greenwood, 1985), 410–11.

14. Powell, *FDR's Folly*, 53–64. My interpretation on banking is more sympathetic to Roosevelt than Powell's. In part, I am assuming the insurance charges the government made on the bankers were adequate to cover the payouts when banks failed. A helpful source is George Benston, *The Separation of Commercial and Investment Banking: The Glass-Steagall Act Revisited and Reconsidered* (New York: Oxford University Press, 1995). Roosevelt, by the way, did not particularly favor deposit insurance.

15. Powell, *FDR's Folly*, 105–12. See also Raymond Moley, *The First New Deal* (New York: Harcourt, Brace, & World, 1966), 306.

Chapter 9: Safety Net or Quagmire?

1. Hadley Arkes, *The Return of George Sutherland: Restoring a Jurisprudence of Natural Rights* (Princeton, N.J.: Princeton University Press, 1994), 12–14; Kermit L. Hall, ed., *The Oxford Companion to the Supreme Court* (New York: Oxford University Press, 1992), 9.

2. Arkes, *The Return of George Sutherland*, 12–14. For information on Willie Lyons, see *Adkins v. Children's Hospital*, 261 U.S. 525 (1923). An excellent history of the early minimum wage laws is Clifford F. Thies, "The First Minimum Wage Laws," *Cato Journal* 10 (Winter 1991), 715–46. Thies argues for some relationship between minimum wages and unemployment.

3. Bernard Bellush, *The Failure of the NRA* (New York: Norton, 1975), 160–79; Robert K. Fleck, "The Marginal Effect of New Deal Relief Work on County-Level Unemployment Statistics," *Journal of Economic History* 59 (September 1999), 659–87; and William A. Sundstrom, "Last Hired, First Fired? Unemployment and Urban Black Workers during the Great Depression," *Journal of Economic History* 52 (June 1992), 415–29.

4. I describe this sectional split on minimum wage in Burton W. Folsom, Jr., "The Minimum Wage's Disreputable Origins," *Wall Street Journal*, May 27, 1998, A22. The material in the next four paragraphs comes from this article.

5. An excellent history of social security is in Carolyn L. Weaver, *The Crisis in Social Security: Economic and Political Origins* (Durham, N.C.: Duke Press Policy Studies, 1982). On Townsend and the relief problem, see Edwin Amenta, *Bold Relief: Institutional Politics and the Origins of Modern American Social Policy* (Princeton, N.J.: Princeton University Press, 1998).

6. Jim Powell, *FDR's Folly: How Roosevelt and His New Deal Prolonged the Great Depression* (New York: Crown Forum, 2003), 180.

7. U.S. Bureau of the Census, *Historical Statistics of the United States: Colonial*

Times to 1970 (Washington, D.C.: U.S. Government Printing Office, 1975), I, 55.

8. "Research Note #3: Details of Ida May Fuller's Payroll Tax Contributions," at www.ssa.gov/history/idapayroll.html.

9. Frank Freidel, *Franklin D. Roosevelt: A Rendezvous with Destiny* (Boston: Little, Brown, 1990), 150.

10. Burton Folsom, "Revive the Clark Amendment to Privatize Social Security," *Human Events*, July 10, 1998, 20. For triggering my interest in the Clark Amendment, and for information on the subject, I am indebted to Weaver, *The Crisis in Social Security*.

11. Folsom, "Revive the Clark Amendment." I am using this article for my next two paragraphs. Chile has a system of private insurance, and in the first twenty-two years of operation, Chile has averaged almost 10 percent return above inflation—a rate that is perhaps unsustainable. For information on the relatively low rate of return for the U.S. social security system, see www.ncpa.org/pub/st/st277 and www.socialsecurity.org/pubs/ssps/ssp31.pdf.

12. For background on labor and "liberty of contract," see Howard Dickman, *Industrial Democracy in America: Ideological Origins of National Labor Relations Policy* (LaSalle, Ill.: Open Court, 1987), 70–77, 227–29. The Pitney quote is in Powell, *FDR's Folly*, 190.

13. Dickman, *Industrial Democracy in America*, 238–41, 327–30. See also James S. Olson, *Historical Dictionary of the 1920s* (Westport, Conn.: Greenwood, 1988), 254–55. A useful recent book is George C. Leef, *Free Choice for Workers: A History of the Right-to-Work Movement* (Ottawa, Ill.: Jameson, 2005).

14. Joseph J. Huthmacher, *Senator Robert F. Wagner and the Rise of Urban Liberalism* (New York: Atheneum, 1971), 157–61; Dickman, *Industrial Democracy in America*, 258–61; and George I. Lovell, *Legislative Deferrals: Statutory Ambiguity, Judicial Power, and American Democracy* (Cambridge, England: Cambridge University Press, 2003). A useful book is Paul Moreno, *Black Americans and Organized Labor: A New History* (Baton Rouge: Louisiana State University Press, 2006).

15. Huthmacher, *Senator Robert F. Wagner and the Rise of Urban Liberalism*, 189–98; Dickman, *Industrial Democracy in America*, 257–86, 337–44.

16. John Barnard, *Walter Reuther and the Rise of the Auto Workers* (Boston: Little, Brown, 1983), 36–53; Melvyn Dubofsky and Warren Van Tine, *John L. Lewis: A Biography* (New York: Quadrangle, 1977), 254–72.

17. *Washington Post*, January 26, 1937, 2, 9, and January 27, 1936, 1.

18. Barnard, *Walter Reuther and the Rise of the Auto Workers*, 36–53, 60, 65–69, 102–09.

19. Moreno, *Black Americans and Organized Labor*, 82–175; Barnard, *Walter*

Reuther and the Rise of the Auto Workers; Dubofsky and Van Tine, *John L. Lewis,* 494–97; and Walter E. Williams, *The State Against Blacks* (New York: McGraw-Hill, 1982).

Chapter 10: No Free Ride

1. An excellent source, written during the New Deal years, on the "tax incidence" of excise and income taxes is Henry C. Simons, *Personal Income Taxation* (Chicago: University of Chicago Press, 1938).
2. U.S. Bureau of the Census, *Historical Statistics of the United States: Colonial Times to 1970* (Washington, D.C.: U.S. Government Printing Office, 1975), II, 1107.
3. U.S. Bureau of the Census, *Historical Statistics,* II, 1107; Mark H. Leff, *The Limits of Symbolic Reform: The New Deal and Taxation, 1933–1939* (London and New York: Cambridge University Press, 1984), 23, 36–37.
4. Leff, *The Limits of Symbolic Reform,* 17. See also Simons, *Personal Income Taxation,* 40. I would like to thank Professor Leff for alerting me to the Simons book.
5. Henry Morgenthau Diary, February 5, 1936, RPL. Other Roosevelt friends also condemned excise taxes as regressive. See Robert Jackson, "The Rich Get Richer," *New Republic,* August 28, 1935, 68–72; and Jackson, "The People's Business: The Truth about Taxes," *Forum* 95 (January 1936), 22–26. For an excellent book on tax rebellion in the 1930s, see David T. Beito, *Taxpayers in Revolt: Tax Resistance during the Great Depression* (Chapel Hill: University of North Carolina Press, 1989).
6. Leff, *The Limits of Symbolic Reform,* 22, 34–35; Tun Yuan Hu, *The Liquor Tax in the United States, 1791–1947* (New York: Columbia University Press, 1950), 84–91; Donald Boudreaux, "The Politics of Prohibition," July 25, 2007, at www.pittsburghlive.com/x/pittsburghtrib/search/print_518872 .html.
7. Morgenthau Diary, February 6, 1936, RPL; Leff, *The Limits of Symbolic Reform,* 40–41; Henry Hazlitt, *Economics in One Lesson* (New Rochelle, N.Y.: Arlington House, 1979), 209–10.
8. Leff, *The Limits of Symbolic Reform,* 27–30. For an example of a jeweler opposing the jewelry tax, see T. A. Hannis to George Norris, April 9, 1932, Norris Papers, LC. In another letter to Senator Norris, Omaha grocer Paul Gallagher wrote, "The tax of 2 [cents] on [bank] checks will also work a direct hardship: not only because of the enormous number of checks that any business organization is forced to issue, but because individuals will hold up bills for months, and pay all at one time, with one check" (June 14, 1932, Norris Papers, LC).

9. "Statements on Taxes by Members of This Administration in 1939," in Morgenthau Diary, January 5, 1939, RPL.

10. Roy G. Blakey and Gladys C. Blakey, *The Federal Income Tax* (London: Longmans, Green, 1940), 366–82.

11. Andrew Mellon, *Taxation: The People's Business* (New York: Macmillan, 1924), 13; Lawrence L. Murray III, "Andrew Mellon: Secretary of the Treasury, 1921–1932: A Study in Policy" (Ph. D. diss., Michigan State University, 1970), 111–17.

12. Mellon, *Taxation*, 16–17; Andrew Mellon, "Taxing Energy and Initiative," *Independent* 112 (March 29, 1924), 168.

13. Mellon, *Taxation*, 9, 51–59 (quotation is on 9).

14. Blakey and Blakey, *The Federal Income Tax*, 270–75, 298–301; Hannah Campbell, *Why Did They Name It?* (New York: Fleet, 1964), 200–7; Alan Reynolds, "What Do We Know about the Great Crash?" *National Review*, November 9, 1979, 1416–21.

15. Benjamin G. Rader, "Federal Taxation in the 1920s: A Re-examination," *Historian* 33 (May 1971), 415–35. I give a summary of the Mellon Plan in *The Myth of the Robber Barons* (Herndon, Va.: Young America's Foundation, 2007), 103–20.

16. Roosevelt was interested in the ideas of prominent British economist John Maynard Keynes, and the two of them even had a meeting once. See Keynes, *The General Theory of Employment, Interest, and Money* (London: Macmillan, 1936). See also Daniel R. Fusfeld, *The Economic Thought of Franklin D. Roosevelt and the Origins of the New Deal* (New York: Columbia University Press, 1954); Samuel I. Rosenman, ed., *The Public Papers and Addresses of Franklin D. Roosevelt* (New York: Random House, 1938), I, 742–56.

17. Gary Dean Best, *Pride, Prejudice, and Politics: Roosevelt versus Recovery, 1933–1938* (Westport, Conn.: Praeger, 1991), 106.

18. Herman E. Krooss, *Executive Opinion: What Business Leaders Said and Thought, 1920s–1960s* (Garden City, N.Y.: Doubleday, 1970); Raymond Moley Journal, May 2 and 3, 1936, Hoover Institution, hereinafter HI.

19. Rosenman, *Public Papers*, IV, 272.

20. Krooss, *Executive Opinion*, 161–63, 173, 188–96.

21. Best, *Pride, Prejudice, and Politics*, 105–6; Krooss, *Executive Opinion*, 182–201; and Robert F. Burk, *The Corporate State and the Broker State: The DuPonts and American National Politics, 1925–1940* (Cambridge, Mass.: Harvard University Press, 1990).

22. Rosenman, *Public Papers*, V, 15–16.

23. Alfred G. Buehler, *The Undistributed Profits Tax* (New York: McGraw-Hill, 1937); and George E. Lent, *The Impact of the Undistributed Profits Tax*,

1936–1937 (New York: Columbia University Press, 1948). See also Lawrence W. Reed, "Great Myths of the Great Depression," Mackinac Center for Public Policy, 2005.

24. Krooss, *Executive Opinion*, 193; Leff, *The Limits of Symbolic Reform*, 173.

25. Leff, *The Limits of Symbolic Reform*, 187; Kirk H. Porter and Donald B. Johnson, *National Party Platforms, 1840–1968* (Urbana: University of Illinois Press, 1970), 360.

26. Raymond Moley Journal, May 2 and 3, 1936, HI.

27. Raymond Moley Journal, May 2 and 3, 1936, HI.

28. Rosenman, *Public Papers* V, 231–35. In drawing his picture of "economic royalists," Roosevelt was influenced by Adolf Berle and Louis Brandeis. See Adolf A. Berle, Jr., and Gardiner Means, *The Modern Corporation and Private Property* (New York: Macmillan, 1932); and Louis Brandeis, *Other People's Money and How the Bankers Use It* (New York: Frederick A. Stokes, 1914).

29. Rosenman, *Public Papers*, V, 568–69.

30. Rosenman, *Public Papers*, V, 566–73, 401–8.

31. Blakey and Blakey, *Federal Income Tax*, 428–35; Leff, *The Limits of Symbolic Reform*, 202; Best, *Pride, Prejudice, and Politics*, 181; Richard K. Vedder and Lowell E. Gallaway, *Out of Work: Unemployment and Government in Twentieth-Century America* (New York: Holmes & Meier, 1993), 77.

32. Donald W. Baker to Roosevelt, November 9, 1937, Roosevelt Papers, OF 172, RPL. In just two days, Roosevelt received the Baker letter, and these as well: W. H. Gehm to Roosevelt, November 10, 1937 ("The present economic recession is predicated on FEAR engendered by words spoken by you"); Frederick H. Thomas to Roosevelt, November 10, 1937 ("GIVE American business back to the people who know how to run it ably and honestly"); and John J. O'Brien to Roosevelt, November 9, 1937 ("I beg you to stop setting up the lowest class in the country against the other two-thirds"), Roosevelt Papers, OF 172, RPL.

33. Adolf Berle to Peter Nehemkis, November 10, 1937. In "Memorandum," April 1, 1938, Berle said, "Practically no business group in the country has escaped investigation or other attack in the last five years. . . . The result has been shattered morale." See also Berle entries of October 13, 1937, and October 25, 1937, in Adolf Berle Diary, RPL.

34. Blakey and Blakey, *Federal Income Tax*, 401–27, 436–53; Raymond Moley Journal, May 2 and May 3, 1936, HI.

35. Morgenthau Diary, November 4, 1937, RPL. One possibility here is that Roosevelt took his 2,000 figure from Berle and Means, *The Modern Corporation*, 46. Berle argued in his book that in 1930 some 2,000 directors of 200 corporations had effective control of American business.

36. Morgenthau Diary, November 8, 1937, RPL.

37. "Memorandum of Secretary Morgenthau's Statement to the President at Cabinet on Thursday, February 16, 1939," in Morgenthau Diary, February 16, 1939, RPL.

38. Morgenthau Diary, March 6, 1939, RPL. See also Bernard Baruch to Harry Hopkins, September 28, 1937, in Hopkins Papers, RPL.

39. Morgenthau Diary, March 6, 1939, RPL.

40. Morgenthau Diary, March 8, 1939, RPL; *New York Times*, March 17, 1939; Vedder and Gallaway, *Out of Work*, 77.

41. Morgenthau Diary, March 8, 1939, RPL.

42. Morgenthau Diary, March 8, 1939, RPL.

43. Morgenthau Diary, March 8, 1939, RPL.

44. Morgenthau Diary, March 8, 1939, RPL.

45. Morgenthau Diary, March 8, 1939, February 16, 1939, and November 8, 1937, RPL.

46. "Re Tax Statement," in Morgenthau Diary, May 4, 1939, RPL.

47. Morgenthau Diary, May 9, 1939, RPL.

48. Krooss, *Executive Opinion*, 189–90.

49. "Strangled Rabbit," *Time*, May 22, 1939; Morgenthau Diary, March 8, 1939, and January 5, 1939, RPL.

50. Leff, *The Limits of Symbolic Reform*, 290.

Chapter 11: The IRS

1. Elliott Roosevelt, *A Rendezvous with Destiny: The Roosevelts of the White House* (New York: G. P. Putnam's Sons, 1975), 102; Roy C. Blakey and Gladys C. Blakey, *The Federal Income Tax* (London: Longmans, Green, 1940); and U.S. Bureau of Census, *Historical Statistics of the United States* (Washington, D.C.: U.S. Government Printing Office, 1975), II, 1107.

2. A good study of Long is in Alan Brinkley, *Voices of Protest: Huey Long, Father Coughlin, and the Great Depression* (New York: Knopf, 1982).

3. T. Harry Williams, *Huey Long* (New York: Knopf, 1969), 635.

4. Williams, *Huey Long*, 795.

5. Williams, *Huey Long*, 639.

6. Williams, *Huey Long*, 638.

7. Williams, *Huey Long*, 692–706; Melvin G. Holli, *The Wizard of Washington: Emil Hurja, Franklin Roosevelt, and the Birth of Public Opinion Polling* (New York: Palgrave, 2002), 66–67.

8. Williams, *Huey Long*, 815–16.

9. Holli, *The Wizard of Washington*, 66–67.

10. Elmer Irey, *Tax Dodgers: The Inside Story of the T-Men's War with America's*

Political and Underworld Hoodlums (New York: Greenberg, 1948), 93–94, 97.

11. An excellent account of Roosevelt, Huey Long, and the IRS is Harnett T. Kane, *Louisiana Hayride* (Gretna, La.: Pelican, 1998 [1941]), 164–87. See also Irey, *Tax Dodgers*, 88–117; Williams, *Huey Long*, 794.

12. Irey, *Tax Dodgers*, 98; Kane, *Louisiana Hayride*, 165–68; David Burnham, *A Law Unto Itself: Power, Politics, and the IRS* (New York: Random House, 1989), 231–36 (quotation on 234); and Edgar Eugene Robinson, *They Voted for Roosevelt: The Presidential Vote, 1932–1944* (Palo Alto, Calif.: Stanford University Press, 1947).

13. Roosevelt, *A Rendezvous with Destiny*, 102.

14. Roosevelt, *A Rendezvous with Destiny*, 97; and Burnham, *A Law Unto Itself*, 235. On Coughlin, see Francis Biddle, *In Brief Authority* (Westport, Conn.: Greenwood, 1976), 238, 243–48; and Thomas Fleming, *The New Dealers' War* (New York: Basic Books, 2001), 113–14. During World War II, Roosevelt finally was able to squelch Coughlin's criticism. U.S. Attorney General Francis Biddle had FDIC director Leo Crowley persuade Edward Mooney to use his position as archbishop of Detroit to silence Coughlin.

15. Roosevelt, *A Rendezvous with Destiny*, 175–76; Burnham, *A Law Unto Itself*, 235; and Jerre Mangione, *An Ethnic at Large: Memoirs of America in the Thirties and Forties* (New York: G. P. Putnam's Sons, 1978), 248.

16. Hamilton Fish, *Memoirs of an American Patriot* (Washington, D.C.: Regnery, 1991), 142–44, 157.

17. Irey, *Tax Dodgers*, 245–70.

18. Irey, *Tax Dodgers*, 269; Robinson, *They Voted for Roosevelt*, 128.

19. Lyle W. Dorsett, *Franklin D. Roosevelt and the City Bosses* (Port Washington, N.Y.: Kennikat Press, 1977), 98–111.

20. Robinson, *They Voted for Roosevelt*, 128–29.

21. Dorsett, *Franklin D. Roosevelt and the City Bosses*, 102, 104–5 (quotation on 102); Robinson, *They Voted for Roosevelt*, 128.

22. Dorsett, *Franklin D. Roosevelt and the City Bosses*, 98, 106.

23. Dorsett, *Franklin D. Roosevelt and the City Bosses*, 104.

24. Dorsett, *Franklin D. Roosevelt and the City Bosses*, 103.

25. Dorsett, *Franklin D. Roosevelt and the City Bosses*, 104.

26. Johnson's background is capably presented by Robert A. Caro, *The Years of Lyndon Johnson: The Path to Power* (New York: Knopf, 1982).

27. Caro, *The Path to Power*, 501, 742–53; Robert A. Caro, *The Years of Lyndon Johnson: Means of Ascent* (New York: Knopf, 1990), 15, 16, 74, 272–75, 285–86.

28. Caro, *The Path to Power*, 742–53. See also Burnham, *A Law Unto Itself*, 222–23.

29. Lyle W. Dorsett, *The Pendergast Machine* (New York: Oxford University Press, 1968).

30. Dorsett, *Franklin D. Roosevelt and the City Bosses*, 76; Robinson, *They Voted for Roosevelt*, 118.

31. Dorsett, *Franklin D. Roosevelt and the City Bosses*, 70–82; Irey, *Tax Dodgers*, 225–44 (quotation on 230).

32. Dorsett, *Franklin D. Roosevelt and the City Bosses*, 70–82.

33. Gary Dean Best, *Pride, Prejudice, and Politics: Roosevelt versus Recovery, 1933–1938* (Westport, Conn.: Praeger, 1991), 151; Morgenthau Diary, May 14, 1937, RPL.

34. David E. Koskoff, *The Mellons* (New York: Thomas Y. Crowell, 1978).

35. Irey, *Tax Dodgers*, xii–xiii; David Cannadine, *Mellon: An American Life* (New York: Knopf, 2006), 509–15; and Burnham, *A Law Unto Itself*, 229–30.

36. John Morton Blum, *From the Morgenthau Diaries: Years of Crisis, 1928–1938* (Boston: Houghton Mifflin, 1959), I, 324–25.

37. Cannadine, *Mellon*, 509–13; Burnham, *A Law Unto Itself*, 229–30.

38. See Christopher Ogden, *Legacy: A Biography of Moses and Walter Annenberg* (Boston: Little, Brown, 1999); and John Cooney, *The Annenbergs: The Salvaging of a Tainted Dynasty* (New York: Simon & Schuster, 1982).

39. *Philadelphia Inquirer*, July 22, 1936, July 19, 1936, (taxpayers are "paying through the nose for New Deal follies, experiments, and extravagances"). See also Ogden, *Legacy*, 191; J. David Stern, *Memoirs of a Maverick Publisher* (New York: Simon & Schuster, 1962), 186–203, 248–50, 257–62.

40. Ogden, *Legacy*, 212–13; Bascom N. Timmons, *Jesse H. Jones: The Man and the Statesman* (Westport, Conn.: Greenwood, 1975 [1956]), 249–50. See also Morgenthau Diary, April 11, 1939, RPL.

41. Ogden, *Legacy*, 212–13, 239. Having put Annenberg in jail, Roosevelt was determined to keep him there. Francis Biddle, the president's attorney general, made sure Annenberg's appeals for parole were denied. Harold Ickes, the secretary of the interior, wrote the president, "In his much smaller sphere, Annenberg has been as cruel, as ruthless and as lawless as Hitler himself." Roosevelt responded, "I think you are right about Mr. Annenberg."

42. Blum, *Morgenthau Diaries*, I, 335.

43. Roosevelt, *A Rendezvous with Destiny*, 174–75.

44. Blum, *Morgenthau Diaries*, I, 327–37; Roosevelt, *A Rendezvous with Destiny*, 175.

45. Blum, *Morgenthau Diaries*, I, 327–29, 333–34; Morgenthau Diary, May 26, 1937, RPL.

46. Roosevelt, *A Rendezvous with Destiny*, 200–1, 213; Leff, *The Limits of Symbolic Reform*, 59.

47. Roosevelt, *A Rendezvous with Destiny*, 175. Roosevelt's tax returns are available for 1934–37 at www.taxhistory.org.

Chapter 12: Patronage Transformed

1. James A. Farley, *Jim Farley's Story* (New York: Whittlesley House, 1948), 35; Melvin G. Holli, *The Wizard of Washington: Emil Hurja, Franklin Roosevelt, and the Birth of Public Opinion Polling* (New York: Palgrave, 2002), 58.
2. Farley, *Jim Farley's Story*, 46–68; Holli, *The Wizard of Washington*, 50–72.
3. Holli, *The Wizard of Washington*, 59–60.
4. Mark Sullivan to Herbert Hoover, October 18, 1934 and Sullivan to Hoover, May 18, 1934, in Sullivan Papers, HI. See also *New York Herald Tribune*, November 1, 1934, 2. Oregon senator Charles McNary, the Republican minority leader, was also somewhat skeptical of the president's economic and political strategy in 1934. See Charles McNary to James Couzens, August 14, 1934, and Couzens to McNary, August 23, 1934, in McNary Papers, LC.
5. Holli, *The Wizard of Washington*, 62.
6. Holli, *The Wizard of Washington*, 62; David Lawrence, *Stumbling into Socialism* (New York: D. Appleton–Century, 1935), 196.
7. *Portland Press Herald*, September 9, 1934, Section B, 10; and September 6, 1934, 6.
8. *Portland Press Herald*, September 6, 1934, 6.
9. "Blame it on Santa Claus," *Baltimore Sun*, September 29, 1934, 10; Harold L. Ickes, *The Secret Diary of Harold L. Ickes* (New York: Simon & Schuster, 1953), I, 189–91. I am indebted to Gary Dean Best for alerting me to the article in the *Baltimore Sun*.
10. *Bangor Daily News*, September 1, 1934, 1; and September 3, 1934, 3.
11. *Baltimore Sun*, September 29, 1934, 10; *Washington Post*, October 31, 1934, 1, 7; *New York Herald Tribune*, November 1, 1934; and *Bangor Daily News*, September 11, 1934, 1. See also Lawrence, *Stumbling into Socialism*, 193.
12. "Astounding Democratic Victory," in *Portland Press Herald*, September 12, 1934, 12, and September 13, 1934, 8.
13. *Daily Kennebec Journal* [Augusta], September 13, 1934, 6; *Chicago Tribune*, October 9, 1934, 7, and October 8, 1934, 8.
14. *Washington Post*, October 24, 1934; and Gary Dean Best, *Pride, Prejudice, and Politics: Roosevelt versus Recovery, 1933–1938* (Westport, Conn.: Praeger, 1991), 77–78.
15. *Chicago Tribune*, October 1, 1934, 1.
16. *New York Herald Tribune*, November 1, 1934, 16; *Washington Post*, October 31, 1934, 1, 7; *Chicago Tribune*, November 3, 1934, 14.

17. "An Audit of Election Returns," *Chicago Tribune*, November 16, 1934, 26; and David M. Kennedy, *Freedom from Fear: The American People in Depression and War, 1929–1945* (New York: Oxford University Press, 1999), 216–17.

18. "Hell Bent for Santa Claus," *New York Herald Tribune*, November 7, 1934, 26, November 1, 1934, 10; and "An Audit of the Election Returns," *Chicago Tribune*, November 16, 1934, 12.

19. "Exploiting Relief," *Washington Post*, October 23, 1935, 2. See also Holli, *The Wizard of Washington*, 62, 64; and Stanley High, *Roosevelt—And Then?* (New York: Harper & Bros., 1937), 64–175.

20. High, *Roosevelt—And Then?* 13–15, 87–88 (quotation on 15).

21. Holli, *The Wizard of Washington*, 77; Philip J. Funigiello, *Toward a National Power Policy: The New Deal and the Electric Utility Industry, 1933–1941* (Pittsburgh: University of Pittsburgh Press, 1973); and George McJimsey, *The Presidency of Franklin Delano Roosevelt* (Lawrence: University Press of Kansas, 2000), 74–75.

22. Holli, *The Wizard of Washington*, 65–66; Anthony Badger, *The New Deal: The Depression Years, 1933–1940* (New York: Hill & Wang, 1989).

23. *New York Times*, August 8, 1935; "The Farmers' View of the AAA," *St. Louis Post-Dispatch*, January 8, 1936. See also Lawrence, *Stumbling into Socialism*, 195.

24. *New York Times*, August 8, 1935.

25. *New York Times*, August 8, 1935.

26. *New York Times*, November 7, 1935, and November 6, 1935; *Washington Post*, November 6, 1935.

27. *New York Times*, November 7, 1935. The *Washington Post*, October 10, 1935, editorialized, "Few more pernicious influences ever enter into politics than the use of Government expenditures as bait to catch votes."

28. William E. Leuchtenburg, *The FDR Years: On Roosevelt and His Legacy* (New York: Columbia University Press, 1995), 101; Holli, *The Wizard of Washington*, 66–67.

29. *New York Herald Tribune*, August 2, 1936, Section II, Part II. Ten states, in fact, had majorities who believed "the acts and policies of the Roosevelt administration may lead to dictatorship." See also Gary Dean Best, *Pride, Prejudice, and Politics*, 127, 133.

30. John M. Blum, *From the Morgenthau Diaries: Years of Crisis, 1928–1938* (Boston: Houghton Mifflin, 1959), I, 242; *New York Times*, March 3, 1936.

31. Frank R. Kent, *Without Grease: Political Behavior, 1934–1936* (New York: William Morrow, 1936), 100.

32. *Washington Post*, June 15, 1935, 2.

33. Holli, *The Wizard of Washington*, 72.

34. Holli, *The Wizard of Washington*, 72.

35. Thomas E. Dewey, *The Case Against the New Deal* (New York: Harper & Bros., 1940), 91.

36. Dewey, *The Case Against the New Deal*, 93.

37. Blum, ed., *Morgenthau Diaries*, I, 277.

38. Morgenthau Diary, September 24, 1936, and Memo from Edna Lonigan to Morgenthau, October 21, 1936, RPL.

39. Morgenthau Diary, August 25, 1936, RPL.

40. *New York Herald Tribune*, November 1, 1934, 1, 2.

41. Donald R. McCoy, *Landon of Kansas* (Lincoln: University of Nebraska Press, 1966), 217, 300, 295.

42. Hiram Johnson to Hiram Johnson, Jr., September 22, 1936, in Johnson Papers, LC. Johnson's point is well illustrated by a county Democrat leader in California who wrote Senator William McAdoo, "[I] feel that the appropriations for and the erection of the [federal post office] building will be of great assistance to our party during the next campaign." See T. G. Patton to William G. McAdoo, in McAdoo Papers, LC.

43. "Address by the honorable Harold L. Ickes, Secretary of the Interior and administrator of public works, on the occasion of the dedication of the new chemistry building at Howard University, October 26, 1936," in Harold Ickes Papers, LC. See also Raymond Wolters, "The New Deal and the Negro," in John Braeman et al., *The New Deal: The National Level* (Columbus: Ohio State University Press, 1975), 170–217.

44. Paul R. Williams to Dr. Robert C. Weaver, November 3, 1936, and Mordecai Johnson to Ickes, October 31, 1936, in Harold Ickes Papers, LC; Wolters, "The New Deal and the Negro," 210.

45. On Landon's weak speaking voice, see George B. Compton to Landon, May 20, 1936, and Rowland L. Davis to Landon, February 6, 1936, File C, D-E in Landon Papers, Kansas State Historical Society. On Landon's political views, see McCoy, *Landon of Kansas*, 334–35; Thomas L. Stokes, *Chip Off My Shoulder* (Princeton, N.J.: Princeton University Press, 1940), 441–44.

46. McCoy, *Landon of Kansas*, 307–8, 313–52. On Landon's political squeeze, see Landon to Frank Altschul, February 13, 1936, and Frank Altschul to Landon, May 21, 1936, Box 52, Collection 10. See also Bruce Barton to Landon, May 22, 1936, and George Bauer to Landon, March 30, 1936, in Landon Papers, Kansas State Historical Society.

47. Eugene H. Roseboom, *A Short History of Presidential Elections* (New York: Collier, 1967), 192–210.

48. David Lawrence, *Who Were the Eleven Million?* (New York: D. Appleton–Century, 1937), 2–3.

49. Lawrence, *Who Were the Eleven Million?* 7–8.

50. Lawrence, *Who Were the Eleven Million?* 7–48.

51. Lawrence, *Who Were the Eleven Million?* 11–12.

52. Lawrence, *Who Were the Eleven Million?* 14–15.

53. Lawrence, *Who Were the Eleven Million?* 20–25.

54. Lawrence, *Who Were the Eleven Million?* 25–27.

55. Sean Savage, *Roosevelt the Party Leader, 1932–1945* (Lexington: University Press of Kentucky, 1991), 50.

56. Savage, *Roosevelt the Party Leader*, 54–55; Lyle W. Dorsett, *Franklin D. Roosevelt and the City Bosses* (Port Washington, N.Y.: Kennikat Press, 1977), 102–7; Edgar E. Robinson, *They Voted for Roosevelt: The Presidential Vote, 1932–1944* (Palo Alto, Calif.: Stanford University Press, 1947), 128.

Chapter 13: FDR Stumbles

1. The standard work on the Court-packing plan is Joseph Alsop and Turner Catledge, *The 168 Days* (Garden City, N.Y.: Doubleday, Doran, 1938). A recent account sympathetic to Roosevelt is William E. Leuchtenburg, *The Supreme Court Reborn: The Constitutional Revolution in the Age of Roosevelt* (New York: Oxford University Press, 1995). An excellent new book is Marian C. McKenna, *Franklin Roosevelt and the Great Constitutional War: The Court-Packing Crisis of 1937* (New York: Fordham University Press, 2002), 280–82.

2. McKenna, *Franklin Roosevelt and the Great Constitutional War*, 280–82; Burton K. Wheeler, *Yankee from the West* (Garden City, N.Y.: Doubleday, 1962), 321–22.

3. James A. Farley, *Jim Farley's Story* (New York: Whittlesley House, 1948), 88.

4. Claude Denson Pepper, *Pepper: Eyewitness to a Century* (New York: Harcourt Brace Jovanovich, 1987), 59.

5. *New York Times*, July 17, 1937, 1; Farley, *Jim Farley's Story*, 87–89; Martha H. Swain, *Pat Harrison: The New Deal Years* (Jackson: University Press of Mississippi, 1978), 156.

6. Swain, *Pat Harrison*, 156; James K. Libbey, *Dear Alben: Mr. Barkley of Kentucky* (Lexington: University Press of Kentucky, 1979), 73–74.

7. Swain, *Pat Harrison*, 158.

8. Swain, *Pat Harrison*, 158; David McCullough, *Truman* (New York: Simon & Schuster, 1992), 227–29.

9. Farley, *Jim Farley's Story*, 92; Harold L. Ickes, *The Secret Diary of Harold L. Ickes* (New York: Simon & Schuster, 1954), II, 170, 174–75; Grace Tully, *F.D.R., My Boss* (New York: Charles Scribner's Sons, 1949), 225; and Swain, *Pat Harrison*, 159, 286.

10. Charles Michelson, *The Ghost Talks* (New York: G. P. Putnam's Sons, 1944), 182; Swain, *Pat Harrison*, 159, 162, 286.

11. Swain, *Pat Harrison*, 162–63.

12. Swain, *Pat Harrison*, 164.

13. Swain, *Pat Harrison*, 164–66; Ickes, *Secret Diary*, II, 187; Frank R. Kent, *Without Grease: Political Behavior, 1934–1936* (New York: William Morrow, 1936), 167.

14. Farley, *Jim Farley's Story*, 120–22; Raymond Clapper Diary, January 9, 1938, LC.

15. Monica L. Niznik, "Thomas G. Corcoran: The Public Service of Franklin Roosevelt's 'Tommy the Cork'" (Ph. D. diss., University of Notre Dame, 1981), 346–47; David McKean, *Peddling Influence: Thomas "Tommy the Cork" Corcoran and the Birth of Modern Lobbying* (Hanover, N.H.: Steerforth Press, 2004), 104–5; Pepper, *Pepper*, 73; and Sean J. Savage, *Roosevelt: The Party Leader, 1932–1945* (Lexington: University Press of Kentucky, 1991), 134–35.

16. Savage, *Roosevelt*, 134–35; Niznik, "Thomas G. Corcoran," 346–47; and Pepper, *Pepper*, 69–73.

17. Niznik, "Thomas G. Corcoran," 348–51; Ickes, *Secret Diary*, II, 500; Savage, *Roosevelt*, 135–37.

18. Russell D. Buhite and David W. Levy, eds., *FDR's Fireside Chats* (New York: Penguin, 1993), 124–35; Farley, *Jim Farley's Story*, 120–36.

19. Libbey, *Dear Alben*, 77–81.

20. Savage, *Roosevelt*, 140–43; Thomas L. Stokes, *Chip Off My Shoulder* (Princeton, N.J.: Princeton University Press, 1940), 534–37.

21. George T. Blakey, *Hard Times and New Deal in Kentucky, 1929–1939* (Lexington: University Press of Kentucky, 1986), 182–88.

22. Blakey, *Hard Times and New Deal in Kentucky*, 183–84. Adolf Berle, a Brains Truster, recorded in his diary that efforts were "being made directly in the president's interest" in "the Kentucky election. My impression, accordingly, is that political deals will be made in connection with P.W.A. grants and certainly with W.P.A. officials—and probably with respect to certain S.E.C. transactions provided these can be made quietly and there is no danger of getting into print." See Adolf Berle Diary, July 16, 1938, RPL.

23. James Eccles, *The Hatch Act and the American Bureaucracy* (New York: Vantage Press, 1981).

24. Stokes, *Chip Off My Shoulder*, 534–37; Blakey, *Hard Times and New Deal in Kentucky*, 186.

25. Savage, *Roosevelt*, 143; Eccles, *The Hatch Act and the American Bureaucracy*, Stokes, *Chip Off My Shoulder*; and Hadley Cantril, ed., *Public Opinion, 1935–1946* (Princeton, N.J.: Princeton University Press, 1951), 192. In the same poll, conducted on January 9, 1939, by the American Institute of Public Opinion, 78 percent "favor[ed] a law prohibiting any person on relief from contributing money to a political campaign." That such a question would even be asked, least of all answered that way, suggests how rampant the problem was.

26. Stokes, *Chip Off My Shoulder*, 492–96; Farley, *Jim Farley's Story*, 96–97. Roosevelt took one cross-country trip in the fall of 1937 and another in mid-1938.

27. Savage, *Roosevelt*, 149; James T. Patterson, *Congressional Conservatism and the New Deal* (Lexington: University Press of Kentucky, 1967), 281.

28. Stokes, *Chip Off My Shoulder*, 492–500; Farley, *Jim Farley's Story*, 127.

29. Caroline Keith, *"For Hell and a Brown Mule": The Biography of Senator Millard E. Tydings* (Lanham, Md.: Madison, 1991), 336–37.

30. *Charleston News and Courier*, August 14, 1938, 4; *Atlanta Constitution*, September 1, 1938, 1; Stokes, *Chip Off My Shoulder*, 497–500; and Savage, *Roosevelt*, 146–50.

31. *Baltimore Sun*, September 16, 1938; Keith, *"For Hell and a Brown Mule,"* 336–40; Savage, *Roosevelt*, 129–58.

32. *Philadelphia Inquirer*, quoted in *Baltimore Sun*, September 14, 1938, 3.

33. *Atlanta Journal*, September 17, 1938, 4.

34. *Atlanta Journal*, September 17, 1938, 4. Clapper, in his diary, noted earlier in the campaign, "Politicians run for election on [the] issue of giving more benefits—used to be tariff or abstract issues but now issue is how large a check will you give me" (Raymond Clapper Diary, May 3, 1938, LC.)

35. Farley, *Jim Farley's Story*, 145–46; Savage, *Roosevelt*, 152–53.

36. Farley, *Jim Farley's Story*, 137, 148–49.

37. McKenna, *Franklin Roosevelt and the Great Constitutional War*.

38. Robert L. Zangrando, *The NAACP Crusade Against Lynching, 1909–1950* (Philadelphia: Temple University Press, 1980), 139–65; Harvard Sitkoff, *A New Deal for Blacks: The Emergence of Civil Rights as a National Issue* (New York: Oxford University Press, 1978), 289–95. For a view more sympathetic to Roosevelt (especially than that of Zangrando's), see Kevin J. McMahon, *Reconsidering Roosevelt on Race* (Chicago: University of Chicago Press, 2004).

39. Zangrando, *The NAACP Crusade Against Lynching*, 6–7; Donald R. McCoy,

Landon of Kansas (Lincoln: University of Nebraska Press, 1966), 311–12; Nancy J. Weiss, *Farewell to the Party of Lincoln: Black Politics in the Age of FDR* (Princeton, N.J.: Princeton University Press, 1983), 250–51. Roosevelt captured most of the black vote in 1940 anyway, but that outcome was not apparent during the antilynching debates of the late 1930s.

40. J. Joseph Huthmacher, *Senator Robert F. Wagner and the Rise of Urban Liberalism* (New York: Atheneum, 1971), 238–43; Sitkoff, *A New Deal for Blacks*, 289–95.

41. Booker T. Washington, *Up from Slavery* (New York: Signet Classic, 2000 [1901]); and Zangrando, *The NAACP Crusade Against Lynching*.

42. Blakey, *Hard Times and New Deal in Kentucky*. In 1945, Chandler became commissioner of major league baseball, and helped Jackie Robinson become the first black to play in the major leagues.

43. Swain, *Pat Harrison*, 202–6.

44. Farley, *Jim Farley's Story*, 219–20.

45. Weiss, *Farewell to the Party of Lincoln*, 250–51; Swain, *Pat Harrison*, 206–8; George Creel, *Rebel at Large: Recollections of Fifty Crowded Years* (New York: G. P. Putnam's Sons, 1947), 338.

46. William J. Baker, *Jesse Owens: An American Life* (New York: Free Press, 1986), 132–38.

47. Joe Louis, *Joe Louis: My Life* (New York: Harcourt Brace Jovanovich, 1978), 158–59, 215; Chris Mead, *Champion Joe Louis: Black Hero in White America* (New York: Charles Scribner's Sons, 1985), 133–34, 223–25; Robert W. Creamer, *Babe: The Legend Comes to Life* (New York: Simon & Schuster, 1974), 318–19.

48. Baker, *Jesse Owens*, 138; Louis, *Joe Louis*, 215.

49. Donald A. Ritchie, *Reporting from Washington: The History of the Washington Press Corps* (New York: Oxford University Press, 2005), 28–31; Marian Anderson, *My Lord, What a Morning* (Madison: University of Wisconsin Press, 1992 [1956]); Mary Bethune, "My Secret Talks with FDR," *Ebony*, April 1949, 42–51; and Dennis S. Nordin, *The New Deal's Black Congressman: A Life of Arthur Wergs Mitchell* (Columbia: University of Missouri Press, 1997), 140–41. Roosevelt's indifference to civil rights seems to have continued into the war years. According to Chris Mead, biographer of Joe Louis, "Secretary of War Henry Stimson believed blacks were inferior soldiers and said the army should not become a 'sociological laboratory.' His policy was to maintain segregation, and FDR initiated his approval of Stimson's recommendations on October 8, 1940." Reluctantly, in response to a threatened march on Washington by labor leader A. Philip Randolph, Roosevelt created the Fair Employment Practices Committee during the

war. See Mead, *Champion Joe Louis*, 223–24; and Paul D. Moreno, *Black Americans and Organized Labor* (Baton Rouge: Louisiana State University Press, 2006), 198–208.

Chapter 14: How FDR's Deception Tarnished the Presidency Forever

1. For the Haiti episode, see Geoffrey Ward, *First-Class Temperament: The Emergence of Franklin Roosevelt* (New York: Harper & Row, 1989), 535–36.
2. Gordon Lloyd, *The Two Faces of Liberalism: How the Hoover-Roosevelt Debate Shapes the 21st Century* (Salem, Mass.: M & M Scrivener Press, 2007), 104–14, 123–39, esp. 129.
3. Samuel I. Rosenman, ed., *The Public Papers and Addresses of Franklin D. Roosevelt* (New York: Random House, 1938), I, 805–8.
4. Rosenman, *Public Papers,* I, 808–10.
5. A useful study of Douglas is Robert P. Browder and Thomas G. Smith, *Independent: A Biography of Lewis W. Douglas* (New York: Knopf, 1986). See also Frank Freidel, *Franklin D. Roosevelt: A Rendezvous with Destiny* (Boston: Little, Brown, 1990), 138. Douglas had just been elected to his fourth term and Roosevelt then appointed him as budget director.
6. Turner Catledge, *My Life and The Times* (New York: Harper & Row, 1971), 83–84.
7. Catledge, *My Life and The Times*, 84–85.
8. Browder and Smith, *Independent*, 114–16. In Douglas's letter of resignation he urged the president to balance his budgets to secure a respectable place in history. See also William Chenery, *So It Seemed* (New York: Harcourt, Brace, 1952), 258. For examples of Morgenthau working his way through deceptions by FDR, see the personal entries in Morgenthau Diary, January 1, 1935, and January 14, 1935, RPL.
9. Morgenthau Diary, January 22, 1935, RPL.
10. Robert Smith Thompson, *A Time for War: Franklin Roosevelt and the Path to Pearl Harbor* (New York: Prentice-Hall, 1991); and Delbert Clark, *Washington Dateline* (New York: Frederick A. Stokes, 1941), 84.
11. Martha H. Swain, *Pat Harrison: The New Deal Years* (Jackson: University Press of Mississippi, 1978), 107–12.
12. Harold Ickes Diary, July 23, 1936, LC.
13. Louis Howe concurred with Roosevelt: "Who in hell around here knows what we will be interested in, six weeks from now." Fulton Oursler, *Behold This Dreamer! An Autobiography* (Boston: Little, Brown, 1964), 390. See also Arthur Krock, *Memoirs: Sixty Years on the Firing Line* (New York: Funk & Wagnalls, 1968), 148; Joe Martin, *My First Fifty Years in Politics* (Westport, Conn.: Greenwood, 1975 [1960]), 72; Catledge, *My Life and The*

Times, 82–83; Walter Trohan, *Political Animals* (Garden City, N.Y.: Doubleday, 1975), 59–60.

14. James Farley, *Jim Farley's Story* (New York: Whittlesley House, 1948), 75–76.

15. Arthur M. Schlesinger, Jr., *The Politics of Upheaval* (Boston: Houghton Mifflin, 1960), 621.

16. Rosenman, *Public Papers*, V, 402–4.

17. Swain, *Pat Harrison*, 113, 130–34.

18. Morgenthau Diary, November 8, 1937; "Memorandum of Secretary Morgenthau's Statement to the President's Cabinet on Tuesday, February 16, 1939," and "Re Tax Statement," May 4, 1939, RPL.

19. Krock, *Memoirs*, 179–80. Even Roosevelt's opponents had to be on guard about Roosevelt's charm. Joe Martin, for example, the Republican minority leader in the House, worked to make sure his fellow Republicans were not swept up by Roosevelt's charisma. See Martin, *My First Fifty Years in Politics*, 72–73.

20. Betty Houchin Winfield, *FDR and the News Media* (Urbana: University of Illinois Press, 1990). Winfield makes the point that the opposition of newspaper publishers to FDR was always present and increased numerically over time.

21. Clark, *Washington Dateline*, 99–100, 108, 124, 131, 135–36, 141, 163.

22. Clark, *Washington Dateline*, 86–88; Ronald Steel, *Walter Lippmann and the American Century* (Boston: Little, Brown, 1980), 316; Ralph G. Martin, *Cissy: The Extraordinary Life of Eleanor Medill Patterson* (New York: Simon & Schuster, 1979), 360; Gary Dean Best, *The Critical Press and the New Deal* (Westport, Conn.: Praeger, 1993).

23. Clark, *Washington Dateline*, 83; John R. Boettiger, *A Love in Shadow* (New York: Norton, 1978), 158; Doris Faber, *The Life of Lorena Hickok, E.R.'s Friend* (New York: William Morrow, 1980), 183. For the close relationship between Lorena Hickok and Eleanor Roosevelt, see Rodger Streitmatter, *Empty Without You: The Intimate Letters of Eleanor Roosevelt and Lorena Hickok* (New York: Free Press, 1998).

24. Oursler, *Behold This Dreamer!* 369–70; Howard K. Smith, *Events Leading Up to My Death* (New York: St. Martin's, 1996), 38.

25. Caroline H. Keith, *"For Hell and a Brown Mule": The Biography of Senator Millard E. Tydings* (Lanham, Md.: Madison, 1991), 337; Martin, *Cissy*, 359, 398. Both Cissy and Joseph Patterson tended to be favorable to FDR, but both also tended to be isolationists and broke with Roosevelt around 1940.

26. *Time*, January 27, 1936.

27. Trohan, *Political Animals*, 75; Bascom N. Timmons, *Jesse H. Jones: The Man*

and the Statesman (Westport, Conn.: Greenwood, 1975 [1956]), 249–50. Roosevelt also secured an RFC loan for his brother-in-law and tried to get an RFC loan for George Fort Milton of the *Chattanooga News*. See Best, *The Critical Press and the New Deal*, 27; and Thomas G. Corcoran, "Rendezvous with Destiny: The Memoirs of Thomas G. Corcoran," *Credo*, 16, LC.

28. Steel, *Walter Lippmann and the American Century*, 316.

29. Trohan, *Political Animals*, 133–35; Martin, *Cissy*, 359–60. Also, columnist Raymond Clapper discussed Roosevelt's affair with Lucy Mercer, "a young Catholic woman," in his diary as early as 1933, but Clapper never mentioned the episode in print. See Raymond Clapper Diary, July 13, 1933, LC.

30. Trohan, *Political Animals*, 133–40; Joseph Alsop, *FDR, 1882–1945: A Centenary Remembrance* (Thorndike, Maine: Thorndike Press, 1982), 79.

31. A. Merriman Smith, *Thank You, Mr. President* (New York: Harper & Bros., 1946), 72–74.

32. Clark, *Washington Dateline*, 74, 90–91. The expelled reporter, columnist Paul Mallon, protested vigorously and his expulsion was rescinded. See also, Winfield, *FDR and the News Media*, 144.

33. Clark, *Washington Dateline*, 121; Thomas L. Stokes, *Chip Off My Shoulder* (Princeton, N.J.: Princeton University Press, 1940), 536–37.

34. Oursler, *Behold This Dreamer!* 391–92.

35. Samuel I. Rosenman, *Public Papers*, VI, 35–66. The most thorough book on the Court-packing episode is Joseph Alsop and Turner Catledge, *The 168 Days* (Garden City, N.Y.: Doubleday, Doran, 1938). See also Marian C. McKenna, *Franklin Roosevelt and the Great Constitutional War: The Court-Packing Crisis of 1937* (New York: Fordham University Press, 2002).

36. Robert Nisbet, *The Present Age* (New York: Harper & Row, 1988), 81. More than two weeks before Roosevelt announced his Court-packing plan, reporter Raymond Clapper wrote in his diary that Donald Richberg, a key presidential advisor, told Clapper that the president was in an "audacious mood and is even thinking of proposing to pack the Supreme Court by enlarging it. He says R[oose]v[el]t is determined to curb the court and put it in its place, and will go ahead even if many people think it unwise." Raymond Clapper Diary, January 20, 1937, LC. See also Clapper Diary, February 8, 1937, and January 14, 1938 (where Clapper quotes Richberg as saying the congestion on the Court argument was "[ph]ony" from the start; and April 28, 1937 (where Clapper quotes Robert Jackson as saying the congestion on the Court argument was a "guise"). On Roosevelt's deceptive motives for packing the Court, Newton Baker, former Democrat secretary of war, said, "We are all dishonored by his [Roosevelt's] lack of frankness. . . . In a matter of such tremendous importance a deliberate effort was made to lull us into

acquiescence by concealing the real purposes for which the [Court-packing] proposal was made." See Newton Baker to Josiah Bailey, March 30, 1937, in Baker Papers, LC.

37. Farley, *Jim Farley's Story*, 77–99.

38. *New York Herald Tribune*, February 9, 1937, and May 6, 1937; Arthur Sears Henning to Herbert Hoover, February 1, 1937, in Hoover Papers, Hoover Presidential Library. See also David Lawrence, "The March of Devils," February 15, 1937, in *The Editorials of David Lawrence: The Era of the New Deal, 1933–1937* (Washington, D.C.: U.S. News & World Report, 1970), 550; and Best, *The Critical Press and the New Deal*, 114, 116, 121. I thank Gary Dean Best for alerting me to the Henning letter to Hoover.

39. *New York Herald Tribune*, August 2, 1936, Section II, Part II. See also Best, *The Critical Press and the New Deal*, 138; and Rosenman, *Public Papers*, VII, 179.

40. Burton K. Wheeler, *Yankee from the West* (Garden City, N.Y.: Doubleday, 1962), 343–46, 356.

41. Best, *The Critical Press and the New Deal*, 23.

42. According to political scientist Tom West, only those radio stations that criticized FDR were threatened with nonrenewal of their licenses. See his discussion of the Yankee Radio Network in Thomas G. West, "Free Speech in the American Founding and in Modern Liberalism," in Ellen Frankel Paul, Fred D. Miller, Jr., and Jeffrey Paul, eds., *Freedom of Speech* (New York: Cambridge University Press, 2004), 310–84. See also Richard W. Steele, *Propaganda in an Open Society: The Roosevelt Administration and the Media, 1933–1941* (Westport, Conn.: Greenwood, 1985), 24–25; Winfield, *FDR and the News Media*, 104. A very helpful essay is Elisha Hanson, "Official Propaganda and the New Deal," *Annals of the American Academy of Political and Social Science* 179 (May 1935), 176–86.

43. Swain, *Pat Harrison*, 147–94.

44. Raymond Moley, *After Seven Years* (New York: Harper & Bros., 1939), 354.

45. James MacGregor Burns, *Roosevelt: The Lion and the Fox* (New York: Harcourt, Brace, & World, 1956), 323.

46. By the end of his second term, Roosevelt's interests had strongly turned to foreign policy, but he continued to lead by deception. In 1940, Roosevelt "changed his mind" and decided to run for a third term because, he said, changing international conditions dictated it. During the 1940 campaign, Roosevelt promised, a week before the election, "I have said this before, but I will say it again and again: Your boys are not going to be sent into any foreign wars." He did not even say, "unless we are attacked," but when we were at-

tacked at Pearl Harbor, Roosevelt, with massive public support, did urge America to go to war and everyone recognized the changed circumstances. See David M. Kennedy, *Freedom from Fear: The American People in Depression and War, 1929–1945* (New York: Oxford University Press, 1999), 463.

Chapter 15: What FDR Should Have Done

1. U.S. Bureau of the Census, *Historical Statistics of the United States: Colonial Times to 1970* (Washington, D.C.: U.S. Government Printing Office, 1975), I, 127, 135; and John V. Denson, ed., *Reassessing the Presidency* (Auburn, Ala.: Mises Institute, 2001).
2. Samuel I. Rosenman, ed., *The Public Papers and Addresses of Franklin D. Roosevelt* (New York: Random House, 1938), I, 760, 798.
3. Rosenman, *Public Papers*, I, 808–9; Kirk H. Porter and Donald B. Johnson, *National Party Platforms, 1840–1968* (Urbana: University of Illinois Press, 1970), 331.
4. Rosenman, *Public Papers*, I, 808; *Historical Statistics*, I, 135.
5. Rosenman, *Public Papers*, I, 724, 764.
6. Rosenman, *Public Papers*, I, 724–26.
7. Douglas A. Irwin, "From Smoot-Hawley to Reciprocal Trade Agreements: Changing the Course of U.S. Trade Policy in the 1930s," in Michael D. Bordo, Claudia Goldin, and Eugene N. White, eds., *The Defining Moment: The Great Depression and the American Economy in the Twentieth Century* (Chicago: University of Chicago Press, 1998), 325–52 (quotation on 344).

Chapter 16: What Finally Did End the Great Depression?

1. John Garraty, *Interpreting American History: Conversations with Historians* (London: Macmillan, 1970), II, 184–85.
2. David M. Kennedy, *Freedom from Fear: The American People in Depression and War, 1929–1945* (New York: Oxford University Press, 1999), 376, 857.
3. Henry Hazlitt, *Economics in One Lesson* (New Rochelle, N.Y.: Arlington House, 1979 [1946]), 25, 27. See also Robert A. Margo, "The Microeconomics of Depression Unemployment," *Journal of Economic History* 51 (June 1991), 333–41.
4. Robert Higgs, "Regime Uncertainty: Why the Great Depression Lasted So Long and Why Prosperity Resumed after the War," *Independent Review* 1 (Spring 1997), 562. See also Robert Higgs, *Depression, War, and Cold War* (New York: Oxford University Press, 2006), 30–80. Professor Higgs has written several books on economic history, and is editor of *The Independent Review*, a prominent journal of political economy.

5. Higgs, "Regime Uncertainty," 585.
6. Higgs, "Regime Uncertainty," 576.
7. Higgs, "Regime Uncertainty," 577.
8. League of Nations, *World Economic Survey, 1938/39* (Geneva, 1939), 56; Irving Fisher to Franklin Roosevelt, June 16, 1936, Roosevelt Papers, RPL.
9. Samuel I. Rosenman, ed., *The Public Papers and Addresses of Franklin D. Roosevelt* (New York: Harper & Bros., 1950), XII, 90; U.S. Bureau of Census, *Historical Statistics of the United States*, I, 126; and Roy G. Blakey and Gladys C. Blakey, *The Federal Income Tax* (London: Longmans, Green, 1940).
10. League of Nations, *World Economic Survey*, 128, 192–93.
11. Burton W. Folsom, Jr., and Robert Higgs, "Crisis and Leviathan: Review and Response," 13 *Continuity* (Spring/Fall 1989), 89. See also Robert Higgs, *Neither Liberty nor Safety* (Oakland, Calif.: Independent Institute, 2007), 84–85.
12. *St. Louis Post-Dispatch*, January 8, 1936.

Chapter 17: Why Historians Have Missed the Mark

1. Charles Beard to Raymond Moley, September 15, 1948, HI. I thank Gary Dean Best showing me this quotation and giving me the citation. See Gary Dean Best, *Retreat from Liberalism: Collectivists versus Progressives in the New Deal Years* (Westport, Conn.: Praeger, 2002).
2. Jim Powell, *FDR's Folly* (New York: Crown Forum, 2003); Amity Shlaes, *The Forgotten Man* (New York: HarperCollins, 2007). Among professional historians, Edgar Eugene Robinson and Gary Dean Best are among the few to write significant books critical of Roosevelt.
3. Clinton Rossiter, ed., *The Federalist Papers* (New York: New American Library, 1961), 110, 301, 322, 323.
4. Thomas Sowell, *A Conflict of Visions* (New York: William Morrow, 1987), 58–62.
5. The quotations in this section are from Ronald J. Pestritto, *Woodrow Wilson: The Essential Political Writings* (Lanham, Md.: Rowman & Littlefield, 2005), 1–27.
6. James MacGregor Burns, *Roosevelt: The Lion and the Fox* (New York: Harcourt, Brace, & World, 1956), 291.
7. Samuel I. Rosenman, ed., *The Public Papers and Addresses of Franklin D. Roosevelt* (New York: Random House, 1938), VI, 127, 130.
8. Arthur M. Schlesinger, Jr., *The Politics of Upheaval* (Boston: Houghton Mifflin, 1988 [1960]), 652.
9. Rosenman, *Public Papers*, XIII, 40–42.

10. John A. Garraty, *Interpreting American History: Conversations with Historians* (London: Macmillan, 1970), 173, 180.
11. Garraty, *Interpreting American History*, 184–85.
12. Garraty, *Interpreting American History*, 181.
13. Irving Bernstein, *A Caring Society: The New Deal, the Worker, and the Great Depression* (Boston: Houghton Mifflin, 1985), 306–7; George McJimsey, *Harry Hopkins: Ally of the Poor and Defender of Democracy* (Cambridge, Mass.: Harvard University Press, 1987).
14. Kennedy, *Freedom from Fear: The American People in Depression and War, 1929–1945* (New York: Oxford University Press, 1999), 365, 378.
15. Allan Nevins, *Grover Cleveland: A Study of Courage* (New York: Dodd, Mead, 1966 [1932]), 763.
16. Rosenman, *Public Papers*, V, 575.
17. Robert Higgs, "Bolingbroke, Nixon, and the Rest of Them," *Independent Review* 2 (Summer 1997), 156–57; Henry Hazlitt, *The Conquest of Poverty* (Irvington, N.Y.: Foundation for Economic Education, 1994), 88.

SELECT BIBLIOGRAPHY

Franklin D. Roosevelt Presidential Library
Adolf Berle Diary
Irving Fisher Papers
Harry Hopkins Papers
Henry Morgenthau Diary
Franklin Roosevelt Papers
Samuel Rosenman Papers
Rexford Tugwell Diary

Library of Congress
Newton Baker Papers
Hugo Black Papers
Raymond Clapper Diary
William Borah Papers
Benjamin Cohen Papers
Thomas Corcoran Papers
Felix Frankfurter Papers
Harold Ickes Diary
Harold Ickes Papers
Hiram Johnson Papers
Frank Knox Papers
William G. McAdoo Papers
Charles McNary Papers
George Norris Papers

Hoover Institution
Raymond Moley Diary
Mark Sullivan Papers

Kansas State Historical Society
Alfred Landon Papers

National Archives
WPA—Political Coercion File—New Jersey

Newspapers
Atlanta Constitution
Atlanta Journal
Baltimore Sun
Bangor [Maine] Daily News
Charleston News and Courier
Chicago Tribune
Daily Kennebec Journal [Maine]
Los Angeles Times
New York Herald Tribune
New York Times
Omaha World-Herald
Philadelphia Inquirer
Portland [Maine] Press Herald
St. Louis Post-Dispatch
Washington Post

INDEX